PILGRIM CITY

Pilgrim City

St Augustine of Hippo and His Innovation in Political Thought

MILES HOLLINGWORTH

t & t clark

Published by T&T Clark International
A Continuum imprint
The Tower Building
11 York Road
London
SE1 7NX

80 Maiden Lane
Suite 704
New York
NY 10038

www.continuumbooks.com

First published 2010

British Library Cataloguing-in-Publication Data
A catalogue record for this book is available from the British Library.

ISBN: 978–0567–31002–6
PB ISBN: 978–0567–48010–1

Designed and typeset by Pindar NZ, Auckland, New Zealand
Printed and bound in Great Britain by MPG Books Group Ltd

Contents

Foreword

As Dr Hollingworth points out, St Augustine's thoughts on the subject of politics are not to be found entire in any one of his many writings. Augustine's concerns are pastoral, theological, exegetical, controversial. He is not primarily a political thinker; even his enormous critique of the moral and political tradition of Rome, *De civitate Dei*, is not in any ordinary sense a political treatise or an essay in 'political philosophy'. Yet it is hardly possible to overstate his significance as a figure in the history of political thought. This significance lies chiefly in a single, though very complex, fact. More than any earlier Christian author, Augustine grasped the implications of the Christian doctrine of Original Sin for the political and ethical beliefs of classical antiquity. In doing so, he furnished the culture of the Latin West with what may be called a new kind of political anthropology: an anthropology of *fallen* man, wholly dependent on Divine Grace and unable to find redemption by any effort of his own or through any kind of merely human contrivance.

This anthropology, and the various interpretations, misinterpretations and revisions of it that have accrued over the centuries, has been immensely important in terms of its influence on the development of various ideological currents in Western thought, but its importance does not lie solely within the province of the historian. Man, according to the famous dictum of Aristotle, is by nature a political animal. Human beings need to find ways of living in constructive association with one another if they are to meet needs – moral and spiritual needs as well as material ones – that are intrinsic to their nature; yet political and social life is everywhere fraught with difficulty and instability. How is this conundrum to be explained? By what means, if any, can it be resolved? Are kingdoms indeed nothing more than great bands of robbers? Can anything make them otherwise? Questions of this kind are as pertinent now as they were at the first beginnings of political thought, and we are no longer as inclined as we once were to suppose that political philosophy is dead. It may be that Augustine's reflections on the human condition are especially relevant to the present day, when so many optimistic Enlightenment assumptions about human nature and motivation have come under scrutiny. Dr Hollingworth has produced a comprehensive, learned and thought-provoking analysis of a body of thought that is of much more than antiquarian interest. His book will be a valuable contribution to the long and still fruitful stream of Augustinian scholarship.

R. W. Dyson
Durham, 2009

Acknowledgements

This book owes a great deal to three scholars. The Right Rev. Professor Stephen Sykes, DD, appointed me to my first post at St John's College, Durham. He also chaired my PhD examination. The college has continued to give me every support under its new Principal, the Rev. Dr David Wilkinson, and I am grateful for such a happy and longstanding association. Dr R. W. Dyson was my postgraduate supervisor at the University of Durham. He has subsequently guided me in my study of St Augustine and I would like to thank him in particular for contributing such an insightful foreword. Professor Nicholas Rengger of the University of St Andrews examined my PhD and has subsequently supported my work in many ways. I would like to thank him for his generous recommendation.

I would like to thank also my publisher, Robin Baird-Smith. Robin commissioned this book and has done much else besides to help my career. He has been a constant source of advice and friendship.

From the very start I have read Augustine's writings with this great advantage: that what Augustine seems to be saying happens to be the same thing that my father has been teaching me all my life. I found many of Augustine's ideas familiar when I encountered them – so familiar that the real work of this book was to locate Augustine in the history of Western political thought, not to reconstruct his outlook, as some may think.

Miles Hollingworth
Valsolda, 2009

A Note on Texts and Translations

On occasion I have chosen to use my own translation from Augustine's Latin. In each case I have added the phrase 'author's translation' in parentheses after the citation to the Latin text in the notes. These translations have been made from the Latin texts in the *Nuova Biblioteca Agostiniana* (Roma, Città Nuova Editrice, 1965–). I have also used the phrase 'author's translation' to indicate my translations from languages other than Latin.

In all other cases, quotations from *De civitate Dei* come from R. W. Dyson's English edition: Augustine (ed. R. W. Dyson), *The City of God against the Pagans* (Cambridge: Cambridge University Press, 2001); quotations from *Confessiones* come from John K. Ryan's English edition: Augustine (tr. John K. Ryan), *The Confessions of Saint Augustine* (New York: Doubleday, 1960); and quotations from *De Genesi ad litteram* come from John Hammond Taylor's English edition: Augustine (tr. John Hammond Taylor, SJ), *The Literal Meaning of Genesis*, 2 Vols. (*Ancient Christian Writers: The Works of the Fathers in Translation*, No. 41 [New York: Newman Press, 1982]).

All biblical quotations come from the King James Version.

Abbreviations

THE WORKS OF AUGUSTINE

Contra Fort.	*Acta seu Disputatio contra Fortunatem Manichaeum*	Debate with Fortunatus, a Manichee
Contra Crescon.	*Ad Cresconium grammaticum partis Donati lib. 4*	To Cresconius, a Donatist Grammarian
Ad Emeritum	*Ad Emeritum Donatistarum episcopum, post collationem Lib. 1*	To Emeritus the Donatist Bishop, after a Meeting
Ad inquis. Ian.	*Ad inquisitiones Ianuarii*	Responses to Januarius (Letters 54–55)
Adn. in Iob	*Adnotationes in Iob lib. 1*	Comments on Job
Adv. Iud.	*Adversus Iudaeos tractatus*	Against the Jews
Brev. coll. cum Don.	*Breviculus conlationis cum Donatistas lib. 3*	A Summary of a Meeting with the Donatists
Confess.	*Confessiones*	Confessions
Coll. cum Maxim.	*Conlatio cum Maximus*	Debate with Maximus

Contra Acad.	*Contra Academicos lib. 3 (De Academicis)*	Against the Skeptics
Contra Adim.	*Contra Adimantum Manichei discipulum lib. 1*	Against Adimantus, a Disciple of Mani
Contra adv. L. et P.	*Contra adversarium Legis et Prophetarum lib. 2*	Against the Adversaries of the Law and the Prophets
Contra duas ep. Pelag.	*Contra duas epistolas Pelagianorum lib. 4*	Against Two Letters of the Pelagians
Contra ep. Don.	*Contra epistolam Donati*	Against the Letter of the Donatists
Contra ep. Man.	*Contra epistolam Manichaei quam vocant fundamenti lib. 1*	Against the 'Foundation Letter' of the Manichees
Contra ep. Parm.	*Contra epistolam Parmeniani lib. 3*	Against the Letter of Parmenian
Contra Faustum	*Contra Faustum Manichaeum lib. 33*	Against Faustus, a Manichee
Contra Felicem	*Contra Felicem Manichaeum lib. 2*	Against Felix, a Manichee
Contra Gaud.	*Contra Gaudentium Donatistarum episcopum lib. 2*	Against Gaudentius, a bishop of the Donatists
Contra Hilarum	*Contra Hilarum lib. 1*	Against Hilarus
Contra Iul.	*Contra Iulianum lib. 6*	Against Julian
Opus imp. c. Iul.	*Contra Iulianum opus imperfectum*	Against Julian, an Unfinished Work
Contra litt. Petil.	*Contra litteras Petiliani lib. 3*	Against the Letter of Petilian
Contra Maxim.	*Contra Maximinum Arianum lib. 2*	Against Maximus, an Arian
Contra mend.	*Contra mendacium lib. 1*	Against Lying

Contra Prisc. et Orig.	*Contra Priscillianistas et Origenistas*	Against the Priscillianists and the Origenists
Contra Secund.	*Contra Secundinem Manichaeum lib. 1*	Against Secundius, a Manichee
Contra Arian.	*Contra sermonem Arianorum lib. 1*	Against an Arian Sermon
De ag. Christ.	*De agone Christiano lib. 1*	On the Christian Struggle
De an. et eius or.	*De anima et eius origine lib. 4 (De natura et origine animae)*	On the Soul and its Origin
De bapt.	*De baptismo lib. 7*	On Baptism
De b. vita	*De beata vita lib. 1*	On the Happy Life
De bono con.	*De bono coniugali lib. 1*	On the Good of Marriage
De bono vid.	*De bono viduitatis*	On the Good of Widowhood
De cath. rud.	*De cathechizandis rudibus lib. 1*	On the Instruction of Beginners
De civ. Dei	*De civitate Dei*	The City of God
De con. adult.	*De coniugiis adulterinis lib. 2*	On Adulterous Marriages
De cons. Evang.	*De consensu Evangelistarum lib. 4*	On Agreement among the Evangelists
De cont.	*De continentia*	On Continence
De corr. Donat.	*De correctione Donatistarum lib. 1*	On the Correction of the Donatists (Letter 185)
De corrept. et gr.	*De correptione et gratia lib. 1*	On Admonition and Grace
De cura pro mort.	*De cura pro mortuis gerenda lib. 1*	On the Care of the Dead
De div. qq. ad Simpl.	*De diversis quaestionibus ad Simplicianum lib. 2*	To Simplicianus, on Various Questions

De div. qq. 83	De diversis quaestionibus 83 lib. 1	On Eighty-Three Varied Questions
De div. daem.	De divinatione daemonum lib. 1	On the Divination of Demons
De doctr. Christ.	De doctrina Christiana lib. 4	On Christian Doctrine
De dono pers.	De dono perseverantiae	On the Gift of Perseverance
De d. anim.	De duabus animabus lib. 1	On the Two Souls
De 8 qq. Dulc.	De 8 Dulcitii quaestionibus lib. 1	On Eight Questions from Dulcitius
De 8 qq. V. T.	De 8 quaestionibus ex Veteri Testamento	Eight Questions on the Old Testament
De fide et op.	De fide et operibus lib. 1	On Faith and Works
De fide et s.	De fide et symbolo lib. 1	On Faith and the Creed
De fide r. quae n. v.	De fide rerum quae non videntur	On Faith in Things Unseen
De Gen. ad litt.	De Genesi ad litteram lib. 12	On the Literal Interpretation of Genesis
De Gen. ad litt. l. imp.	De Genesi ad litteram liber imperfectus	On the Literal Interpretation of Genesis, an Unfinished Book
De Gen. c. Man.	De Genesi contra Manichaeos lib. 2	On Genesis against the Manichees
De gestis cum Em.	De gestis cum Emerito Lib. 1	On the Proceedings with Emeritus
De gestis Pel.	De gestis Pelagii lib. 1	On the Deeds of Pelagius
De gr. Chr.	De gratia Christi et de peccato originali lib. 2	On the Grace of Christ and Original Sin
De gr. et l. arb.	De gratia et libero arbitrio lib. 1	On Grace and Free Will

De gr. N. T.	*De gratia Novi Testamenti lib. 1*	On the Grace of the New Testament (Letter 140)
De haer.	*De haeresibus*	On Heresies (Letters 221–224)
De immort. an.	*De immortalitate animae lib. 1*	On the Immortality of the Soul
De lib. arb.	*De libero arbitrio lib. 3*	On Free Will
De Mag.	*De Magistro lib. 1*	The Teacher
De mend.	*De mendacio lib. 1*	On Lying
De mor. Eccl. cath.	*De moribus ecclesiae catholicae et de moribus Manichaeorum*	On the Morals of the Catholic Church and the Morals of the Manichees
De mus.	*De musica lib. 6*	On Music
De nat. boni	*De natura boni lib. 1*	On the Nature of the Good
De nat. et gr.	*De natura et gratia lib. 1*	On Nature and Grace
De nupt. et conc.	*De nuptiis et concupiscentia lib. 2*	On Marriage and Concupiscence
De op. mon.	*De opere monachorum lib. 1*	The Works of Monks
De ord.	*De ordine lib. 2*	On Order
De o. an. et de sent. Iac.	*De origine animae et de sententia Iacobi lib. 2*	On the Origins of the Soul, and Some Thoughts on a Verse in James (Letters 166–167)
De pat.	*De patientia*	On Patience
De pecc. mer. et rem.	*De peccatorum meritis et remissione lib. 3*	On the Merits and Forgiveness of Sins
De perf. iust. hom.	*De perfectione iustitiae hominis*	On the Perfection of Man's Righteousness
De praed. sanct.	*De praedestinatione sanctorum*	On the Predestination of the Saints

De praes. Dei	*De praesentia Dei lib. 1*	On the Presence of God (Letter 187)
De quant. an.	*De quantitate animae lib. 1*	On the Greatness of the Soul
De s. virg.	*De sancta virginitate lib. 1*	On Holy Virginity
De serm. Dom. in m.	*De sermone Domini in monte lib. 2*	Discourse on the Sermon on the Mount
De sp. et litt.	*De Spiritu et littera lib. 1*	On the Spirit and the Letter
De Trin.	*De Trinitate lib. 15*	On the Trinity
De un. bapt. c. Petil.	*De unico baptismo contra Petilianum lib. 1*	On the One Baptism against Petilian
De un. Eccl.	*De unitate Ecclesiae lib. 1*	On the Unity of the Church
De util. cred.	*De utilitate credendi lib. 1*	On the Utility of Belief
De vera rel.	*De vera religione lib. 1*	On the True Religion
De vid. Deo	*De videndo Deo lib. 1*	On the Vision of God (Letters 147–148)
En. in Ps.	*Enarrationes in Psalmos*	Commentaries on the Psalms
Ench.	*Enchiridion ad Laurentium lib. 1*	A Manual on Faith, Hope, and Charity
Ep.	*Epistolae*	Letters
Exp. i. ep. ad Rom.	*Epistolae ad Romanos inchoata expositio lib. 1*	Unfinished Commentary on the Letter to the Romans
Exp. ep. ad Gal.	*Expositio epistolae ad Galatas*	Commentary on the Letter to the Galatians
Exp. ep. Iac. ad d. t.	*Expositio epistolae Iacobi ad duodecim tribus*	Commentary on James' Letter to the Twelve Tribes

Exp. q. p. ep. ad Rom.	*Expositio quarumdam propositionum ex epistola ad Romanos*	Statements in the Letter to the Romans
Loc. in Hept.	*Locutionem in Heptateuchum lib. 7*	Sayings in the Heptateuch
Post coll. c. Don.	*Post collationem contra Donatistas lib. 1*	After the Meeting with the Donatists
Pr. et test. c. Don.	*Probationum et testimoniorum contra Donatistas lib. 1*	Proofs and Testimonials against the Donatists
Ps. c. p. Don.	*Psalmus contra partem Donati*	Psalm against the Donatist Sect
Quaest. Evang.	*Quaestiones Evangiolorum lib. 2*	Questions on the Gospels
Quaest. c. pagani	*Quaestiones expositae contra Paganos numero sex*	Six Questions against the Pagans (Letter 102)
Quaest. in Hept.	*Quaestiones in Heptateuchum*	Questions on the Heptateuch
Quaest in Mt.	*Quaestiones sedecim in Evangelium secundum Matthaeum lib. 1*	Sixteen Questions on the Gospel according to Matthew
Regula	*Regula ad servos Dei*	Rule of the Servants of God
Retract.	*Retractiones*	Retractions
Ad Caes. eccl.	*Sermo ad Caesariensis Ecclesiae Plebem*	A Sermon to the People of the Church of Caesariensis
Ad cat. de symb.	*Sermo ad catechumenos de symbolo*	On the Creed, to the Catechumens
De disc. Chr.	*Sermo de disciplina Christiana*	On Christian Discipline
De urbis exc.	*Sermo de urbis excidio*	Sermon on the Sack of Rome

De util. ieiunii	*Sermo de utilitate ieiunii*	Sermon on the Utility of Fasting
Serm.	*Sermones*	Sermons
Solil.	*Soliloquiorum lib. 2*	Soliloquies
De s. Script.	*Speculum de sacra Scriptura*	The Mirror of Scripture
In Io. ev. tr.	*Tractatus in Ioannis Evangelium*	Tractates on the First Letter Of John

OTHER STANDARD ABBREVIATIONS

AS *Augustinian Studies*

ATA *Augustine through the Ages: An Encyclopedia*, Ed. Allan D. Fitzgerald, OSA (Grand Rapids, Michigan: William B. Eerdmans, 1999).

CS *Church and State through the Centuries*, Eds. Sidney Z. Ehler and John B. Morrall (London: Burns & Oates, 1954).

DECT *Documents in Early Christian Thought*, Eds. Maurice Wiles and Mark Santer (Cambridge: Cambridge University Press, 1975).

HMPTW *A History of Mediaeval Political Theory in the West*, 6 Vols., Sir R. W. Carlyle and A. J. Carlyle (Edinburgh and London: William Blackwood & Sons, 1962).

IJE *International Journal of Ethics*

Chronology of the Main Events in Augustine's Life up to His Baptism

354   Augustine is born to the pagan Patricius and the
                    Christian Monica at Thagaste, in Roman North Africa.
                    The day is 13 November, a Sunday. On the insistence of
                    his mother, he is signed with the sign of the Cross and
                    seasoned with salt as he leaves her womb.
354–365   Infancy and begins to undergo his first studies.
ca 365–369   Goes to study in Madauros, a small but relatively well-
                    known intellectual centre, also in Roman North Africa.
370   Returns to Thagaste, where he is forced to spend a
                    frustrating year in idleness while Patricius gathers the
                    funds to send him to the University of Carthage.
371   With the help of Romanianus, a rich relative and
                    patron, Patricius obtains the funds and Augustine
                    travels to Carthage for the first time. He is struck by the
                    licentiousness of the big city.
372   The death of Patricius. Augustine takes a concubine.
373   Reads Cicero's *Hortensius* and is inspired by it to a
                    love of wisdom. Probable date for the birth of his
                    son, Adeodatus. At this time he also comes under the
                    influence of the Manichees, becoming an auditor in their
                    sect. He will retain this status for 11 years.
375   Returns from Carthage to Thagaste with the plan of
                    teaching there.

376   The death of a great friend hastens his return to
           Carthage.
380   Writes *De pulchro et apto*, which has since been lost.
383   Faustus of Milevis, the famous Manichean teacher,
           arrives at Carthage to meet Augustine and answer some
           of his more pressing questions on Manichean doctrine.
           Augustine likes the man but finds his answers very
           unsatisfactory. Later in the same year he departs to teach
           at Rome.
384   In the autumn, under the aegis of the pagan Prefect
           of Rome, Symmachus, he is nominated Professor of
           Rhetoric at Milan. Begins to formally dissociate himself
           from the Manichees and starts to take a professional
           interest in the sermons of Ambrose, the brilliant and
           charismatic Bishop of Milan.
385   In the late spring Monica arrives at Milan. Encouraged
           by Monica, Augustine begins to come under the
           influence of Ambrose's teaching and personality. Having
           completely given up his Manicheism, and now, as it
           were, faithless, he begins to style himself as something of
           a skeptic after Cicero and the Academics.
386   Probably in June, he reads the books of the Platonists
           for the first time. These equip him with the language and
           concepts of idealism. With their help he begins to clear
           his mind of its former materialism and starts to see sense
           in Christian philosophy. By supplementing these books
           with the writings of St Paul, he learns of the necessity
           of Grace and conceives new hope of finding the truth.
           Towards the end of June he receives Ponticianus, and
           shortly after that he is converted in the garden of the villa
           he is renting from a friend in Milan. In September he
           travels to Cassiciacum with his mother, son, other close
           relatives and like-minded friends to establish his new
           life as a Christian intellectual. In November he writes

Contra Academicos and *De beata vita*. He also promises his patron, Romanianus, a book on *De vera religione*. In December he writes *De ordine*. Some time in winter he writes the *Soliloquia*.

387   He returns to Milan at the beginning of March. On 24 April he is baptized alongside Adeodatus by Ambrose.

Introduction

In this work we are to concern ourselves with the contribution that St Augustine of Hippo makes to the history of political thought in the West. In the first instance, this will involve us in analysing the processes by which his political ideas were received and interpreted in that history from his death onwards. We will see how generally his thoughts on man, society and the state have been misrepresented by thinkers motivated by agendas other than his own, and in addition to this we will learn how ambiguities in many of his more important ideas have only encouraged this tendency. In the second instance, our concern to correctly represent his political ideas will cause us to propose a novel approach to them. We will argue that the formative events of his life are a kind of master key to them: that in his own struggle to make terms with God, Augustine laid down the prototype for his later doctrine of the Two Cities, and that at the heart of this doctrine is an unexpected understanding of discipleship which makes obedience to the spoken word of God the requirement of human freedom. It may also be stated at the outset that it is this understanding of discipleship, and its chief institutional form, the Pilgrim City, that we will eventually propose as Augustine's innovation in political thought. For of course it was to a very different kind of freedom that Augustine first aspired as a young man. In the philosophical literature of pagan antiquity he encountered freedoms that were predominately based in intellectualist conceptions of law. From the presocratic philosophers onwards, the idea of a law of nature would come to dominate

1

the Western mind: in fact it would effectively become the paradigm of wisdom and salvation. The idea that the observable laws of the natural and human worlds anticipate a similarly ordered intelligence, and that this intelligence is the location of the enlightening principles of wisdom, would go on to inspire diverse schemes of salvation. It is well known that Augustine dabbled in some of these as a young man. However, unlike many of his contemporaries, he possessed a personality that made it impossible for him to be entirely content with the idealism of these schemes. As we will have occasion to observe in later chapters, Augustine's outstanding characteristic, from boyhood to old age, was his lack of sentimentality. Where so many others before and after him found comfort in sentimentalizing their intellectual experiences, he did not. His suspicion of the human condition and the motives that drive it was profound, and he would remain its sternest critic until his death. His own salvation was, when it came, his complete rejection of the narratives of human progress and development that he had been taught as a child and then as a man. In the account of his conversion that he would leave in his *Confessiones*, Augustine would identify these narratives with the potent myth of the 'two natures': the idea that good and evil originate in two distinct natures within us, and the corresponding idea that, inasmuch as our evil nature implicates us in the general corruption of the universe, our good nature is a spark of the Divine within us and intimates the possibility of an intellectual meeting place with God.[1]

Given that the purpose of this book is to present Augustine's political ideas in their original, pristine disposition, we should briefly say something on the need for this. Anyone who chooses to write on Augustine's political ideas faces an immediate and well-documented problem. It is that in approximately 5 million words of books, treatises, sermons and letters, he never once wrote to an explicitly political purpose. It is a problem that has been most acutely felt by those who teach him. Herbert A. Deane is a good example of this:

In no single work by Augustine, comparable to Plato's *Republic*, Aristotle's *Politics*, Hobbe's *Leviathan*, or Hegel's *Rechtsphilosophie*, can his leading ideas about man, society, and the state be found. Nor can the student be sent to a work where Augustine expounds his entire philosophy, including his teachings on these subjects. He never produced a synthesis of his thought like the *Summa Theologica* of St. Thomas, which contains orderly, systematic treatments of such topics as law, justice, and obedience.[2]

Unsurprisingly, the absence of such an authoritative work has decisively influenced the transmission and reception of Augustine's political ideas down to the present day. For nearly 1,600 years they have been subject to all manner of mercenary treatment at the hands of thinkers committed to making capital out of their ambiguity. That makes for an extremely complicated tradition of interpretation – far too complicated to be considered in any serious detail in the course of our enquiry. However, in Chapter 4, we do nonetheless commit ourselves to making some attempt to consider it, if only under its three main aspects: first, political Augustinianism;[3] second, Augustinian political-theology; and third, Augustinian political theory. We should point out, of course, that these aspects follow a rather loose chronological order: loose in the sense that there is in reality a great deal of overlap between them. Nonetheless it is an order that is worth persisting with for the clarity that it brings to such a complicated tradition. The expectation is that each of these aspects will stand for a period in which elements of Augustine's thought were harnessed to promote political agendas other than his own. In this sense they are a little like lenses that when held up against his writings bring certain areas of them into sharper focus than others. Making for these peculiar qualities of refraction are the political and religious preoccupations of each period, and in a way this really highlights the nub of the issue. In the absence of an authoritative Augustinian work on politics one must always view his political ideas through someone else's lens. That is to say, it is very hard to get at their original disposition in his mind. Of course it goes without saying that some lenses are significantly less distorting than others, but ground into each is a distinctly un-Augustinian agenda, and that is the problem. In Chapters 1, 2 and 3 we deal with some of the important

preliminary matter to Chapter 4. In Chapter 1 we summarize the effect of
Augustine's influence on the Western political tradition in terms of main
themes and trends; in Chapter 2 we introduce some of the key features
of the transition from classical to medieval political philosophy; and
finally, in Chapter 3, we draw attention to Augustine's specific rôle in this
transition as well as outlining the shape of his political ideas as we intend
to unlock them through the formative events of his life. This ends the
first part of our enquiry. In the second, we pursue a kind of intellectual
biography of Augustine from his early years to his conversion and retreat
to Cassiciacum. For our perspective on these formative years we take the
political category of 'citizenship'. We follow Augustine as he is initiated
into his citizenship of the Earthly City in the bourgeois[4] ambitions and
kindnesses of his parents; we then observe how the persistent ironies of
the Earthly City cause him to seek salvation in an idealistic embrace of
all that it is not; and finally, we learn how his withering assessment of
his efforts to engineer his own salvation brings him, humbled and speaking the truth about himself, before God. The high-water mark of our
intellectual biography is naturally Augustine's conversion. We should
briefly say something here about the approach that we plan to take
to it.

Augustine's conversion has attracted a great deal of attention from
scholars over the years. Generally, they have tended to regard it in terms
of an event of immediate and isolated significance, constructing debates
around what it was that Augustine was actually converted to: orthodox
Catholicism or some Neoplatonic compromise?[5] In a departure from
this tendency we are going to maintain that in the light of Augustine's
subsequent theology, that is, his understanding of discipleship, this is not
the correct approach to take. All the passion of Augustine's conversion in
the garden at Milan – the tears he shed, the hair he tore – was everything
to do with the old man that he was committing himself to giving up, not
some new set of beliefs that he was professing to adopt. Tellingly, there is
absolutely nothing in his account of it to suggest that it was a particularly
happy or joyous occasion for him. To the contrary, he describes genuine
terror and uncertainty as he nerved himself to face a future without the

securities, hopes and habits of old. Conversion of this sort is the promise to persevere in becoming a new creation: to learn to do without the compromises that characterize living in the Earthly City. It is the promise, in other words, to do what at the time must seem utterly impossible: nothing less than to give up the private morality of one's previous existence: that is, to abandon the mode of life that one pioneered against the unique and unasked-for circumstances of one's birth. As such, the mark of this sort of conversion is the way that it completely undoes a man; the way that it leads him to face what his fallen heart holds most dear, and the cruelty with which it asks him to give it up. And the point, as Augustine is so often at pains to make, is that it cannot just be given up once in a symbolic act; it has to be continuously given up in the 'actual present'[6] of a man's life, in what can fairly be regarded as repeated acts of death and resurrection.[7] These features make conversion an intensely political act. Not a naturalization ceremony, however, where the intention is to publicly signify oneself once and for ever, by a new set of beliefs, but a complete and continuing reorientation of heart.

Such considerations as these invite a fresh perspective on the greatest and most troubling mystery of Augustine's doctrine of the Two Cities: namely, questioning what '. . . kind of life the citizens of the City of God must lead during this pilgrimage'.[8] Due to the demands placed upon him as a Catholic bishop in Roman North Africa, Augustine was only able to address this question through the rigid constructions of his polemical and apologetic works.[9] This, as Dyson has pointed out in the Introduction to his translation of *De civitate Dei*, has made it all too easy for his characteristic doctrines to be dismissed as products of their time:

Because of the original sin, then, each one of us comes into the world worthy of damnation: subject to the 'necessity of death'. This, to Augustine's mind, is the dominant fact of our individual and social existence. He does not really explain to us why or how the original sin has such consequences for all mankind, rather than merely for those who committed it; and he does not discuss the obvious difficulties which his view encounters. God's dispensation is hidden from us, but we are not entitled to question its fairness. It is, he considers, a matter of faith that the subsequent condition – moral, social and political – of mankind has been determined by the sin of our first parents.[10]

And yet this conviction was not merely a 'matter of faith' for Augustine: his *Confessiones* show that he was convicted of it in every act of his life, however trivial. As W. J. Sparrow Simpson pointed out, it was precisely for its '. . . inability to correspond with the facts of human experience . . .'[11] that Augustine was not satisfied by Neoplatonism. Consequently if we are apt to be fascinated by the combinations of reason and faith in his thought, then it is largely because we are not taking the events of his life seriously enough or, at any rate, as seriously as he seems to have wanted us to take them:

> The profit [*fructus*] of my confession is that I confess not what I have been, but of what I am; and that I confess this not only before Your Face in secret, rejoicing and trembling, and fearing but hopeful [Ps. 2.11], but also in the ears of believing sons of men: those who partake of my joy and share in my mortality: my fellow citizens and pilgrims with me . . .[12]

We plan, then, to approach as nearly as possible to the original disposition of Augustine's political ideas in his mind by exploiting the insight that his formative intellectual experiences are a striking analogue of his doctrine of the Two Cities. And of course we cannot claim to be surprised by this correspondence between the events of his life and his most enduring political statement. For after all, the latter was never written with any political intention in mind: it was from first to last a work of theology, or discipleship. Indeed this general point could be made of all Augustine's so-called 'political ideas'. For the fact is that Augustine, though customarily given a position of great importance in the Western political tradition, was not, strictly speaking, a political thinker. He was a thinker (that is, a fifth-century Church theologian) some of whose ideas went on to have considerable political repercussions. This means that it is, strictly speaking, inaccurate to talk of Augustine's 'political ideas' or of his 'political theory'; though it need not, as Dyson has pointed out on a number of occasions, be in any serious sense misleading.[13] For from the historical point of view, the factors that go into making a particular idea 'political' are complex, and often it is the case that context turns out to be of far greater moment than the author's original intentions. This has largely been Augustine's fate. As we will go on to discover, his political ideas are singularly depressing in their original disposition; indeed, it is difficult to imagine a less inspiring set of remarks on man, society and the state. Upon further reflection, it becomes possible to imagine that, had a definitive Augustinian political treatise been circulating in the medieval period, the history of Western political thought might have followed a very different line of development.[14] For instance, the papacy would have found it extremely difficult to enlist Augustine for its ambitious political program and, consequently, Pope Gregory the Great's (AD 540–604) policy of deference towards the temporal authorities might have come to set the terms of debate.

We have one additional methodological point to consider. It concerns our preference to understand the Western intellectual tradition on the principle of the laws of nature. That intelligence consists, essentially, in acts of discrimination, and that these acts of discrimination determine that knowledge takes the form of classes as well as the laws that govern the members of each class is a longstanding observation.[15] It is almost always attached to the corresponding thought that such a benignly-ordered universe can be no accident; that in his apprehension of this, man occupies a unique and flattering position in the animate world and, therefore, that his progress and development *vis-à-vis* the powers that be, whether supernatural (theology) or natural (science), is assured.[16] From the point of view of political historiography, these are, to use J. G. A. Pocock's term, 'cardinal assumptions'. In our case they are cardinal assumptions that transcend the merely political thought of the West because they have influenced 'all or several of its modes of organized thought'. Pocock's term for such cardinal assumptions is '*Weltanschauung*', and for the

narrative history written on their basis, '*Weltanschauungsgeschichte*'.[17]
That Augustine's political ideas – in particular his idea of the voluntarist
Will or Law of God – place him outside this narrative history will emerge
as one of the main themes of our enquiry.

Earlier we mentioned that the customary arrangement of Augustine's
leading political ideas is ambiguous at certain key points. Let us now
briefly elaborate what we mean by this. First, then, Augustine's leading
political ideas in his own words:

> We find that, in each man, as the apostle says, 'that *was* not first
> which is spiritual, but that which is natural; and afterward that
> which is spiritual' [1 Cor. 15.46]. Accordingly, each man is at first
> necessarily evil and fleshly after Adam, because he arises from his
> condemned stock. However, if he is reborn, and from that time
> on continues in Christ, he will afterwards be good and spiritual.
> We find this to be so also with the whole human race. When those
> two cities [founded by Cain and Abel] began to run their course
> by means of birth and death, the first to be born was a citizen of
> this age, while the second was merely a pilgrim in this age, belong-
> ing to the City of God. The latter was predestined by Grace and
> elected by Grace; by Grace he was a pilgrim below, and by Grace
> he was a citizen above. It is by Grace because, so far as he himself
> is concerned, he is of the same lump which was wholly condemned
> originally; but God, like a potter (and this simile is not impudent,
> but carefully chosen by the Apostle) made '[of the same lump] one
> vessel unto honour, and another unto dishonour' [cf. Rom. 9.21].
> But the vessel unto dishonour was made first, and afterwards came
> the vessel unto honour; this was done because, as we have said
> already, man is first false. From this derives the necessity that we
> begin thus as well as the necessity that we do not remain thus; for
> there later comes a state of virtue towards which we may advance,
> and in which we may abide when we have attained it. Hence, though
> not every bad man will become good, it is nonetheless true that no
> one will be good who was not originally bad.[18]

That, effectively, is Augustine's doctrine of the Two Cities. Because of Adam's Original Sin and expulsion from Paradise, all men are born into the necessity of paying a price they do not owe:[19] they arrive into this fallen world apart from God and condemned to die. Augustine characteristically calls them a *massa peccati* 'mass of sin'.[20] These two punishments are the conditions of their citizenship of the first, Earthly City,[21] and we notice that it is out of their nature especially that the first causes for ambiguity arise.

The claim that every human being pays the price for Adam's Original Sin in a corrupted nature generates obvious philosophical difficulties. Aside from it seeming terribly unfair that everyone should be implicated in a crime of such antiquity, there is the question whether this apparently unqualified assertion should invalidate Augustine's conception of human nature, the premiss for his bleak diagnosis of the human condition and all that follows from it.[22] Traditionally, the most successful political pessimists have sought to ground their conclusions about human nature in something more quantifiable than religious dogma (observed behaviour or scientific reductionism, for example),[23] and at a first glance it seems that Augustine does indeed derive the full authority for his conclusions from the Christian Scriptures. From the scholarly point of view this is difficult to accept. However, thanks in no small part to his keen powers of observation and description, Augustine has left behind him a conception of human nature that is still considered respectable today.[24] It may well have been the case that *he* had to believe before he could understand,[25] but the modern student of his political ideas has the luxury of being able to pass belief and go straight to understanding, so compelling, entertaining and numerous are the insights that he furnishes into human psychology. Many of these insights bear no obvious traces of their scriptural origins and, when gathered together, present a surprisingly contemporary perspective on the human condition. To this end it has often been remarked by scholars how peculiarly modern many of Augustine's social and political ideas are. As Stephen Sykes points out,

. . . Augustine is by turns startlingly post-modern and disturbingly

theological on the subject of justice. He seriously considers that the
proper definition of a 'people' and 'commonwealth' is the neutral
concept of an 'assembled multitude of rational creatures bound
together by a common agreement as to the objects of their love'. But
his preferred standpoint on 'justice' is that it can only exist when
the true God is acknowledged and worshipped.[26]

Later on there will be an opportunity for us to comment on the modernity
of his theory of political justice as well as his sociology of the Roman
religion.

Nearer to Augustine's own time, issues tended to congregate more
around the logistics and practicalities of the term Earthly City. For
instance, if everyone is at birth a citizen of the Earthly City, what serious
political significance can the term possibly have? Does such a definition
make it so wide as to be practically meaningless? Perhaps Augustine
merely intended for it to refer to the greatest or most notorious of the
cities or empires on earth at any one time? And from here it would be
easy to go on unfolding the possible difficulties of interpretation. Suffice
it to say, then, that Augustine's medieval interpreters, both ecclesiastical
and secular, and many of his later ones too, found it extremely difficult
to take his studied indifference to the various forms of politics seriously.
This indifference issued, as MacQueen has explained, in a broadening of
the standard classical connotation of the term *civitas* 'citizenship':

> Within the Roman Empire, [citizenship] had been based upon cir-
> cumstances of birth or upon a grant made by the Roman people:
> in the *Civitas Dei*, however, as also in its opposition, citizenship
> depends upon a deliberate act of free will involving the acceptance
> or rejection of Divine Grace.[27]

Far more mysterious than these ambiguities, however, are those sur-
rounding the second, Heavenly City. Augustine does not say that men are
condemned to their first citizenship without hope: there is the possibility
for them to take up new citizenship of the Pilgrim City (that portion of the

Heavenly City still sojourning on earth – Augustine variously calls them *peregrini* or *viatores*[28]). Once again there are problems of practicality and logistics, but these pale in insignificance beside those that surround the conditions of the new citizenship. In order to become a citizen of the Heavenly City, a man must be reborn; literally, as he was born into his first, earthly citizenship, so he must be reborn into his second, heavenly citizenship. But this time, of course, it is not through his mother's womb but by Divine Grace that he is born. However, and here is the most mysterious thing, this Divine Grace is not given according to merit; it is given entirely according to a hidden but perfect justice, and then only to certain men.[29] In other words, it absolutely cannot be earned by good deeds, and this, of course, is tantamount to saying that those undeserving men who receive Divine Grace are pre-selected or predestined to receive it. From the general human wreck God chooses to save them for reasons known only to Himself. He sends them the power to will to obey His sovereign commands and thus to persist as pilgrims of the Heavenly City while they are on earth.[30] As Bertrand Russell (1872–1970) concluded in his exposition of this aspect of Augustine's thought, 'Damnation proves God's justice; salvation, His mercy. Both equally display His goodness'.[31]

As it stands, this doctrine is clearly a scheme of salvation: it is political in what could only be regarded as a metaphorical sense. But the distinction begins to break down when one considers how often politics has claimed to be the salvation of mankind. The classical Greeks believed that politics was an ethical enterprise; that human fullness of nature could only be achieved in political community.[32] Since then there have been any number of attempts to realize fullness of nature or freedom or enlightenment or whatever one might prefer to call it through political means and, by the same token, schemes of salvation have just as often claimed to be political.[33] In the case being considered here, Augustine was writing as a bishop of the Catholic Church in the Christian Roman Empire; it was somewhat inevitable, then, that his thoughts should raise important questions concerning the actual correspondence between his doctrine and real earthly institutions, both secular and spiritual.

First of all we should point out that Augustine's Two Cities are not

really cities in the ordinary sense of the word. They are more like categories or classes of person; F. C. Copleston has helpfully called them
'camps'.[34] But at the same time this wide meaning need not preclude
them from providing the framework for detailed and insightful political
theory. As students of Augustine's political ideas have discovered, if the
limitations of his doctrine of the Two Cities are borne in mind, it can
still give a pleasing and intuitive shape to his political ideas. But what
sort of shape exactly?

Starting with the Earthly City, it makes it the setting for an uncompromising form of political pessimism. Broadly speaking, Augustine's
political thinking is reductionist in the extreme: that is, he derives all
political practices and institutions, from the smallest to the largest,
out of a particular conception of human nature. Needless to say it is
an extremely ungenerous conception. Augustine thinks that on their
own, outside of God's continuing Grace, men are unable not to sin.[35]
Correspondingly his definition of sin is so wide as to seem practically
meaningless: sin is, for Augustine, any action committed apart from
God's Will. This means that in their natural fallen state, men are unable
not to sin as the logical consequence of their being born apart from God.[36]
For Augustine, this fact leads to the difficulties that call politics into
being. As part of the rational creation, men are gifted with the ability to
choose what it is that they think will bring them true happiness and to
direct their wills towards its attainment.[37] This ability is a gift because
it allows their love to be the expression of their entire orientation as a
being.[38] Augustine thinks that, naturally, they choose to seek happiness
in all manner of things other than God, and that this brings them out of
alignment with His Will and the created order, and into conflict with each
other.[39] For him, then, 'politics' is the term that traditionally describes
the attempt to reconcile these competing interests in a conception of
the common life, and, insofar as by doing so it seeks to provide a stable
structure within which different 'experiments of living'[40] can play out, he
considers it the most articulate expression of fallen human nature: '. . .
for he who wishes to glory in his own lordship must surely see his power
diminished by the addition of a rival . . . Therefore the wicked contend

among themselves and with the good; likewise, the good contend with the wicked'.[41]

In short, Augustine thinks that there was no politics in Paradise. The ethical problem that politics is the preferred solution to – the question of what everyone should be doing at every point in order to bring about a useful and meaningful combination of interests[42] – could not have arisen in Paradise where Adam and Eve knew God and devolved all responsibility for the conduct of the actual present to His infinite wisdom. This means that for Augustine, politics never refers to some best constitution or theory; it is at one and the same time more and less than that: it is the condition of life in this fallen world.[43] Without its remedial effects, he thinks that men would simply fight each other to extinction. It is this important insight that allows him to be astonishingly indifferent to the various forms of government, for so long as each does the job of maintaining the apparatus of civilized life, he cannot legitimately fault it. As Deane points out,

> When [Augustine] tells a Christian ruler or magistrate that he ought to use his power not only to secure peace and prosperity for the people but also to promote and foster true religion and piety among them, he is reminding him of his duties as a Christian who is seeking to win eternal salvation – he is not discussing what a state must do if it is to be a state, nor is he advising the ruler to neglect the fundamental functions of the political and legal order.[44]

Moving now to the Heavenly City, one could say that it is what the Earthly City would desperately like to be but cannot. That is to say, it is in the Heavenly City that Augustine places all the virtues normally associated with the best kinds of political activity – peace, justice, freedom, happiness, enlightenment and so on.[45] When the Earthly City imagines that it has realized these virtues, it has in fact realized only imperfect imitations of them. That it can strive to realize them at all is because God allows men to retain an impression of the laws of nature on their hearts.[46] In practice this operates by a process of anamnesis as a faint recollection of what they once had but have since lost.[47] All of this has an important implication for the political theorist: the Heavenly City can have no exact counterpart on earth; that is, no city or empire, however great or saintly, and not even the institutional Church can presume to take on its rôle. The Heavenly City cannot, in other words, be the inspiration for anything made with hands, whether secular or spiritual. It is remembered in the common morality of men and forgotten in the imagination of their hearts. As Dorothy F. Donnelly writes,

> The appointed end of the City of God is an ideal life where man will enjoy everlasting and perfect peace, no longer subject to the wretchedness of mortal life. Thus unlike the utopists' description of an ideal organization of the state, Augustine's conception of an ideal existence is a vision of a mystical or spiritual state of being – in no sense is it an idealization of temporal life.[48]

Now there have, of course, been many 'heavenly cities' in history, each one judged on its outstanding virtues and proclaimed the leaven of civilization,[49] but for Augustine, it is precisely the fact that they are 'heavenly cities in history' that disqualifies them from consideration as such. For to his mind, human history as it has unfolded since the Fall is very different to what it might have been had Adam obeyed God. Since Adam's Original Sin, men have been walking apart from God, fashioning this world according to their own fallen understanding. In the imagination of their hearts, they are apt to think that, in its finest points, it is a paradise comparable to that which they left behind all those years ago. This leads them into regarding this world of their own construction as a perfectly legitimate point of reference for their thoughts on larger things.[50] For Augustine it seems that no weight of fact concerning their insignificant position in the grand scheme of things can dent this presumption, or convince them that their wills cannot influence the universal run of affairs:

> Just because human affairs appear all awry, let it not seem to us that they are ungoverned. For every man has been appointed to his

place; and yet to each it seems that there is no order. You just see what you want to be: for no matter what it is, the Master knows just where to put you. Imagine a painter: before him are placed various colours and he knows where to put each one. The sinner, of course, is determined to be the colour black; is the painter then at a loss to know where to put him? What things can be done with the colour black? What adornments can the painter make from it? From it he can make the hair, the beard, the eyebrows; though not, of course the face, for which he must use white. You just see what you want to be, then: do not concern yourself with where He puts you Who cannot err, for He knows just what He will do with you. And so it is that we see this accomplished in the common laws of the world. Some man (I do not know who) wants to be a house-breaker: the law of the judge knows that he has acted contrary to the law; the law of the judge knows where to place him; and it orders him most properly. He indeed has lived evilly; but not evilly has the law ordered him. From a house-breaker he will become a miner: and from the labour of the mines, how great works are constructed?[51]

To Augustine, considerations such as these make it pointless (but not altogether unhelpful) to speculate how history might have progressed had Adam not sinned in the Garden of Eden: for speculation is not the privileged, objective activity that men imagine it to be. To Augustine it simply cannot be when the conditions of life are the categories that help men to understand it. A striking example of what he surely meant by this is the birth of Western philosophy in Greece, in the sixth century BC. For then the Greeks set the habit of the Western mind by projecting the customary arrangements of the *polis* onto the universe:[52] in other words, they presumed that justice must pervade the universe and give a certain harmony to its parts because this is what it manifestly does in the *polis*.[53] But against this intellectual trajectory, the trajectory of Western science, Augustine would teach that there is no possibility of an independent perspective *vis-à-vis* God.[54] Categories like justice and goodness cannot legislate for the mind of God because by the logic of creation they are anterior to Him. Contrary to popular opinion, reason is just as much fallen as the rest of man, for the categories that it must operate by are not shared by God but are given by Him: 'I did not know that [reason] must be enlightened by another light in order to be a partaker in the truth, since it is not itself the essence of truth . . .'[55] Correspondingly, at any points at which this world seems pellucid to the human mind, it is only because it has been constructed by human hands. Otherwise, in its deepest and most mysterious aspects, the aspects that Augustine accounts for out of the greatness of God's Mercy, it is utterly impenetrable. We notice how this is partly borne out by modern moral philosophy. The finest efforts of the philosophers over the ages have shown that there is, for instance, no accounting by reason for the traditional lights of conscience; that is, for platitudes such as 'treat others as you would have them treat you', 'don't take another man's wife', and so on: the so-called laws of nature. This epistemological distance between man and God is one of the least-appreciated aspects of Augustine's thought; it is intimated in a great deal of what he has written but never stated explicitly, and as a number of distinguished Augustinian scholars have helped to show, including R. P. Mandonnet, Étienne Gilson and H.-X. Arquillière,[56] some of the most persistent misinterpretations of Augustine's political ideas have been justified on this perceived ambiguity in his understanding of the difference between what Mandonnet has called '. . . the order of rational truth and that of revealed truth'.[57] As such, one of the main aims of Chapters 1 to 4 will be to confirm this fact as the dominant or recurring theme in the history of the reception and interpretation of Augustine's political ideas. And further to this, it will also be one of our main aims to show that Augustine's political thought in particular, but also his entire mature outlook, is based in a firm and clearly worked-out distinction between the truths of reason and revelation, verification and illumination.[58]

To the political theorist surveying this scene, there must appear a troubling theoretical lacuna in the space between the political pessimism represented by the Earthly City, and what Henry Paolucci calls the 'prophetic utopianism' of the Heavenly City.[59] For ultimately, politics is a practical activity – the art and the science of government[60] – and yet there seems little in Augustine's doctrine of the Two Cities to support a practical arrangement of his leading political ideas. And that this is indeed a problem becomes apparent when one considers how many of them (the Sociable Nature of Man, Natural Law, the Spiritual and Temporal Spheres, The Christian Ruler, Just War and Religious Persecution, to name only the most obvious) do seem to point beyond the bleak diagnosis of his political realism to some cure, some positive reconciliation, however tentative, between politics and theology. It is this area of overlap and interaction between the Two Cities – the space effectively occupied by the Pilgrim City – that is of immediate concern to students of Augustine's political ideas. Understandably, then, they do not find it helpful to discover that the Pilgrim City's characteristic feature is a citizenship defined by a mysteriously administered Grace, and consequently it has been Augustine's fate to have his political ideas put into practical form by generations of scholars, many of them determined to claim his genius and authority for some or other cause. The crux of the problem, as we have identified, is the lack of an authoritative Augustinian political treatise or, what is really the same thing, a systematic presentation of his understanding of discipleship. Evidently such a work would challenge many of the assumptions governing the use of Augustine in political theory today, as well as calling into question his customary position in the history of Western political thought. What really is the relationship between the laws of nature and the Will of God in Augustine's thought? If the former are, as Dyson suggests, the backbone of the 'pagan theories of moral action',[61] how are they incorporated by Augustine into his Christian political philosophy? Is he simply prompted by dogma into a point-by-point rejection of all that is idealistic in classical political philosophy or does his alternative consist in something more substantial? When he gave up the books of the Neoplatonists for St Paul, how were his expectations about salvation affected? It has long been accepted by scholars that Augustine's was the mind that ended ancient thought and began medieval thought;[62] however, it is in the answers to these questions that the true significance of his rôle in this process lies.

Notes

1 *See* in particular *Confess.*, VIII, 10, 22: 'Let them be lost to Your Face, O God [cf. Ps. 67.1], in the same way as vain talkers and deceivers [*See* Tit. 1.10] of men's minds are lost who discern two wills in the act of deliberation; and who then go on to assert the existence of two natures of two minds, the one for good, the other for evil. They themselves are truly evil who think such evil. They will become good if they become familiar with the truth and consent to it, so that Your apostle may say to them, "For ye were sometimes darkness, but now *are ye* light in the Lord." [Eph. 5.8] However, thinking the soul's nature to be akin to God's, they wish to be light, not in the Lord, but in themselves. Thus they are made into a more pressing darkness, for, in a horrid pride, they have departed further from You Who are ". . . the true light which lighteth every man that cometh into the world."' [Jn 1.9] (author's translation).

2 Herbert A. Deane, *The Political and Social Ideas of St. Augustine* (New York: London, Columbia University Press, 1963), p. vii. Cf. Robert Dyson, *St. Augustine of Hippo: The Christian Transformation of Political Philosophy* (London: Continuum, 2005), pp. 4–5; Norman H. Baynes, *The Political Ideas of St. Augustine's* De civitate Dei (London: Historical Association, 1936), pp. 3–4; D. J. MacQueen, 'The origin and dynamics of society and the state according to Saint Augustine: part I', *AS*, Vol. 4 (1973), pp. 72–5; and Henry Paolucci (Ed.), *Political Writings of St. Augustine* (Chicago: Henry Regnery Company, 1962), pp. vii–ix.

3 This term is, of course, H.-X. Arquillière's, from his *L'augustinisme politique: Essai sur la formation des theories politiques du moyen-age* (Paris: Librairie Philosophique J. Vrin, 1972), p. 19.

4 It is Dyson who uses the term 'bourgeois' to describe the limitations of Patricius' outlook (Dyson, *St. Augustine of Hippo*, p. 1).

5 Joanne McWilliam's article, 'Cassiciacum dialogues', in *ATA*, pp. 135–43, is a cautious assessment of the debate.

6 We will continue to use this term to stand for the point of obedience to God's commands – commands that God gives *ad personam pro tempore expressa iussione* 'to a particular person at a particular point in time' (*De civ. Dei*, I, 21). Augustine distinguishes these commands from the *lex data* 'general, or covering, law' (*ibid.*). Obedience to God's commands is *in creatura rationali mater quodammodo est omnium custosque virtutem* 'the mother and guardian of all other virtues in a rational creature' (*ibid.*, XIV, 12). The philosophical implications of this scheme are obvious. George MacDonald was one who compared it to the felicity of the animals: 'The bliss of the animals lies in this, that, on their lower level, they shadow the bliss of those – few at any moment on earth – who do not "look before and

after, and pine for what is not" but live in the holy carelessness of the eternal *now*'. (quoted in C. S. Lewis (Ed.), *George MacDonald: An Anthology: 365 Readings* (New York: Touchstone, 1990), reading 314, p. 130. Cf. *De op. mon.*, XXVII, 35: '. . . since not for the sake of temporal things which pertain to tomorrow, but for the sake of those eternal things where it is ever-more today, have we proved ourselves to Him . . .' (author's translation).

7 See *De Trin.*, XIV, 5, 22–23; *Serm.*, IX, 13; *Serm.*, IV, 9; *Serm.*, CCCXLIV, 4.

8 *De civ. Dei*, XIV, 9.

9 That is, in dogmatic statements such as at *ibid.*: '. . . they must live according to the spirit and not according to the flesh; that is, according to God, and not according to man'.

10 R. W. Dyson, in the Introduction to his translation of the Cambridge edition of *The City of God against the Pagans* (Cambridge: Cambridge University Press, 2001), p. xvii.

11 W. J. Sparrow Simpson, *St. Augustine's Conversion* (London: SPCK, 1930), p. 91.

12 *Confess.*, X, 4, 6. (author's translation).

13 His latest statement to this effect comes in his *St. Augustine of Hippo*, p. 5. But *see* also his *The Pilgrim City: Social and Political Ideas in the Writings of St. Augustine of Hippo* (Suffolk: The Boydell Press, 2001), pp. xi–xii. Dino Bigongiari calls Augustine's social and political ideas 'by-products' of his theology; though he is careful to point out that they are 'fully as important as the theological ideas themselves'. (Dino Bigongiari, 'The political ideas of St. Augustine', in Paolucci [Ed.], *Political Writings of St. Augustine*, p. 343).

14 This is a point that Ernest Barker (1874–1960) draws special attention to in his Introduction to the reissued 1931 edition of John Healey's translation of *De civitate Dei*. He quotes Professor Harnack's (1851–1930) remark that, 'The history of Church doctrine in the West is a much disguised struggle against Augustinianism'. (Ernest Barker, in his Introduction to John Healey's translation of *The City of God* [London: J. M. Dent & Sons, 1931], p. iv).

15 Take, for example, R. G. Collingwood (1889–1943): 'In studying the world of nature, we begin by getting acquainted with the particular things and particular events that exist and go on there; then we proceed to understand them, by seeing how they fall into general types and how these general types are interrelated. These interrelations we call laws of nature; and it is by ascertaining such laws that we understand the things and events to which they apply'. (R. G. Collingwood, *The Idea of History* (Oxford: Clarendon Press, 1951), pp. 205–6).

16 In this case our example comes from Henry Drummond: 'The Natural Laws
   then are great lines running not only through the world, but, as we now
   know, through the universe, reducing it like parallels of latitude to intelli-
   gent order. In themselves, be it once more repeated, they may have no more
   absolute existence than parallels of latitude. But they exist for us. They are
   drawn for us to understand the part by some Hand that drew the whole; so
   drawn, perhaps, that, understanding the part, we too in time may learn to
   understand the whole'. (Henry Drummond, *Natural Law in the Spiritual
   World* [London: Hodder & Stoughton, 1884], p. 6)

17 *See* J. G. A. Pocock, 'The history of political thought', in Peter Laslett &
   W. G. Runcimann (Eds.), *Philosophy, Politics, and Society* (Oxford: Basil
   Blackwell, 1972), pp. 187–8.

18 *De civ. Dei*, XV, 1. (author's translation).

19 *De vera rel.*, XXVII, 50. Cf. *De civ. Dei.*, XII, 22; *Contra Faustum*, XXXII,
   14; *Contra Iul.*, IV, 16, 83.

20 *De div. qq. ad Simpl.*, I, 2, 16. Cf. *De div. qq. 83*, LXVIII, 3; *Confess.*, I, 7;
   Ep., CXC, 3, 12; *De civ. Dei*, XXI, 12; XIII, 3.

21 *Ench.*, VIII, 26; *De nat. et gr.*, III, 3.

22 *See* Dyson's comment that 'This view of human nature is . . . the major
   obstacle that Christianity encountered in coming to terms with pagan theories of moral action. Augustine is the first Christian author to confront this
   obstacle with a view to specifying in detail its implications for social and
   political life and relationships. It is this fact above all that gives his political
   thought its character'. (Dyson, *St. Augustine of Hippo*, p. 12).

23 *See* for instance how G. H. Sabine chooses to describe Niccolò Machiavelli
   as possessing the thought of '. . . a true empiric, the result of a wide range
   of political observation and a still wider reading in political history . . .' (G.
   H. Sabine, *A History of Political Theory* [London: George G. Harrap &
   Co., 1949], p. 301).

24 Probably the most enduring statement of this view, though tainted somewhat (unfairly) by its proximity to certain world events, was Deane's. *See*
   his *The Political and Social Ideas of St. Augustine*, p. 242.

25 *See In Io. ev. tr.* XXIX, 6.

26 Stephen Sykes, *Power and Christian Theology* (London: Continuum, 2006),
   p. 52.

27 MacQueen, 'The origin and dynamics of society and the state', 80.

28 See *En in ps.*, CXLIX, 5.

29 *De dono pers.*, XIII, 33. Cf. *Ench.*, XXV, 99; *Contra duas ep. Pelag.*, IV, 6,
   16.

30 For an analysis of Augustine's political ideas from the point of view of
   his doctrine of Predestination, see Dino Bigongiari, 'The political ideas

of St. Augustine', in Paolucci (Ed.), *Political Writings of Saint Augustine*, pp. 343–58. Bigongiari's comment that the facts of Augustine's doctrine of Predestination are 'hard to scrutinize' is generous: most thinking men would find them unconscionable insofar as they seem to preclude human freedom of will. However, as Dyson has neatly pointed out, the logic of Augustine's position can be softened at the expense of grammar: '. . . God knows eternally that Adam would sin'. (Dyson, *St. Augustine of Hippo*, p. 27). Augustine himself explained this on a number of occasions, most notably at *De civ. Dei*, V, 9–10 and *De lib. arb.*, III, 1, 1 – III, 4, 11. The crux of Augustine's argument was always that God effectively chooses, or predestinates, only those men whom He foreknows will freely choose to face Him with the truth of their hearts. See *Exp. q. p. ep. ad Rom.*, LV. Cf. *De div. qq. ad Simpl.*, I, 2, 13; *De corrept. et gr.*, IX, 23; *De praed. sanct.*, XVIII, 36 & 37; *Ep.*, CII, 2.

31 Bertrand Russell, *A History of Western Philosophy* (London: George Allen & Unwin, 1946), p. 383. Cf. *De civ. Dei*, XIV, 27: 'However, God preferred not to remove [Adam and Eve's] capacity for disobedience; and by this means He showed how great is the power of their pride for evil, and of His Grace for good'. (author's translation); *Opus imp. c. Iul.*, I, 22: 'In the same way, sin, however we choose to attribute it to infants, is the work of the devil; while man, however we choose to attribute to him the birth of sin, is the work of God'. (author's translation); *De nupt. et conc.*, I, 1.

32 Emblematic of this attitude is Aristotle's dictum, 'He who is without a polis, by reason of his own nature and not of some accident, is either a poor sort of being, or a being higher than man . . .' (Aristotle [tr. Ernest Barker], *Politics* [Oxford: Clarendon Press, 1960], 1253*a*, p. 6).

33 This strange determination is, in the opinion of Erich Fromm (1900–1980), explicable from the point of view of individual psychology: 'We see that the process of growing human freedom has the same dialectic character that we have noticed in the process of individual growth. On the one hand it is a process of growing strength and integration, mastery of nature, growing power of human reason, and growing solidarity with other human beings. But on the other hand this growing individuation means growing isolation, insecurity, and thereby growing doubt concerning one's rôle in the universe, the meaning of one's life, and with all that a growing feeling of one's own powerlessness and insignificance as an individual'. (Erich Fromm, *The Fear of Freedom* [London: Kegan Paul, 1945], p. 29). Cf. *De civ. Dei*, XIV, 15: 'For although, in Paradise, before his sin, man could not do everything, he did not at that time wish to do anything that he could not do, and therefore he could do all that he wished'.

34 In his *A History of Philosophy*, Vol. 2 (New York: Doubleday, 1962),
    p. 100. *See* also MacQueen's comment that, 'For Augustine the beginnings
    of the *civitas*, as an organised expression of man's social and political life,
    antedate the earliest records of secular history. Nevertheless this institution
    stems from a unity itself prior even to the most ancient forms of communal
    existence. The unity here in question is actually one of "racial stock" (*genus*)
    or origin, and the fellowship to which it has given rise precedes and in a
    sense transcends the entire human domain of the social and of the secular
    politics'. (MacQueen, 'The origin and dynamics of society and the state',
    pp. 78–9).

35 See *Contra duas ep. Pelag.*, II, 5, 9. Cf. *De pat.*, XXI, 19. *See* also J. N.
    Figgis' conclusion that '. . . a man can choose between ambition and self-
    indulgence, between the pride of heroism and the meanness of cowardice'.
    (J. N. Figgis, *The Political Aspects of St. Augustine's 'City of God'* [London:
    Longmans, Green, 1921], p. 46, quoted in Deane, *The Political and Social
    Ideas of St. Augustine*, n. 15, p. 251).

36 See *De civ. Dei*, XIV, 27: 'By the experience which followed from that
    [Original] sin, however, He demonstrated to all rational creatures, angels
    and humans alike, how great is the difference between each creature's pre-
    sumption and God's direction'. (author's translation) Cf. *Confess.*, VII, 20,
    26.

37 The non-rational creation do not possess this ability. In their case, instinct
    determines what will make them happy, and not possessing reason, they
    cannot question its judgement. *See* what Augustine has to say about this at
    Serm., VIII, 8.

38 This thought is a commonplace of Augustine's mature theology and a major
    plank of his political thinking. A man reveals his character most clearly in
    what he loves – so does a people – and it is this fact that Augustine draws
    on when making his most famous distinction between the Two Cities: 'Two
    cities, then, have been created by two loves: that is, the earthly by love of
    self extending even to contempt of God, and the Heavenly by love of God
    extending to contempt of self'. (*De civ. Dei*, XIV, 28. Cf. *En. in Ps.*, LXIV, 2;
    XXXIII, 2, 10; *In Io. ep. tr.*, VII, 8; VII, 7; *Confess.*, XIII, 9, 10; XI, 2, 3; II,
    1, 1; II, 5, 11; *ep.* CXL, 18, 45; *Serm.* CCCI, 11, 11. For a general discussion
    of the theme of 'love' in Augustine's thought *see* Giovanni Reale, *Agostino:
    amore assoluto* [Milano: Bompiani, 2001]). As we will explain in Chapter 1,
    this unsentimental approach to the human condition allowed Augustine to
    dispense with the philosophical problems traditionally associated with the
    concept of 'justice' – a fact which has long been recognized by scholars.
    See for instance, *HMPTW*, Vol. I, pp. 165–70. To this longstanding fact of
    scholarship, we will contribute the insight that the Western conception of

political justice is dispensed with by Augustine because it is implicated in the attempt to close the epistemological distance between man and God.

39 Augustine characteristically describes this disposition by means of a distinction between *frui* 'enjoying; serving' and *uti* 'using'. Only God is to be enjoyed or served as the *summum bonum* 'Greatest Good'. Man, however, insists on choosing other things for the *summum bonum*, and in this lies one of the chief practical manifestations of his estrangement from God. See *De doctr. Christ.*, I, 4, 4; *En. in Ps.*, XCV, 14. Cf. *Confess.*, IV, 12, 18; *De civ. Dei*, XV, 5.

40 This useful term is, of course, borrowed from John Stuart Mill (1806–1873). *See* John Stuart Mill (Ed. Geraint Williams), *Utilitarianism; On Liberty; Considerations on Representative Government* (London: J. M. Dent, 1993), p. 124.

41 *De civ. Dei*, XV, 5. (author's translation).

42 In Augustine's words, '. . . the Earthly City . . . establishes . . . a kind of co-operation of men's wills for the sake of attaining the things which belong to this mortal life'. (*ibid.*, XIX, 17).

43 See *De doctr. Christ.*, II, 39, 58; II, 25, 40.

44 Deane, *The Social and Political Ideas of St. Augustine*, p. 133.

45 See *De civ. Dei*, XV, 1–2.

46 *Ep.*, CLVII, 15; *De div. qq. 83*, LIII, 2; *De sp. et litt.*, XXVIII, 48; *De div. qq. ad Simpl.*, I, 2, 16; *De div. qq. 83*, LXXXII, 2; *In Io. ev. tr.*, XIX, 11–12; *Serm.*, IV, 6–7; *En. in Ps.*, LXI, 21.

47 See *De Trin.*, XIV, 15, 21.

48 Dorothy F. Donnelly, 'The City of God and utopia: a revaluation', *AS*, Vol. 8 (1977), pp. 122–3.

49 *See* Ernest Barker's discussion of them in the Appendix to his *Greek Political Theory: Plato and His Predecessors* (London: Methuen, 1960), pp. 445–52.

50 See *In Io. ev. tr.*, VI, 8, 16; *Serm.*, CXXIV, 3; *De civ. Dei*, X, 7; *Serm.*, CCCXVI, 16; *De div. qq. ad Simpl.*, I, 2, 16; I, 2, 22.

51 *Serm.*, CXXV, 5. (author's translation). Cf. *De civ. Dei*, V, 11; XIV, 27; XXII, 2; *De cath. rud.*, XIX, 31.

52 *See* Bernard Bosanquet's comments in his *The Philosophical Theory of the State* (London: Macmillan, 1925), pp. 1–15; and most especially his observation that, 'The [Greek] mind which can recognise itself practically in the order of the commonwealth, can recognise itself theoretically in the order of nature'. (p. 5).

53 For further general discussion of this subject *see* Sabine, *A History of Political Theory*, pp. 35–8; T. A. Sinclair, *A History of Greek Political Thought* (London: Routledge & Kegan Paul, 1967), pp. 10–19; Barker, *Greek Political Theory*, pp. 47–63; Sheldon S. Wolin, *Politics and Vision:*

Continuity and Innovation in Western Political Thought (London: George Allen & Unwin, 1961), pp. 28–34; Raymond G. Gettell, *History of Political Thought* (London: George Allen & Unwin, 1932), pp. 39–41; Malcolm Schofield, 'The Presocratics', in David Sedley (Ed.), *The Cambridge Companion to Greek and Roman Philosophy* (Cambridge: Cambridge University Press, 2006), pp. 42–73; John Burnet, 'Law and nature in Greek ethics', *IJE*, Vol. 7, No. 3 (April, 1897), pp. 328–33; Anthony Kenny, *Ancient Philosophy* (Oxford: Clarendon Press, 2004); and especially Ernst Cassirer, *The Myth of the State* (New Haven: Yale University Press, 1963), pp. 53–61.

54 See *De civ. Dei*, XIV, 11: 'God is, indeed, said to change His decrees; and we even read in the Scriptures that, figuratively speaking, God "repented" [Gen. 6.6; Exod. 32.14; 1 Sam. 15.11; 2 Sam. 24.16; cf. *De doctr. Christ.*, III, 40]. But such statements reflect a merely human perspective . . .'

55 *Confess.*, IV, 15, 25.

56 Others are Mathias Joseph Scheeben (*Dogmatique* [tr. Belet], t. III, p. 495), Paul Dumont ('Le supernatural dans la théologie de saint Augustin', in *Revue des Sciences Religieuses*, XLIV [1931], p. 515) and Charles Boyer (*Essais sur la doctrine de saint Augustin* [Paris, 1933], p. 184).

57 P. Mandonnet, *Siger de Brabant et l'Averroïsme latin au XIII siècle* (Louvain: Institut supérieur de philosophie, 1911), p. 55.

58 From what has just been said, it is clear that our argument is going to turn on a particular understanding of Augustine's illumination theory of truth. What is particular about it and how does it differ from conventional wisdom on the matter? Very briefly, it contends that Augustine's illumination theory of truth accommodates two types of knowledge: 1) knowledge of *a priori* analytical or logical principles (the kind of knowledge that is traditionally associated with illumination theories) and 2) knowledge of God's spoken commands in the actual present. Standard treatments of Augustine's episte- mology tend to focus on the former, because in the course of his writings, he did indeed develop an impressive theory of knowledge in the Neoplatonic tradition, claiming that principal ideas – that is, the ideas that stand behind the realities of the world and make a universal appeal to reason – reside in the mind of God and from there illuminate human minds. It is this theory of knowledge that Augustine applied to understand the laws of nature, and which he presents most clearly in his dialogue *De Magistro*. A very clear exposition of it is Bruce Bubacz, *St. Augustine's Theory of Knowledge: A Contemporary Analysis* (New York: Edwin Mellen Press, 1981), pp. 133– 62. However, our point is that this theory cannot account for the knowledge that Augustine associated with God's Will – the knowledge that sustained Adam and Eve in Paradise – and which was also a form of illumination. In

this respect this work is in large part an attempt to show that of Augustine's two understandings of illumination, it was the second that was the more politically significant, for it came to represent, in a purely negative and technical way, the achievement of the Pilgrim City in separating itself from the ordinary course of human history. The attempt to refer all of Augustine's remarks on Divine illumination to a single type of knowledge is hazardous, and has led scholars into great difficulties in the past. Of these, Gilson is the least misleading insofar as he attributes a merely formal quality to Divine illumination in Augustine's thought: it accounts for only the certainty of human judgements (Étienne Gilson, *The Christian Philosophy of St. Augustine* [New York, Random House, 1961], pp. 79–91). Ronald H. Nash, on the other hand, makes the error of presuming that Neoplatonism inspired Augustine's interpretation of the *Imago Dei*: 'The knowledge possessed by man can be regarded as a reflection of the truth originating in the mind of God. To be more specific, God has endowed man with a structure of rationality patterned after the Divine ideas in His own mind'. (Ronald H. Nash, 'Some philosophic sources of Augustine's illumination theory', *AS*, Vol. 2 (1971), p. 49. We might summarize these thoughts by saying that the effect of referring Augustine's remarks on Divine illumination to a single type of knowledge is always to close the epistemological distance between man and God to a point where it runs up against his numerous, characteristic statements about Divine omniscience in all matters (for instance, his declaration at *En. in Ps.*, XXXVI, 3 that, 'The Will of God is the Law of God).

59 Paolucci (Ed.), *The Political Writings of St. Augustine*, p. vii. In a note, Paolucci quotes Étienne Gilson to amplify what he means by this phrase: 'In [Augustine's] notion of a universal religious society is to be sought the origin of that ideal of a world society haunting the minds of so many today'. (Étienne Gilson, in his foreword to the *Fathers of the Church* edition of the *City of God* [New York: Catholic University of America Press, 1950], Vol. 1, p. xi) and *see* also *Les metamorphoses de la Cité de Dieu* (Louvain: Publications Universitaíres de Louvain, 1952), p. 288.

60 The phrase preserved in Justinian's (ca 483–565) *Digest*, though actually referring to law, is *ars boni et aequi* 'the art of what is good and equitable' (*Digest.*, liber I, titulus I, *De Iustitia et Iure*).

61 Dyson, *St. Augustine of Hippo*, p. 12.

62 *See* G. G. Coulton, 'Augustine', in *Studies in Medieval Thought* (London: Thomas Nelson, 1940), p. 24.

1

Augustine's influence on the Western political tradition

It is generally accepted that the history of Western political thought begins with the start of serious philosophical thinking in Greece in the sixth century BC, and that from there it runs roughly parallel with the history of philosophy, initially existing only as the practical aspect of moral philosophy but later emerging as a subject in its own right in accordance with the general secularization of European thought in the sixteenth century.[1] During this time it is shaped by three significant events.

TEMPORALITY, ETERNALITY AND THE IDEA OF A LAW OF NATURE

The first of these events is the intellectual preoccupation with absolute truth conceived as a function of the reasonable and benign ordering of the universe – the intellectual preoccupation first associated with the presocratic philosophers and their curious determination to explain the universe on a principle of natural justice.[2] This scientific approach immediately supersedes the mythopoeic outlook of old and makes possible the conception of politics as a practical activity chiefly concerned with the correct rational ordering of the community. Furthermore, by suggesting the pregnant association of 'correct rational ordering' with the moral language of terms such as δίϰε 'the way of righteousness' and λόγος 'the justifying word', it also equips the mind to think of politics as a possible vehicle for human fullness of nature:[3] that is, the prototype for all subsequent thinking on ideal states, utopias and heavenly cities.[4]

The second event consists in the concerted efforts of Plato (BC 427–347) and Aristotle (BC 384–322) to see in the form of the Greek city-state and its unique institutions the possibility of political perfection on the lines laid down above. Although the momentum of events about them is moving against the viability of the city-state as a discrete political unit (and towards the federated empire of Alexander (BC 356–323), they persist in allowing its language and customs to frame their thoughts on such perennial political themes as 'justice', 'equality', 'obligation', 'law' and 'freedom'.[5] This romantic approach causes them to neglect the rôle of human nature in society and to overstate the possibilities of politics.[6] Consequently the keynote of classical moral and political philosophy is its justification '. . . of the *polis* as a community ordered to a common and rational good'.[7] Only politics can fully form a man in accordance with his better nature and place him in alignment with the universal scheme of things.

The third event is Augustine's systematic dismantling of this enthusiasm as he receives it in the form of the pagan Roman Empire. To the Greek political tradition that it inherits wholesale, Rome adds a characteristic note of hard-nosed pragmatism. For to the Roman mind the essence of politics must lie in what is practically possible: political thought must address real problems of rule and order. This difference of disposition shifts political thought away from the question of the good or ideal life and towards problems of efficiency and organization, and the chief expression of this becomes the Roman preoccupation with law.[8] Furthermore, the need to govern a growing empire of diverse peoples sees a corresponding emphasis in Roman political practice on the individual and his rights. For traditionally recognized by the Roman people as an institution of necessity, as one of the conditions of civilized life, the Roman state is never called upon to furnish the good life as in Greece. To the contrary, it comes to conceive its great gift to the world as the imposition and administration of the proper apparatus of life. This apparatus eventually finds its characteristic expression in the convictions of the Roman lawyers about certain foundational principles of right, and of their embodiment in the outstanding examples of Roman political practice.[9] However this practical approach does not mark a break with the chief assumption of classical political philosophy: the assumption that a kind of universal justice *will* vindicate the best efforts of men: the assumption, in other words, that the universe must submit to human categories of understanding, and that in this submission lies the key to human freedom and enlightenment. Correspondingly, the characteristic feature of Roman moral and political philosophy (even if it is very seldom stated explicitly by the authors in abstract terms), comes to be the conviction that ethical truth *is* practical wisdom revealed in time by the natural growth of the best (that is, Roman) institutions.[10] And this allows us to notice with A. J. Carlyle this instructive similarity between the Roman approach to politics and that pioneered in England towards the end of the eighteenth century and represented chiefly by the ideas of Edmund Burke (1729–1797): '. . . the conception of the constitution of a state as an organic growth in contradistinction to the conception of it as a mechanical product'.[11]

We can summarize these developments by saying that to the theoretical universe constellated by the Greek words δίχε, λόγος, νόμος 'political right' and εὐδαιμονία 'happiness', the Romans add *ius naturale*, *lex naturale* and *re publica* 'commonwealth'. Of the last of these terms, *re publica*, we have something more to say; this is by focusing attention on the strategy of Augustine's attack on the Roman moral and political tradition.

HUMAN NATURE, REASON AND POLITICAL EXPECTATIONS

The main theme of our narrative to this point has been the commitment of the Western political tradition to a recognizably scientific understanding of justice. From the presocratics onwards, political right becomes permanently associated with a quality that we might fairly call 'cosmic alignment'. The best and most outstanding political arrangements are those that are demonstrably 'natural'; where to the Greeks demonstration might consist in abstract theory, and to the Romans, successful practice. And of course it goes without saying that this has continued to be the trajectory of the Western political tradition up to the present day; though now the criteria of truth are rather more exacting, as even the most cursory examination of recent landmark works on political justice will show.[12] It is against this particular understanding of political right and its utopian tendencies that Augustine directs his attack. What is it about the traditional Western approach to political justice that is so inimical to his understanding of the human condition?

The straightforward answer emerges as we consider what is effectively the suppressed premiss to the Western approach to political justice: the belief that men can achieve and maintain perfection in their social arrangements – a perfection that must by its very nature stand for the consummation and vindication of the universe and its processes. For in the first three books of Genesis, books that Augustine is apt to believe furnish a complete and accurate diagnosis of the human condition, God plainly teaches that men are born fallen, and, as such, can bring nothing truly good or just into being by the use of their wills. Indeed he thinks that even to qualify human endeavour by reference to goodness or justice or, as it has been rather clumsily termed above, cosmic alignment is to ignore the metaphysical restrictions of life under temporal conditions. For if it is the case that God conceives His plan for the universe in the eternity of His Mind, then it is logically impossible for its goodness and justice to translate into any kind of morality. It is logically impossible because moralities are by their nature constraining devices, designed to bring future actions under the jurisdiction of past priorities. This means that they can only exist in situations where the future is the subject of active speculation and the past the only possible point of reference. Moralities, in other words, were no part of Adam and Eve's experience in Paradise. For there they had only to look to God's Face in the actual present,

> . . . and without syllables of time they read upon it what Your eternal Will commands. They read Your Will; and choosing it they

love it. They read it always, and what they read never passes away [for it is without syllables that must depart in order to give up their meaning]. For by choosing, and therefore by loving, they read the actual immutability of Your Counsel [cf. Mt. 18.10].[13]

As we suggested in the Introduction, this outlook prevents Augustine from imagining that ethical terms such as 'goodness' and 'justice' intimate the possibility of an intellectual meeting place with God. The truths of reason and revelation are categorically different because men live in temporality and God lives in eternity: '. . . for though our knowledge is under the sway of those three varieties of time, namely, past, present and future, they do not affect that of Him "with Whom is no variableness, neither shadow of turning" [Jas 1.17]'.[14] Augustine's point is made by saying that reason is just as much fallen as the rest of man. Of course it is in man's best interests to believe that it is not; that it exists as a kind of spark of the Divine substance, but Augustine seems genuinely to think that fallen human reason offers no way to understanding God and His Wisdom.[15]

This amounts to a very different approach to politics than that pioneered in the Western tradition. The expectations that we customarily associate with political thinking are absent from Augustine's analysis of man, society and the state for, unlike other canonical political thinkers in the West, he is under no obligation to redeem politics.[16] Expressed in its most general configuration, the motif of the Two Cities has been an element in the political thought of the West since its inception. To justify the good life by referring it to some Weberian 'ideal type' – some heavenly city – was the genius of the classical Greeks. Since then, the West has been more or less continually committed to justifying its most cherished convictions about justice, freedom and rights on a principle of cosmic alignment. In today's intellectual climate this commitment has issued in a powerful irony. As Dyson puts it, '. . . the ambiguities and dangers of the "postmodern" world have both intensified the desire to believe in a universal morality and undermined the persuasive power of the "grand narratives" about reason and human nature upon which such belief depends'.[17] This disquieting clash between the moral and

intellectual consciences[18] of man is addressed directly by Augustine and
made the centerpiece of his political vision. In his willingness to take the
Genesis narrative seriously, that is, in his willingness to see in it a possible diagnosis of the most troubling aspects of his life (chief among these
being his propensity to do evil for evil's sake), Augustine liberates himself
from the desire to seek a comforting correspondence between the Earthly
City and the Heavenly City. The result is an unexpected independence of
perspective and a true objectivity that raises serious questions about his
position in the history of Western political thought.

CICERO, AUGUSTINE AND THE ASSUMPTIONS
OF CLASSICAL POLITICAL PHILOSOPHY

It is this outlook that informs Augustine's unequivocal definition of political justice at book XIX, 21 of his *De civitate Dei*, the definition that he
produces in response to Cicero's (BC 106–43) qualification of the Roman
re publica. Against Cicero's contention that a *re publica* is *rem populi*
'the property of the people',[19] where the people are *coetum multitudinis
iuris consensu et utilitatis communione sociatum* 'a multitude united in
fellowship by common agreement as to what is right and by a community
of interest',[20] Augustine proposes the following:

> In the course of the discussion, [Cicero] explains what he means
> by 'common agreement as to what is right', showing that a com-
> monwealth cannot be maintained without justice. Where, therefore,
> there is no true justice there can be no right. For that which is done
> according to what is right is invariably a just act, whereas nothing
> that is done unjustly can be done according to right. But the unjust
> institutions of men are neither to be called right nor supposed to be
> such . . . Where there is no true justice, then, there can be no associa-
> tion of men 'united in fellowship by common agreement as to what
> is right', and therefore no people according to the definition of Scipio
> or Cicero . . . If, therefore, a commonwealth is 'the property of a

people', and there is no 'people' where there is no 'common agreement as to what is right', and if there is no right where there is no justice, then it follows beyond doubt that where there is no justice there is no commonwealth. Moreover, justice is that virtue which gives to each his due. What kind of justice is it, then, that takes a man away from the true God and subjects him to impure demons?[21]

By claiming that the pagan Roman commonwealth cannot be the natural and perfect embodiment of justice because it manifestly does not grant to the one true God the praise that is due Him by rights, Augustine proclaims his intention to break with the Western political tradition. It is not that he is suggesting that 'justice' and words like it should be struck from the political vocabulary, but rather that they should refer to the reality of life in a fallen world. This is the logic that leads him to make his infamous suggestion that with '. . . justice removed, then, what are kingdoms but great robber bands?'[22] If true justice on earth is impossible because the truths of reason are categorically different to the truths of revelation,[23] then politics should not be considered a privileged activity – the vehicle for human fullness of nature, or any such thing. The virtues that politics produces and perpetuates are real and valuable in the sense that they furnish the conditions of life in a world turned from God,[24] but, by the same token, they cannot intimate the first principles of God's Will. They cannot be both the conditions of life in a fallen world and the source of its renovation and renewal. For as Augustine points out,

> . . . we must seek our good by faith as we cannot yet see it . . . By contrast the philosophers have imagined that the Final Good and Evil are to be found in this life . . . Out of a wondrous pride, these philosophers have correspondingly desired to be happy in this life, and to attain perfection by their own efforts. The Truth has derided such philosophers in the words of the prophet: 'The Lord knoweth the thoughts of man' [Ps. 94.11] – or, in the words of the apostle Paul, 'The Lord knoweth the thoughts of the wise, that they are vain' [1 Cor. 3.20].[25]

AUGUSTINE'S REALISM IN THE HISTORY
OF WESTERN POLITICAL THOUGHT

In terms of the subsequent trajectory of Western political thought, this realism is not Augustine's legacy. He lived through the sack of Rome in AD 410 and died just as the barbarians were starting to make good their hold on the Roman Empire. Political history from this point onwards would be dominated by the growing ascendancy of the Catholic Church relative to the newly developing barbarian kingdoms and, in time, the emergence of the new geopolitical concept of Latin Christendom: two coordinate powers, Church and State, triumphantly ruling a territory conceived in terms of the old Roman Empire. Nothing could be further removed from the stark image of the Pilgrim City, a sojourner in a hostile world, '. . . ambushed and beset by fugitives and deserters, under their leader, the lion and the dragon'.[26] Yet throughout the papacy's rise as a viable political enterprise, during the political-theology of the Reformation, and after that, for the time in which political theory developed as a distinct, secular discipline, Augustine continued to exert a significant influence; to inspire thinkers with his language and ideas, and to set the terms of debate in many areas of political discourse. How can we explain this discrepancy between his ideas and their misuse?

We might begin by adapting Professor Harnack's contention, 'that the history of Church doctrine in the West is a much disguised struggle against Augustinianism'.[27] The inspiration for this thought was evidently Harnack's consideration of the fact that Augustine took seriously the fallen nature of this world: that he remained convinced that although it is absolutely subject to God's sovereign Will, and thus pursues an end that men are obliged to call good and just, the logic of this state of affairs will very seldom be reflected in its arrangements (or at least in those arrangements subject to fallen human volition).[28] Consequently the Church has often been tempted to step into this breach and establish doctrinal grounds for a more positive understanding of God's plan for the world. Naturally, these grounds have involved it in thinking of itself and Christian society as something substantially more than Augustine's Pilgrim City.

By the same token, might we not then interpret the history of Western political thought after Augustine as 'a [not so] much disguised struggle against Augustinianism'? For after all, it was always Augustine's intention that his bleak diagnosis of the human condition should furnish the antidote to the moral optimism of the fallen imagination, and nowhere is this more clear than in his damning indictment of Rome's claim to be the leaven of civilization. His contention that individual and social perfection is only possible in a world where all are unceasingly illuminated by the Will of God places him outside the mainstream of developments in Western intellectual history. As a kind of political utopia, his City of God is unique for being a paradise where all share equally in the knowledge that makes true peace and justice possible.[29] Unlike in Plato's Republic, it is not just the philosopher-kings who can apprehend truth and act on it; all citizens of the City of God, whether they are pilgrims below or saints above, behold God's Face, hear His Voice and act on His Will. As a political proposition this goes squarely against the habits of the Western mind. Either it is the case that one man should rule on the basis of his claim to privileged knowledge, or it is the case that the possibility of such privileged knowledge should be discounted altogether, and a system of government established on the principle that all being equally ignorant of absolute truth, all should have an equal input into the decision making processes of the community. The former state of affairs has traditionally gone by the name of 'monarchy' or 'dictatorship'; the latter by the name of 'democracy'. Together they encompass the unique predicament of the Western political tradition: that short of taking fallen human nature and its effects seriously, one is impelled towards romantic expectations about politics.

In conclusion, then, the extent of Augustine's influence over the development of Western political thought should not in the first instance be measured in positive terms. Instead, attention should focus on how his uncompromising vision of the human condition gave the West its first clear picture of the reality that it must at all costs reject:

> They should not imagine to rejoice in the Final Good in this mortal
> age; for the traditional virtues [out of which the philosophers con-
> struct the good life] testify more to man's misery by the assistance
> that they give him in the face of dangers, hardships, and sorrows,
> than they do to his capacity to be sufficient to himself.[30]

As we will demonstrate, the so-called political Augustinianism of the
medieval period was the most cynical attempt to reject this vision insofar
as it greedily prostituted the carefully wrought distinctions of Augustine's
leading political ideas in the name of temporal power. In contrast, the
political theology of the Reformation fares rather better. Generally
speaking, the new context of the smaller, centralized European kingdoms
meant that less was at stake; consequently the political schemes of men
such as Luther (1483–1546) and Calvin (1509–1564) were able to miss
the point in more subtle ways. However, the rise of political theory as
a discipline in its own right, coupled with the rapid development of
Western science and technology, sparked new interest in the possibilities
of politics. During a period that the historian Carl L. Becker chose to
characterize with the phrase 'the heavenly city of the eighteenth-century
philosophers',[31] the Augustinian vision of the human condition would
come under renewed attack. This, after all, was the time when men like
Emmanuel Kant (1724–1804) were waking from their 'dogmatic slum-
bers'[32] to proclaim that,

> *Enlightenment is man's emergence from his self-incurred imma-*
> *turity. Immaturity* is the inability to use one's own understanding
> without the guidance of another. This immaturity is *self-incurred*
> if its cause is not lack of understanding, but lack of resolution and
> courage to use it without the guidance of another. The motto of the
> Enlightenment is therefore: *Sapere aude!* Have courage to use your
> own understanding![33]

It was somewhat inevitable, then, that this new scientific optimism about the human condition, about nature and its laws, and the capacity of human reason to understand them, would seek to position itself more aggressively than ever against an Augustinian vision proclaiming the ineffability of God, the poverty of reason and the inability of man to follow even his most basic calling as a social creature:

> As our salvation refers to hope, it is therefore in hope that we have been made happy. Moreover, as we do not in this sense possess the present means to our salvation, but rather await its arrival in some future state, we do not also enjoy the present means to our happiness, but look forward to a future happiness, and patiently. For we live amidst evils which we are enjoined to tolerate with patience; but this only until we arrive at those good things that will bestow immeasurable delight upon us, and where there will no longer be anything for us to tolerate. This is the nature of the salvation that awaits us in the age to come; it will also, as it were, be our final happiness. Yet these philosophers will not believe in something they cannot see. Thus, they endeavour to confect a happiness for themselves out of a virtue which is as false as it is proud.[34]

At Jer. 2.13, Augustine would have read the following: 'For my people have committed two evils; they have forsaken Me the fountain of living waters, *and* hewed them out cisterns, broken cisterns, that can hold no water'. It may be that it was against this way of living that Augustine chose to position the Pilgrim City.

Notes

1 Niccolò Machiavelli's (1469–1527) *Il Principe* and Thomas Hobbes' (1588–1679) *Leviathan* are landmark attempts to begin political thinking from the consideration of facts and experience rather than revelation and received wisdom.

2 *See* what F. M. Cornford has to say about this in his *From Religion to Philosophy: A Study in the Origins of Western Speculation* (London: Edward

Arnold, 1912), pp. 1–7. Cf. Henri Frankfort *et al.*, *Before Philosophy: The Intellectual Adventure of Ancient Man* (Harmondsworth: Penguin, 1961), pp. 250–4.

3 For an excellent introductory discussion of classical Greek political language *see* Sinclair, *A History of Greek Political Thought*, pp. 10–33; and Barker, *The Politics of Aristotle*, pp. xi–xxvii.

4 As John Bowle writes, '. . . far from theorizing *in vacuo*, that curse of much Western European and Eastern practice, the Greek thinkers tried to find out what the good life was, and to act upon it'. (John Bowle, *Western Political Thought: From the Origins to Rousseau* [London: Methuen, 1961], pp. 36–7).

5 Very briefly, the presumptions and preoccupations of the classical Greek political tradition as represented by Plato and Aristotle include the following:
   • that through an application of abstract reason to the problems of living, man can reduce the 'good life' to a science called politics (accepted by both Plato and Aristotle);
   • that the science of politics achieves its practical expression in law, the distillation by abstract reason of social truth from custom and myth (rejected by Plato in the *Republic*, but accepted with qualifications in the *Statesman* and the *Laws*. Accepted by Aristotle);
   • that this makes politics an ethical enterprise, and ethics a political one (accepted by both Plato and Aristotle);
   • that the symbol of this convergence is the state: the one true vehicle for human perfection (accepted by both Plato and Aristotle);
   • that the state mobilizes the good life through its division of labour, which furnishes the various stations of life (accepted by both Plato and Aristotle);
   • that these stations correspond to foundational differences in human nature (accepted by both Plato and Aristotle);
   • that because of this, the state is ontologically prior to man: it is the whole within which his life, as part, makes sense (accepted by Plato, exemplified in Aristotle);
   • that this makes a) classical Greek political thought ideological in the extreme, the archetype of all political doctrines that conflate the best interests of the individual and the community; and b) the supreme expression of political idealism, the romantic belief that politics represents both means and end (exemplified in both Plato and Aristotle).

6 As Barker points out, 'Politics is a matter for thought, and government is a concern of the wise. But wisdom is not the conclusion of the whole matter; nor can we afford to forget – what Socrates, and Plato after him, too, often tended to forget – those elements of will and of instinct which

count for so much in political affairs'. (Barker, *Greek Political Theory*, p. 112).

7 R. W. Dyson, *Natural Law and Political Realism in the History of Political Thought: Vol. I* (New York: Peter Lang, 2005b), p. 101.

8 As Cicero would seem to confirm in the opening declaration of his *De re publica* (I, 2, 2).

9 These convictions are expressed in the Roman lawyers' language of *ius* or *lex naturale* ('natural justice' or 'natural law'). For general discussions of their efforts at clarifying these ideas see A. P. d'Entrèves, *Natural Law: An Introduction to Legal Philosophy* (London: Hutchinson University Library, 1970), pp. 22–50; *HMPTW*, Vol. I, pp. 33–44 & 71–9.

10 A good example is Cicero's approving use of Cato's (BC 94–46) dictum at *De re publica*, II, 1, 2.

11 *HMPTW*, Vol. I, p. 14.

12 The most famous of these is, of course, John Rawls' (1921–2002) *A Theory of Justice* (London: Oxford University Press, 1973); but *see* also Robert Nozick, *Anarchy, State and Utopia* (Oxford: Basil Blackwell, 1974); Michael Walzer, *Spheres of Justice* (New York: Basic Books, 1983); and for something of a general overview, *see* the relevant chapters in Brian Barry, *Political Argument* (New York: Harvester Wheatsheaf, 1990).

13 *Confess.* XIII, 15, 18 (author's translation). This is, of course, Augustine's description of the *supercaelestes* 'supercelestials', or 'angels', but there is ample evidence to suggest that it was a description that he would also have applied to Adam and Eve's epistemological condition in Paradise. For instance, at *De civitate Dei*, XI, 12, he states his belief that '. . . the angels are not the only parts of the rational and intellectual creation whom we think it proper to call blessed. For who will venture to deny that the first human beings in Paradise were blessed before they sinned . . .' Generally speaking, Augustine defined the *rationalem vel intellectualem creaturam* as a class by their capacity to be illuminated, and thus formed, by the Light of God's Countenance. See his description of this process at *De Gen. ad litt.*, I, 1, 17: 'For when the eternal and unchangeable Wisdom, Who is not created but begotten, enters into spiritual and rational creatures, as He is wont to come into Holy souls, so that with His Light they may shine, then in the reason which has been illuminated there is a new state introduced . . .' Cf. *Serm.*, IV, 4.

14 *De civ. Dei*, XI, 21 (author's translation).

15 See *Serm.*, LII, 16: . . . *si cepisti, non est Deus* . . . 'If you have understood him, he is not God'.

16 This immediately places him at odds with the medieval political tradition which he is said to have initiated, for insofar as that tradition is represented

by the 'two swords' language of Pope Gelasius I (AD 492–496) (*see* his letter
to the Byzantine Emperor Anastasius I [ca AD 430–518], in *CS*, pp. 10–11),
that is, by the conviction that Church and State can play a coordinated rôle
in achieving the rational good of mankind, then he can be no part of it. He
can be no part of it because to his mind, it is precisely the desire to achieve
the rational good of mankind that taints all pagan philosophy – that makes
its exponents 'vain in the imagination of their hearts'. Correspondingly,
whenever Augustine recommends that secular rule should, in Dyson's
formulation, 'be conducted according to universal spiritual imperatives',
(Dyson, *St. Augustine of Hippo*, p. 142) he is not expressing a conviction
that could be justified in theory. He rather has in mind the Christian ruler
standing as an individual before God, prompted by God's Will in the actual
present and unencumbered by any ideological considerations.

17 Dyson, *Natural Law and Political Realism in the History of Political
    Thought: Vol. II*, p. 228.

18 This distinction between the moral and intellectual consciences is first made
    by Olaf Stapledon in his article, 'Mr. Bertrand Russell's ethical beliefs', *IJE*,
    Vol. 37, No. 4 (Jul., 1927), pp. 390–402.

19 Cicero, *De re publica*, I, 25, 39.

20 *Ibid.*; Cf. *Ep.*, CXXXVIII, 2, 10.

21 *De civ. Dei*, XIX, 21.

22 *Ibid.*, IV, 4. To amplify his point, Augustine mentions with approval the
    story of Alexander and the pirate, which Dyson thinks would probably
    have been known to him in the version given at book III of Cicero's *De re
    publica*. When asked by Alexander what he meant by infesting the seas, the
    pirate apparently answered: 'the same thing as you mean by infesting the
    world; but because you do it with a great fleet, you are called an emperor,
    and because I do it with a small ship, I am called a pirate!'

23 See *ibid.*, XI, 21: '. . . [God] views things in a way that is in every sense
    different to our customary manner of thinking. For His thought does not
    need to change as it passes from one thing to another: it beholds all things
    at once [without syllables of time]'. (author's translation).

24 See what he has to say about this at *ibid.*, XV, 4.

25 *Ibid.*, XIX, 4 (author's translation).

26 *Confess.*, VII, 21, 27.

27 See n. 14 above.

28 The last point in parentheses refers to Augustine's 'privation theory of evil':
    his understanding that all created things being good as a condition of their
    existence, evil can have no existence in itself, but is the consequence of voli-
    tion apart from God. See *De civ. Dei*, XI, 17: 'For there is no doubt that
    wickedness can be a blemish or flaw only in a nature that was not previously

flawed'. Cf. *Confess.*, II, 5, 10; *De civ. Dei*, XV, 22; *De Gen. ad litt.*, VIII, 14, 31.

29 *See* his description of this epistemological state at *De civ. Dei*, XV, 3.

30 *Ibid.*, XIX, 4 (author's translation).

31 This is, in fact, the title of his book on the subject: Carl L. Becker, *The Heavenly City of the Eighteenth-Century Philosophers* (New Haven: Yale University Press, 1969).

32 Kant always claimed that it was David Hume (1711–1776) whose thought first 'woke him'.

33 Emmanuel Kant, 'An answer to the question: what is enlightenment?', essay dated 30 September 1784, quoted in David Williams (Ed.), *The Enlightenment* (Cambridge: Cambridge University Press, 1999), p. 2.

34 *De civ. Dei*, XIX, 4 (author's translation).

2

From classical to medieval political philosophy

What political and religious preoccupations influenced the transmission and reception of Augustine's political ideas during the medieval period? Without any serious risk of oversimplification it is possible for us to represent them at the outset as three interrelated themes:

1. The persistence of the concept of *imperium* (empire) as the major focus of political hope and ambition;
2. The persistence of the concept of the *res publica Christiana* (Christian commonwealth) as the major focus of religious hope and ambition;
3. The large question of *auctoritas* (authority) thrown up by the over-lapping of these two jurisdictions.

Taken together they represent a cast of mind – a medieval cast of mind. This last fact becomes apparent once we note the suppressed premiss to all three themes, namely, the belief that '. . . secular rule can and should be conducted according to universal spiritual imperatives'.[1] In many ways this simple but heartfelt conviction, rendered neatly here by Dyson (for it was in practice a most untidy idea), proved to be the greatest political consequence of Christian monotheism. And it was a revolutionary con-sequence. The medieval, according to John B. Morrall, was,

> . . . the broad period within which the classical world's approach
> to the problem of political life was reversed, 'stood on its head', as

43

Marx would have put it. Instead of religion, as hitherto, forming the buttress for a communal political tradition, it was now elevated essentially above the political sphere and from this position of transcendence it bestowed on political authority whatever limited justification the latter possessed.[2]

ROME, COSMOPOLITANISM AND THE IDEA OF THE NATURAL EQUALITY OF MAN

As might be expected of such a momentous reverse, it was some time in the making. First the post-Aristotelian philosophies helped to establish freedom as an individual pursuit: that is to say, men were no longer obliged to look upon the state or the community as the one true vehicle for fullness of nature. Then Rome helped to reclaim this vision for politics. Where the city-states of Greece had proved too small for the new cosmopolitanism in religion and philosophy, Rome with her Empire was big enough to provide it with a meaningful political expression. To her must go the credit for pioneering a new conception of politics as the science and art of government: in other words, for making it self-conscious. For initially, it had simply been the consequence of a group religious practice. The original cities of Greece and Latium had been congregations of families, choosing to unite under some common worship and organizing themselves according to its rites and customs.[3] There was government of a fashion and there were even activities that we as moderns might recognize as political, but the point was that none of it was comprehended in abstraction from the overbearing religious context. There was, in other words, no political theory.

By the time of the Roman Empire this state of affairs had been comprehensively upset by the development of the philosophical criterion of truth and the collection of new anthropological data.[4] Men became accustomed to seeking better authorities than tradition for their customs and beliefs, a habit that the discovery of new cultures did nothing to discourage.[5] In most cases this effort to establish certainty took the normal course. Men began increasingly to look upon their particular experiences as intimations of a more general reality.[6] In a natural movement of the human mind they began to '. . . place certain principles beyond discussion, by raising them to a different plane altogether'.[7] This intellectual fashion was the beginning of what has come to be called the natural law tradition, but it would have to undergo a great many revisions before it was taken up by the lawyers of the Roman Empire and turned into a coherent principle of political right.[8] However, once this work was done, Rome would be left with an accurate idiom in which to express the reality of her political achievements and ambitions. For her gift to the antique world had been its first truly universal system of rule; that is, a system of rule founded on efficiency and effectiveness rather than the narrow morality of a particular people. As Zeller continues:

> Stoic apathy, Epicurean self-contentment, and Sceptic imperturbability, were the doctrines which suited the political helplessness of the age. They were therefore the doctrines which met with the most general acceptance. Suited, too, was that sinking of national distinctions in the feeling of a common humanity, that severance of morals from politics which characterise the philosophy of the Alexandrian and Roman period. Together with national independence, the barriers between nations had been swept away. East and West, Greeks and barbarians, were united in large empires, placed in communication, and compared in most important respects. In declaring that all men are of one blood and equally privileged citizens of one empire, that morality rests on the relation of man to man independently of his nationality and his position in the state, philosophy was only explicitly stating a truth which had been already partly realised in actual fact, and which was certainly implied within.[9]

It was A. J. Carlyle who first suggested that if there were to be such a thing as a rupture in the early history of Western political thought, then it had better be conceived as occurring somewhere between Aristotle and Cicero. For in the history of ideas, there is surely no more dramatic sea change than Cicero's insistence, against Aristotle and the whole tradition that he stands for, on the fundamental equality of man.[10] In Cicero's mind this sentiment becomes elevated and established as a kind of logical principle: it stands *a priori* behind all that he has to say about man, society and the state, and its recognition and recovery is, he thinks, Rome's outstanding gift to mankind:

> For one might say that whoever has been given reason by nature has also been given law: for reason is the same thing as right reason, and right reason consists in commanding and prohibiting. Wherever you see law, then, see justice also; and if you remember that reason has been given to all, then you will realise that justice has also been given to all.[11]

Indeed over a century and a half later, notwithstanding the greed and corruption of the intervening years, it was still possible to find a Stoic Emperor like Marcus Aurelius (AD 121–180) engaged in the following reflection:

> If the thinking faculty is common to us all, so also is that reason in virtue of which we are rational beings. If this is common, so also is that reason which prescribes what we should, and should not, do. Grant this, and it follows that law is common; if so, we are all fellow-citizens and share alike in a certain form of government. It follows that the World is as a State or City. For in what other City will it be said that the whole human race shares in common? Hence, therefore, from this common City comes the very thinking faculty, as well as the reasoning faculty and the force of law: else whence should they come?[12]

It was largely upon sentiments such as these – intimations of a new undiscriminating ethic – that Rome would stake her claim to be the leaven of civilization. In the words of A. J. Carlyle:

The Latin brought indeed, in his genius for law and administration, his own contribution to the cosmopolitan culture of the world, but that was all he brought. It was impossible for him to imagine himself to be the man possessed of reason and capable of virtue and deny these qualities to others. The Roman Empire continued and carried on the work of the Macedonian Empire in welding the countries of the Mediterranean basin into one homogenous whole. The homogeneity of the human race was in the Roman Empire no mere theory of the philosophers, but an actual fact of experience, a reality in social and political conditions. If the philosopher had learned to believe in the homogeneity of mankind under the Macedonian Empire, he was confirmed and strengthened in his belief by the experience of the Roman.[13]

Educated Romans genuinely felt that they had been gifted the chief responsibility for sustaining and promoting this new wide morality among men. And reality only served to confirm them in this belief. For where once a man had been a citizen of his city, with all the charge of parochialism that that brought, he now found himself a citizen of the world. And the point, of course, was that the world had become Roman. As Professor Flint puts it, 'Rome had made the world Roman and become herself cosmopolitan'.[14]

INDIVIDUALISM, RELATIVISM AND THE INADEQUACY OF A MUNICIPAL POLITICS

But what would need to change for it to become Christian? That this is no obvious question to ask is attested to by the fact that a scholar like Augustine devoted considerable time to answering it. During his gradual conversion to Christianity he had initially been impressed by how close certain of the Neoplatonist philosophers had come to anticipating some of the fundamental truths of Christian doctrine,[15] and during the course of his work as a bishop he found himself continually pressed to establish the proper relationship between reason and faith.[16] This was to be expected in a time when the Church was still working to establish herself in distinction from the intellectual and moral traditions of classical antiquity. Augustine's letters give a full indication of the trouble he had with the lingering pagan practices of his parishioners. In his *Confessiones*, he tells the story of how his mother, a devout Christian, used to take pottage, bread and wine to the memorial shrines of the saints in imitation of pagan practice. In the end she was stopped by the authority of Bishop Ambrose (ca AD 340–397), whom she adored.[17] Some eight centuries later St Thomas Aquinas (1225–1274) would take up the same question. Like Augustine he would conclude that it is possible for unaided human reason to anticipate a great many of the more important Christian teachings.[18] Where he would differ from him would be on the question of the epistemological distance between man and God and its implications for the doctrine of Divine sovereignty. Once again it is in the *Confessiones* that we find a list of the Christian truths that Augustine was able to discover by studying the Neoplatonists alone. It is impressively full and tells us much about the favourable intellectual climate that Christianity encountered in the classical world:[19]

You first desired to show me how You 'resisteth the proud, but giveth Grace unto the humble.' [Jas 4.6] In addition, You desired to show me out of what great mercy You gifted men the way of humility, for which reason Your 'Word was made flesh, and dwelt among us.' [Jn 1.14] To this end You obtained for me certain books of the Platonists that had been translated out of the Greek into Latin; and You did this by means of a man inflated with a monstrous pride. In them I read, not indeed in these words, but commended to reason with various arguments, that, 'In the beginning was the Word, and the Word was with God, and the Word was God. The same was in the beginning with God. All things were made by Him; and without Him was not any thing made that was made. In Him was life; and the life was the light of men. And the light shineth in darkness; and the darkness comprehended it not.' [Jn 1.1–5] I read that the soul of man, although it gives testimony of the Light, is not itself the Light, but the Word, God Himself, was 'the true Light, which lighteth every man that cometh into the world,' [Jn 1.9] and that, 'He was in the world, and the world was made by Him, and the world knew Him not.' [Jn 1.10] . . . Again, I read there that the Word, God, was born, not of the flesh, nor of blood, 'nor of the will of the flesh, nor of the will of man, but of God.' [Jn 1.13] . . . I found out in those books, though it was said differently and in many ways, that the Son, 'being in the form of God, thought it not robbery to be equal with God,' [Phil. 2.6] for by nature He is the same with Him.[20]

Conspicuously absent from this list was, of course, the person of Christ. In Augustine's words, 'I did not read there that "the Word was made flesh, and dwelt among us"' [Jn 1.14].[21] As he continues:

But those books do not have it that He 'made Himself of no reputation, and took upon Him the form of a servant, and was made in the likeness of men,' and that 'being found in a fashion as a man, He humbled Himself, and became obedient unto death, even the death of the cross. Wherefore God also hath highly exalted Him, and given Him a name which is above every name: That at the name of Jesus every knee should bow, of *things* in Heaven, and *things* in earth, and *things* under the earth; and *that* every tongue should confess *that* Jesus Christ *is* Lord, to the glory of God the Father.' [Phil. 2.7–11][22]

In later chapters we will learn why it is characteristic of Augustine to describe the impact of Christianity in the ancient world in terms of the person of Christ.

The fact remains that, however we choose to look at it, Christianity arrived into a world peculiarly ready to receive it. Rome had established a moral and intellectual tradition sympathetic to its general outlook, while in scope and organization the Empire presented the perfect vehicle for its proselytizing mission. Yet for its first 300 or so years, Christianity stubbornly refused to exploit these facts, and, even with the semi-official

Christianization of the Empire upon the Emperor Constantine (ca AD 274–337) becoming a catechumen in AD 323,[23] this modest policy did not immediately change. As to the reasons why, Numa Denis Fustel de Coulanges provides a full and accurate answer:

> As to the government of the state, we cannot say that Christianity essentially altered that, precisely because it did not occupy itself with the state. In the ancient ages, religion and the state made but one; every people adored its own god, and every god governed his own people; the same code regulated the relations among men, and their duties towards the gods of the city. Religion then governed the state, and designated its chiefs by the voice of the lot, or by that of the auspices. The state, in its turn, interfered with the domains of the conscience, and punished every infraction of the rites and the worship of the city. Instead of this, Christ teaches that His kingdom is not of this world. He separates religion from government. Religion, being no longer of the earth, now interferes the least possible in terrestrial affairs. Christ adds, 'Render to Caesar the things that are Caesar's, and to God the things that are God's.' It is the first time that God and the state are so clearly distinguished . . . Now Christ breaks the alliance which paganism and the empire wished to renew. He proclaims that religion is no longer the state, and that to obey Caesar is no longer the same thing as to obey God.[24]

It would not be putting it too strongly to suggest that the world had never before encountered such a radical set of political ideas. In particular, the implied divorce between religion and state caused much disquiet, for this had been a cherished association in the mind of the ancient. Then there was the equally provocative delimiting of the state's ethical portfolio: to advertise human fullness of nature by some route other than the laws of the civil authority was unprecedented. It cut deeply at the root of the ancient world's conception of freedom, a positive conception that conflated the interests of the individual with those of the state.[25] Yet once again Rome had done something to prepare the ground – as T. R.

Glover explains, she had ended up with a government that was simply too good, too efficient, too bureaucratic. Looking back it is impossible not to appreciate how modern it was; to the ancients, however, this made it only impersonal and cynical. 'Rome gave them peace,' writes Glover,

> 'but could not restore their energy [sapped by the centuries of warfare and luxury that followed the break up of the Greek city-states and their ideal of the good life]; and she lost her own, sick of the self-seeking of her own demagogues and military adventurers. "Indifference to the state as if it were no concern of theirs" made men ready to accept the Imperial government; and, as the indifference grew, the civil service rose, and the ancient world declined into bondage and despair. "Do not hope for Plato's Republic", wrote Marcus Aurelius in his diary.'[26]

In the early days of the Empire it was already possible to find social commentators like Polybius (ca BC 203–122) sounding the keynotes of despair. For by then, the ancient Roman religion had already begun its descent into cynicism and farce.[27] It was the play of politics and power that really held the imagination of the Roman statesman; religion was simply a relic from the past – even the language of its rites and formulations was now a subject for the specialist. He tolerated it in much the same way that many tolerate religion in today's secular states. That is, he treated it like a superstition: useless in itself, but potentially of some use in managing the psychology of the masses.[28] To men as astute as Polybius it was clear what was happening, and in time it would help them towards believing that '. . . religion in general was nothing more than a deep political scheme devised by early rulers and moralists to awe their subjects into good behaviour when human devices for detecting and punishing their irregularities were not likely to succeed'.[29] As for the ordinary man, it was too easy for him to get lost in the vast, impersonal state apparatus of Rome. The freedom that the Greek might have taken for granted when ensconced in his city-state, in his 'charmed circle of law and custom', to use Burnett's phrase,[30] was increasingly the subject of nostalgia and longing. For most it was all too clear that the destiny of the individual was coming apart from that of the state.[31] Men suffered because the political vision of Rome was so far in advance of its time. It would have to wait until the libertarianism of the eighteenth and nineteenth centuries before such a robust understanding of the public and private spheres would once again be at the heart of a government. As Raymond Gettell explains:

> In Roman thought the state did not absorb the individual, as in the theory of Plato, nor was the state considered non-essential, as in the teachings of the Epicureans. The Romans separated state and individual, each having definite rights and duties. The state was a necessary and natural framework for social existence; but the individual, rather than the state, was made the center of legal thought, and the protection of the rights of the individual was the main purpose for which the state existed. The state was thus viewed as a legal person, exercising its authority within definite limits; and the citizen was viewed as a legal person, having rights which were to be safeguarded against other persons and against illegal encroachment by the government itself. On the basis of this conception, the elaborate system of Roman private law was created.[32]

It is a testament to Rome's practical wisdom[33] that she was able to pioneer such a conception of positive law, and in many respects it became her chief qualification to rule the world. For so long as law remained the expression and codification of a particular people's ethic it could play no rôle in the promotion of cosmopolitanism. And cosmopolitanism needed law: it needed the stability of some lowest common denominator if it was to take root and grow. In the end this is exactly what Rome was able to provide. Culture and learning she largely left to the Greek; law, government and administration she made her own; and by her success she completely altered the intellectual equipment of the ancient. Government is not this or that constitution or state or religion; it is, to use one of Carlyle's phrases, 'the method of life'.[34]

In sum we could say that Rome helped to turn politics from a first into a second-order activity. In her hands it became firmly established as the science and art of government. That is, rule through *divinarum atque humanarum notitia* 'the science of divine and human things' and *ars boni et aequi* 'the art of what is good and equitable'.[35] Yet crucially none of this took in the feelings of the ordinary man. In the midst of all this change, and without the comforts and pleasures that make individualism such an attractive prospect to the modern, he was left pondering to what he should give his heart and his mind, if not to the state and its gods as before.[36] Rome had carved out a new ideal for the state – centralized power established through administrative efficiency – but in doing so she had neglected to bring the ideal of the good life into line with her achievement.[37] Men generally were happy to accept the new orientation in secular affairs, indeed they praised and acknowledged the peace and stability of Roman rule, but the widening spiritual lacuna worried them.[38] Polybius writes of disillusioned Greeks who, losing their nerve completely, were driven to commit appalling acts of race suicide.[39]

THE CHRISTIAN SOLUTION TO THE PROBLEM OF POLITICAL LIFE

Then Christianity arrived on the scene with its novel solution to the problem of political life in these new and troubling times. There is not really one city but two: the Earthly City and the Heavenly City. The Earthly City is concerned solely with the material conditions of life; it is quite right, in other words, that Rome attempts no more than a superficial and external justice – the friend of merchants and shopkeepers, trade and commerce, but never the companion of the soul – for there is another city altogether to provide for the needs of man's inner, spiritual life. This is the Heavenly City. Its law is true justice and its end is true peace and, like the Greek cities of old, a man can only be born into its citizenship. And yet this birth is open to all, even those who have already been born citizens of the Earthly City. So long as a man is given the necessary gift

of Grace – a kind of Divine dispensation – he can be 'born again', as it
were.[40] What earns him this gift is, however, another matter altogether,
for it is absolutely not given on the basis of reward or merit. It is not
given on the basis of reward or merit because the moral categories that
ordinarily decide these things do not translate the sovereign Will of the
Heavenly City's King. In a disquieting way, He remains wholly incomprehensible.[41] Now this is certainly something different to arrangements
in the Earthly City, where the kings do not generally rule by such a voluntarist conception of law. If we recall Cicero's remarks, law is nothing
other than right reason (*recta ratio*), which nature gives in common to
all men. The city is really a public thing (*res publica*) or commonwealth,
because its law, and therefore its justice, is really the common possession
of its citizens. Insofar as they have been given rational faculties by nature
they are, each of them, the authors of the laws that they obey. And laws,
as Aquinas would explain some 13 centuries later, are in this sense always
'ordinances of reason'.[42]

Stated in these terms the Christian solution to the problem of political
life could not fail to impress, for it seemed to be able to account for all the
least satisfactory aspects of Roman government. It offered the unmatched
liberation of seeing a thing for what it really is. To the man looking to
Roman rule for ethical leadership and spiritual direction, it could only be
a profound disappointment, but to the same man looking to it to provide
a stable apparatus of civilized life, why should it not appear satisfactory,
exemplary even?[43] It seems that what Christianity was able to offer the
ordinary man was a truly fulfilling private sphere, an individualism so
rugged that it might proof him against any disappointment with arrangements in the Earthly City. We should not doubt, then, that the motif of
the 'unquiet heart', later to be made so famous by Augustine, was already
at the core of this vision: 'You [Lord] have made us for Yourself, and our
heart is unquiet until it rests in You'.[44] In Henry Tudor's words,

> The Christian felt no . . . identity, either with the city in which he
> lived or with the natural order, the cosmopolis of which the Stoics
> asserted that all men were citizens. He was the total outcast whose

lot was death unless he could establish a relationship with God in Whom alone there was life.[45]

However, this simple vision could not on its own account for the numerous practical problems thrown up by the establishment of Christianity in the Roman Empire. For the most part these concerned the Church more than they did the Emperor, for he could always frame his thinking by the enlightened cynicism of his forefathers – the enlightened cynicism that it is customary to associate with the municipal religions of pagan antiquity. To the contrary, the Church was faced with a crisis that Wolin has characterized in the following questions:

> . . . how could Christianity support the state and be supported by it and yet avoid becoming yet another civic religion? what was the identity of the state in an historical situation where the Church had grown steadily more political in organization and outlook? what was the identity of the Church when the state undertook to advance the faith and police the behaviour of the believers? could this hurry the Last Judgment? where did both the Church and the political community stand in relation to the time-dimension of history?[46]

These questions, avoided by so many in their philosophical and metaphysical complexity, were taken up decisively by Augustine. His answers form the subject of the next chapter.

Notes

1 Dyson, *St. Augustine of Hippo*, p. 142. In practice this implied that all serious thinking about socio-political matters should carry on within a framework established by the Catholic Church.
2 John B. Morrall, *Political Thought in Medieval Times* (London: Hutchinson University Library, 1960), pp. 10–11. Perhaps the clearest effect of this revolution was in law. *See* Cassirer, *The Myth of the State*, p. 81.
3 *See* Lewis H. Morgan, *Ancient Society* (Chicago: Charles H. Kerr & Company, 1877), pp. 222–3.
4 Herodotus (born sometime between BC 490 and 480) produced one of the most well-known collections in the form of his *Histories*. On Herodotus'

regard for custom and convention, and the skepticism that underlaid it, *see* John Burnet, *Greek Philosophy* (London: Macmillan, 1943), p. 107.

5 *See* Heinrich A. Rommen (tr. Thomas R. Hanley, OSB), *The Natural Law: A Study in Legal and Social History and Philosophy* (London: B. Herder Book Co., 1955), pp. 3–5.

6 Herbert Spencer (1820–1903) gives a very good definition of this view of intelligence: 'From the lowest to the highest creatures', he writes, 'intelligence progresses by acts of discrimination; and it continues so to progress among men, from the ignorant to the most cultured. To class rightly – to put in the same group things which are of essentially the same natures, and in other groups things of natures essentially different – is the fundamental condition to right guidance of actions'. (Herbert Spencer, 'The new Toryism', in *The Man Versus the State, With Six Essays on Government, Society, and Freedom* [Indianapolis, IN: Liberty Fund 1982], p. 11). Cf. William James: 'The first thing the intellect does with any object is to class it along with something else'. (William James, *The Varieties of Religious Experience: A Study in Human Nature* [London: Longmans Green & Co., 1913], p. 9).

7 A. P. d'Entrèves, *Natural Law*, p. 16.

8 The work accomplished by the Roman lawyers was significant. An excellent short summary of their achievements can be found at Gettell, *History of Political Thought* (George Allen & Unwin, 1932), pp. 69–72. A fuller treatment, incorporating a great deal of original material can be found at *HMPTW*, Vol. I, pp. 33–77.

9 Eduard Zeller (tr. Rev. Oswald J. Reichel), *The Stoics, Epicureans and Sceptics* (London: Longmans, Green, and Co., 1880), p. 17.

10 *HMPTW*, Vol. I, p. 8.

11 Cicero, *De Legibus*, I, 10. 28–12. 33 (author's translation).

12 Marcus Aurelius Antoninus, *Meditationes*, IV, 4; tr. Hastings Crossley.

13 *HMPTW*, Vol. I, pp. 10–11.

14 Robert Flint, *History of the Philosophy of History* (New York: Charles Scribner's Sons, 1894), p. 56.

15 See *Confess.*, VII, 9–21, for Augustine's account of how the books of the Neoplatonists first affected him. Much has been written on the extent to which he was influenced by the Neoplatonists, and which of their books he read. The relevant articles in *ATA* contain the most up-to-date wisdom on the matter. *See* also the narrative treatments in Agostino Trapè, *Agostino: l'uomo, il pastore, il mistico* (Roma: Città Nuova Editrice, 2001), pp. 109–16; and Brown, *Augustine of Hippo*, pp. 79–92.

16 Very nearly one of Augustine's first public acts as Bishop of Hippo was to pronounce on the Faith and the Creed at the General Council of Africa, in December AD 393. The address is preserved as his *De fide et symbolo*.

17 See *Confess.*, VI, 2, 2. Cf. *Ep.*, 36, 14, 32; *Ep.*, 54, 2, 3.

18 *See* Aquinas, *Summa contra gentiles*, I, 3, 4, 7, 8.

19 On this subject, see Brooke Foss Westcott, *Essays in the History of Religious Thought in the West* (London: Macmillan, 1891), pp. 1–194. Cf. T. R. Glover, *The Influence of Christ in the Ancient World* (Cambridge: Cambridge University Press, 1929), pp. 1–20. Vergil's Fourth Eclogue, with its apparent allusion to the coming of Christ, has ever been the most tantalizing piece of evidence for the preparation of the human mind for Christianity. *See* the essay in E. V. Rieu (tr.), *Virgil: The Pastoral Poems* (Harmondsworth: Penguin, 1961), pp. 136–43.

20 *Confess.*, VII, 9, 13–14 (author's translation). *See* also the extended discussion of this subject in book X of *De civ. Dei*.

21 *Ibid.*, VII, 9, 13–14.

22 *Ibid.* (author's translation). Cf. *Ibid.*, VII, 9, 14

23 In keeping with a practice not at all uncommon among early Christians, Constantine was only baptized on his deathbed, in AD 337. The logic was that it allowed the least possible time for a sinful relapse to occur. As Sheldon S. Wolin sensibly puts it, 'The nature of Constantine's conversion is a vexed issue which need not detain us, for the important point was that his policies retained much that was reminiscent of older modes of thought concerning the relationship between religion and the political order. The danger came not so much from the favoured position enjoyed by Christianity, but rather from its being converted into a chosen instrument for political regeneration, a "civil religion" shaped to the old classical model'. (Wolin, *Politics and Vision*, p. 120).

24 Numa Denis Fustel de Coulanges, *The Ancient City: A Classic Study of the Religious and Civil Institutions of Ancient Greece and Rome* (New York: Doubleday & Company, 1956), p. 393.

25 It was, of course, Isaiah Berlin (1909–1997) who first described the freedom of the ancients as 'positive'. In his famous paper 'Two concepts of Liberty', given as the inaugural lecture for the Chichele Chair of Social and Political Theory at the University of Oxford, on 31 March 1958, he argued that the history of ideas has furnished two main conceptualizations of 'freedom' or 'liberty'. The first, 'positive liberty', is the more ancient. It is, Berlin explains, '. . . involved in the answer to the question "What, or who, is the source of control or interference that can determine someone to do, or be, this rather than that?"' The second, 'negative liberty', is more modern, for '. . . it is involved in the answer to the question "What is the area within which the subject – a person or group of persons – is or should be left to do or be what he is able to do or be, without interference by other persons?"' In large part this paper was a vehicle for Berlin's strong views on the dangers of ethical

monism in modern industrial societies. He had himself lived through the St Petersburg Revolution of 1917 and, as a Jew, was personally touched by the horrors of the Second World War. Suffice to say that for Berlin, 'positive liberty' was and continues to be the intellectual justification for tyranny, while 'negative liberty' stands against it as the supreme argument for the value of public and private spheres in the business of government. For as he concludes his famous discussion of the two concepts of liberty: 'Pluralism, with the measure of "negative liberty" that it entails, seems to me a truer and more human ideal than the goals of those who seek in the great, disciplined, authoritarian structures the ideal of "positive" self-mastery by classes, or peoples, or the whole of mankind. It is truer because it does, at least, recognize the fact that human goals are many, not all of them commensurable, and in perpetual rivalry with one another. To assume that all values can be graded on one scale, so that it is a mere matter of inspection to determine the highest, seems to me to falsify our knowledge that men are free agents, to represent moral decision as an operation which a slide-rule could, in principle, perform'. (Isaiah Berlin, 'Two concepts of liberty', in *Four Essays on Liberty* [Oxford: Oxford University Press, 1969], p. 171).

26 Glover, *The Influence of Christ in the Ancient World*, p. 33. The quotation from Marcus Aurelius can be found at Book IX, 29 of his *Meditationes*: 'How puny are these little public men, wisely practical as they believe themselves to be. They are like children with running noses. What then is a man to do? Do what nature now requires. Start now, if this be granted to you; do not look around to see whether anyone will know about it. *Do not expect Plato's ideal republic*; be satisfied with the smallest step forward, and consider this no small achievement'.

27 It is possible to speculate that by its form and character the Roman religion was always destined to this fate. For like everything else they did, the Romans approached religion in a strictly business-like manner. The gods were there to provide extraordinary services to individuals, families and the state, and as such they were transacted with according to strict customs and rites. Talking of the Roman propensity to ancestor-worship, J. B. Jevons comments that, 'The early Greeks and Romans, like the Chinese of the present day, were more interested in the way in which they themselves might be affected by the spirits of their dead than they were in the fortunes of the departed, or the nature of their abode'. (J. B. Jevons, *Comparative Religion* [Cambridge: Cambridge University Press, 1913], p. 65). This mercenary aspect became, over time, much the greater part of the Roman religion. There is correspondingly a great deal of truth in the following observation from A. N. Whitehead: 'The cult of the Empire was the sort of religion which might be constructed to-day by the Law School of a

University, laudably impressed by the notion that mere penal repression is not the way to avert a crime wave [!] (A. N. Whitehead, *Religion in the Making* [Cambridge: Cambridge University Press, 1927], p. 31).

28 Augustine has something to say about this. At *De civ. Dei*, IV, 32, he accuses certain evil 'princes' of having '. . . persuaded the people to accept falsities dressed up as truths. They have done this in the name of religion in order to bind men more tightly, as it were, in civil society, in order that they might likewise possess them as subjects'. (author's translation).

29 H. J. Rose, *Religion in Greece and Rome*, p. 248.

30 Burnet, 'Law and nature in Greek ethics', p. 332.

31 See Jérôme Carcopino (Ed. Henry T. Rowell & tr. E. O. Lorimer), *Daily Life in Ancient Rome: The People and the City at the Height of the Empire* (London: George Routledge & Sons, 1943), pp. 121–2).

32 Gettell, *History of Political Thought*, pp. 67–8.

33 S. S. Laurie produces a very perceptive sketch of the practical Roman character in his *Historical Survey of Pre-Christian Education* (London: Longmans, Green, & Co., 1907), pp. 315–16.

34 *HMPTW*, Vol. I, p. 14. As E. C. Dewick points out, '. . . the Roman of old (like the average Englishman of to-day) was not, as a rule, much interested in the abstract truth of this or that religion. He viewed these mainly from the political angle, as useful – or, it may be, mischievous – factors in the administration of the Empire. He had little desire to impose his religion on others, beyond requiring all subjects of the Emperor to show veneration to the imperial image. Nor did he interfere with foreign beliefs or modes of worship, unless these tended to stimulate sedition, or violated Roman ideals of decency and morals'. (E. C. Dewick, *The Gospel and Other Faiths* [London: Canterbury Press, 1948], p. 32).

35 Justinian, *Digest*, liber I, titulus 1.

36 On this point see Herbert A. Deane, 'Classical and Christian political thought', *Political Theory*, Vol. 1, No. 4 (Nov., 1973), p. 416.

37 Wolin sees this change reflected most spectacularly in the fortunes of the concept of Roman citizenship. *See* his *Politics and Vision*, pp. 91–2.

38 *See* Ernst Troeltsch (tr. Olive Wyon), *The Social Teachings of the Christian Churches*, Vol. I (London: George Allen & Unwin, 1931), p. 41.

39 Polybius, *Histories*, xxxvi, 17.

40 See *De civ. Dei*, XV, 2.

41 Once again, Troeltsch is the authority on these matters. *See* his *The Social Teachings of the Christian Churches*, Vol. I, pp. 39–40.

42 *Summa theologica*, Ia, IIae, 90, 4. Cf. *De civ. Dei*, IV, 33: '. . . God is God, not Fortune . . . He acts according to an order of things and times that is completely known to Him but hidden from us. However, we are not to

imagine that this order accounts for His actions; for in fact He rules it as Lord and expresses Himself in its disposition'. (author's translation).

43 Nearly all the early Christian apologists praised and esteemed the Roman Empire as a God-given source of peace and prosperity to men. See Gillian Clark's comments in her article, 'Let every soul be subject: the fathers and the empire', in Loveday Alexander (Ed.), *Images of Empire* (Sheffield: Sheffield Academic Press, 1991), pp. 251–75.

44 *Confess.*, I, 1, 1 (author's translation). Cf. *En. in Ps.*, XXV, 5: 'For dismissed by You from Paradise, and having taken my journey into a far country [cf. Lk. 15.13], I cannot by myself return, unless You meet the wanderer: for my return has been sustained by Your mercy throughout the whole tract of this age's time'. (author's translation).

45 Henry Tudor, *Political Myth* (London: Pall Mall Press, 1972), p. 94.

46 Wolin, *Politics and Vision*, p. 121.

3

Augustine's doctrine of the Two Cities

We should point out that the Christian solution to the problem of political life would not immediately have been stated in terms of two cities. The doctrine of the Two Cities proper was Augustine's creation in the fifth century, yet the language is not at all misleading. From the first, Christianity was forced to defend itself from the charge that it was a politicizing religion – in other words, that it sought to challenge the imperial authority of Rome, or at least to dilute men's allegiance to it by teaching them not to deify the Emperor. If never made explicit, then, the language of the Two Cities was certainly implied in all the Church's early dealings with Rome, and it is significant in this respect that a great deal of the apologetic material from the period is directed towards allaying fears about Christianity's subversive and seditious character. Here, for instance, is what Tertullian (ca AD 160–220) has to say in defense of those Christians who will not worship the Emperor:

> Another charge against us concerns treason with respect to the person of the Emperor. Yet Christians have never been found among the followers of Albinus or Niger or Cassius. Those who have actually been found in practice to be enemies of the Emperor are the very same people who only a day before had been swearing by his genius, had been solemnly offering sacrifices for his safety, and not infrequently had been condemning Christians as well. A Christian is an enemy to no man – certainly not to the Emperor, for he knows

that it is by God that the Emperor has been appointed. He is bound therefore to love him, to revere him, to honour him and to desire the safety not only of the Emperor but of the whole Roman empire as long as the world endures – for as long as the world endures, so also will the Roman empire. So then we do 'worship' the Emperor in such manner as is both permissible to us and beneficial to him, namely as a man second only to God. All that he is he has received from God, and it is God alone Whom he ranks below. This surely is what the Emperor himself will desire. He ranks above all else; it is the true God whom he ranks below.[1]

THE HISTORICAL CONTEXT
OF *DE CIVITATE DEI*

In Augustine's time the charges being leveled at the Church were slightly different. When he began his *De civitate Dei*, in AD 413, a newly Christian Rome had only recently been sacked by Alaric and the Visigoths (AD 410), an unprecedented event that had deeply scarred the Roman psyche. The Romans had simply not thought it possible that their 'eternal' city could be so easily overrun by uncivilized barbarians. As so often happens in these situations, a scapegoat was sought and quickly found in Rome's recent adoption of Christianity as its official religion by the edict *Cunctos populos*, signed by the Emperor Theodosius I (ca AD 346–395) in AD 384. Among other proscriptions, this edict comprehensively abolished the worship of Rome's ancient gods, traditionally her protection and help. To many this was an open invitation to lay the blame for the recent outrage squarely at Christianity's door. In his *Retractiones*, Augustine gives a clear indication of the height at which feelings were running:

Meanwhile, Rome suffered a powerful invasion of Goths under their leader, Alaric, and with an attack of great devastation was overthrown. The worshippers of the false and many gods whom by custom we call by the name of pagans, trying to refer this disaster to the Christian religion, commenced to blaspheme the true God with more than usual acerbity and bitterness. This inflaming me to love with zeal the City of God, I began to write the books of *De civitate Dei* against their blasphemies, or what is really the same thing, their errors.[2]

These circumstances explain the immense labour that Augustine would pour into this, his most celebrated work. Christianity was at the crossroads. The recently converted Empire had suffered a defeat of symbolic dimensions, and now it seemed as if the gains of the last four centuries might be lost in a moment of panic and superstition. It was imperative that someone in a position of intellectual authority speak out against the general scaremongering before the conservative elements in Roman society turn it to their advantage. And so Augustine took up the task. In the first ten books of his *De civitate Dei* he would argue meticulously against Rome's claim that her gods had always protected her from calamity; that by giving them up for the one Christian God, she had forfeited their protection and help; and that subsequently the Christian God, that is, the Christian God who teaches meekness and submission, had been unable to divert the impending disaster.

But of course *De civitate Dei* contains more than ten books. While Augustine was still shaping up the main lines of this argument he received a letter from a friend and fellow Christian named Marcellinus. This man had been given the complicated task of trying to resolve the dispute between the Christians and the Donatists in Africa, but now he had come into the circle of a number of educated pagans who had begun to probe his Christianity with difficult and searching questions. He was unsettled, and wanted to know whether Augustine might be able to help. In the Introduction to his translation of *De civitate Dei*, Dyson gives this useful paraphrase of the more difficult questions that Marcellinus was facing:

Why are the miracles of Christianity regarded as anything special? Paganism has many more miracles to boast of, some of them more

spectacular than the miracles of Christ. If God was pleased with the
sacrifices offered to Him by the people of the Old Testament, and if
He is immutable, why is He not pleased with such sacrifices now?
What good has Christianity brought to Rome? Is it not true that,
ever since the old religion was abandoned and Christianity taken
up, the political and military fortunes of the empire have gone from
bad to worse?[3]

Initially Augustine gave Marcellinus what help he could in two letters
(*Ep.* 137 and 138), but at some point he realized that a more comprehensive treatment was required and promised this in the form of either
another letter or a book. Busy as he always was, it must have occurred
to him that the best solution would simply be to extend the original plan
of *De civitate Dei* along the lines suggested by Marcellinus' questions.
The result, after some 13 years of work, was *De civitate Dei* as it now
stands, in 22 books.[4]

DE CIVITATE DEI AS A WORK
OF POLITICAL THEORY

As a work of Christian apologetics *De civitate Dei* is prosecuted according to an unusually wide, ambitious and passionate plan. Its many editors
and translators have all commented on the formidable challenges posed
by its fluidity of style and structure. It is written, as almost everything
was in Augustine's day, to be read aloud, and it is helpful to bear this in
mind when reading it today. Augustine, ever the rhetorician, was writing
to an educated pagan audience. All the repetition, every laboured point,
is for their benefit: it is to help them as they come to terms with the shock
of having their whole moral, intellectual and political tradition turned
against them. Not until Karl Marx (1818–1883) in the nineteenth century
would the West have its most cherished ideals so spectacularly decon-
structed. Against Rome's claim to be the moral and political education of
mankind, Augustine likens her to a robber band; in place of her ancient

gods, he substitutes a humiliating sociology of religion.[5]

But these considerable achievements do not describe the enduring interest of *De civitate Dei* to historians of ideas. Credit for this must rather go to the clarity and constancy of its central thesis. In the argument that Church and State each have their rôle to play in a coordinated plan for the general good, Augustine lays down what would go on to become the main lines of the solution to the problem of political life in the Christian era. But in his further insistence that the general good cannot account for the true and most fulfilling end of man – that politics and the whole apparatus of civilized life can only touch it in external and superficial ways – he inserts an unexpected and troubling caveat.[6]

AUGUSTINE AND CHRISTIAN REALISM

Augustine is the beginning and the end of a unique form of Christian realism. It is unique because it marks the complete separation of politics from history. Unlike the two other great philosophers of history with whom he is often compared, Augustine's vision of history does not redeem politics. For both Friedrich Hegel (1770–1831) and Karl Marx, politics labours as the unwitting servant of history before eventually winning its freedom. With Augustine it is not so lucky. For him politics can never be redeemed because it is the archetypal sinful activity. It is the archetypal sinful activity because it is the ultimate expression of man's willed estrangement from God. Had Adam not sinned in the Garden of Eden, he would have continued to look to God for all his understanding, discerning and acting on His sovereign Will in the actual present of his life. So too would his offspring, and so on, until there would have arisen a community of men and women united in their obedience to the sovereign Will of God, '. . . because man was created righteous, to live according to His Maker and not according to himself, doing his Maker's Will and not his own . . .'[7]

From this perspective politics becomes the inevitable conclusion to man's original decision in the Garden of Eden. In its hopes and ambitions, it stands symbolic of his refusal to participate in its utopian history. But it is symbolic, too, of God's Grace:[8] for politics is, after all, only possible because God has allowed man to retain an echo of Paradise in his heart. This 'still small voice'[9] is his conscience, and it equips him to fulfill his calling as a sociable creature by speaking out against his fallen nature. In the simplest sense it does this by imploring him to put the needs of others first. In the words that Shakespeare put into the mouth of Cardinal Wolsey: 'Love thyself last: cherish those hearts that hate thee . . .'[10] As we will later on discover, these lights of conscience are one of the main instruments in the Augustinian economy of salvation. They furnish a standard by which all men can examine their conduct and be reproved by it, and by the same token they are the proof of man's dependence upon God's Mercy for illumination:[11]

As if to an audience made up of the whole human race the Truth cries: 'Do ye indeed speak righteousness, O congregation? Do ye judge uprightly, O ye sons of men?' [Ps. 58.1] For even to the unjust man is it not easy to speak of justice? For instance, what man is there who would not be able to say what is just if his motives were not under suspicion? It is like this because the Hand that formed us has written this truth into our hearts: 'Therefore all things whatsoever ye would that men should do to you, do ye even so to them . . .' [Mt. 7.12] This truth was such that even before the law [of Moses] was given no one was suffered to be ignorant of it. This was done in order that those to whom no formal law had been given might yet be judged. But in the event that men should complain that something was wanting to them, what they cannot read in their hearts has been set down on tablets; for the fact is that it is in their hearts for them to read, but some choose not to. There has, in this sense, been placed before their eyes only the very thing that would strike them in their conscience . . . For after all, who has taught you that you do not want other men to make advances to your wife? Who has taught you that you do not want to have someone rob you? Who has taught you that you do not want to suffer injustice? And indeed, what other examples of this, both universal and particular, might you adduce? You see that there are many like questions to which any man would reply in a clear voice: 'I do not want to suffer it.' Come now, are you really the only man who does not want to suffer these things? Do you not live in the society of the human race? Whoever has been made together with you is your fellow; unless, that is, you have worn out on earthly desires that by which you were made in the image of God . . . For you judge that there is evil in that which you do not wish to suffer; and you are held to this by an inward law written into your heart.[12]

Augustine never does try to understand the mechanics of how morality makes this claim on the minds of men; indeed to do so would be to contradict his illumination theory of truth.[13] For after all, if it is the case that God has gifted men the higher-order moral precepts fully formed, what is the point in trying to reduce them to first principles? One should instead accept that they are premisses rather than conclusions: that there is no getting beyond them to something more fundamental:

A man who knows that he owns a tree and attributes its fruit to You, but cannot say how many cubits high it is or how wide it spreads, is better than he who measures it and counts all its branches, but does not own it and does not know or love its Creator.[14]

Illustrations such as these are well chosen by Augustine to express his epistemological position. Truth is always God's prerogative; a man grasps only so much of it as he is allowed to, and little should it be wondered at, then, when attempts to overstep this mark end in farce:

It is just as if a man wishing to give rules for walking should warn you not to lift your back foot before you have placed your front one; and then go on to describe minutely how you should move the hinges of your joints. What he says is undoubtedly true, and it would be difficult to walk in any other way; but we generally find it easier to walk by executing these movements than to self-consciously attend to them while we are walking, or, indeed, to try to understand them in isolation from the activity.[15]

These considerations make politics a desperate and paradoxical business. It exists because men are thoroughly wretched by nature and it persists only so long as they do not attempt to interfere with its first principles. The best that we should hope for, says Augustine, is a ruler who is happy to acquiesce in the order of things: that is, a ruler who is prepared to take up his position beneath the laws of nature, and to seek to increase their sway in his kingdom. By contrast, all the most tragic episodes in human history have been initiated by rulers who, refusing to accept this limiting premiss, imagined that they might express a higher and more perfect law in their will. These facts point towards an unexceptional place for politics in the grand scheme of things. However different and interesting the many outward forms are that it might take, they are merely so many variations on a single unflattering theme.[16] This theme is the continual collision of venial human nature and unmerited Grace:

> Now the kingdom of death so held men that all would have deserved to be driven headlong into that second death to which there is no end had God's unmerited Grace not redeemed some of them. Thus it is that all the many nations of the earth can be arranged under just two so-called orders of human society – this notwithstanding their different rites and customs, and their different forms of language, arms, and dress. What is more, if we follow our Scriptures, we may properly speak of these as two cities [cf. Eph. 2.19; Phil. 3.20].[17]

The effect of this outlook on history is what we might expect: it goes on, but human affairs no longer play an active part in it, for the theme has now changed from 'utopia' to 'salvation'. Man has fallen and must be rescued; God decides to do this by cultivating and sustaining a community of pilgrims, and, so this community can have its love and faithfulness tested in the face of adversity, human society is spared as a kind of proving ground, a veil of tears, as Augustine often calls it.[18] This, insists

Augustine, is the true value and significance of human affairs. They have been established by God as a kind of gauntlet for the pilgrims to run:

> Woe is me! 'Hear, O Lord, and have mercy upon me . . . [Ps. 30.10]'
> Woe is me! Behold, I do not hide my wounds. You are my Physician;
> I am a sick man. You are merciful; I am in need of mercy. Are not
> man's days on earth '. . . like the days of an hireling?' [Job 7.1][19]

This is unquestionably an extreme position to take up. By timely and judicious injections of morality, God keeps the human compound alive,[20] but only while there remain souls to be saved from the general wreck. We should not be surprised, then, to learn that such outlooks generally support undemanding philosophies of history. Oscar Cullmann calls them by the name *Heilsgeschichte* 'salvation history', after the fact that they relegate the purpose of history to the end of salvation.[21] For this reason they often appear disarmingly simple, the usual complexities of human history dismissed as sirens to draw the faithful onto the rocks.[22] But can Augustine really mean to be so dismissive of politics? Does he seriously think that, at best, it has the crude utility of a life-saving device: something for men to cling to before they sink beneath the waves? And then what of the context of these unflattering and provocative opinions? We would do well to remember that Augustine was writing with the Roman Empire expressly in mind and, what is more, a Roman Empire in which public feelings against Christianity were running high. *Pluvia defit, causa Christiani sunt* 'No rain: blame the Christians'[23] was already a popular slogan when he began *De civitate Dei* and, given that the primary purpose of this work was apologetic, was it wise for him to do such violence to Rome's moral and political pretensions?

   At first glance we have to agree that he might have done better to adopt a more conciliatory tone.[24] But then closer inspection reveals his Christian realism to be a rather good advertisement for the Christian citizen. Ordinarily, the main cause of unrest in a political community is the lust for power. Augustine calls it *libido dominandi* 'lust of ruling'. This lust causes instability by encouraging citizens to vie with each other for influence over the affairs of the community. At various places in *De civitate Dei*, Augustine paints vivid pictures of the damage done to Rome by her many civil wars[25] and, more generally, of the effects of war and strife on the Earthly City as a whole.[26] Yet if we think seriously about it, the Christian citizen is positively disqualified by his religion from taking part in such subversive activities. As a man he is just as much afflicted by the itchy sore of *libido dominandi*, but as a Christian he is enjoined not to scratch it.[27] What is more, his religion actually encourages him towards a model citizenship that might even extend to fighting for his city:[28]

> If our religion were heard with proper dignity, it would establish, consecrate, fortify, and enlarge the commonwealth in a manner that Romulus, Numa, Brutus and all the other outstanding men of the Roman people never managed . . . Let those who declare that the doctrine of Christ does not promote the welfare of the common-wealth then produce an army of soldiers such as Christ's doctrine enjoins soldiers to be. Or for that matter, let them give us such citizens, such husbands, such wives, such parents, such children, such masters, such servants, such kings, such judges, in fact even such tax payers and tax collectors, as the Christian religion enjoins us to be. Let them do this and then dare to maintain that the doctrine of Christ does not promote the welfare of the commonwealth. Instead they should not hesitate to confess that if it were obeyed, this doctrine would greatly aid the health of the commonwealth.[29]

Augustine found it difficult to imagine how this message to the kings and princes of the world could be made any clearer:

> Do not fear the Christians; they do not conspire to threaten your worldly aspirations. The things that you seek happiness in, namely, power, wealth, and glory, do not interest them in the same way.[30] They prefer to direct these earthly goods, and others, towards a dif-ferent type of happiness and peace;[31] and because it is a happiness

and peace that touches the inner, spiritual part of man, it need not interfere with your designs on the outer, civil part.[32] Even if you attempt to lord it over the Christians they will not complain, or rise up in rebellion against you; for again, their religion teaches them that all power has its origin and purpose in God; that it is, as it were, a foundation of civilized life in this fallen world.[33] By their grand scheme of things, it matters not whether they are ruled with tyranny or justice; though like any man they prefer justice to tyranny, and Christian rule best.[34] As such, they can be expected to acquiesce in all aspects of your rule and execute their citizenship with an outstanding virtue, while asking only one thing in return. This is that you do not attempt to interfere in or regulate their religion.[35] They are ready to admit that this marks a dramatic departure from the days of old, when religion and politics were united in a single conception, but they ask you only to try to think in terms of the great material benefits which their citizenship will surely confer on your rule.

In Augustine's own words:

. . . while this Heavenly City is a pilgrim on earth, she calls citizens from all nations and every tongue, neither discriminating between their customs, laws, or institutions. She does this because these contrivances all tend toward the same end of earthly peace. By thus respecting the merely conventional differences between men she brings together a society of pilgrims. But she does more than respect these differences: she actually preserves and promotes them, provided only that they do not impede the religion by which we are taught that the One supreme and true God is to be worshipped. This is the sense in which we say that the Heavenly City makes use of earthly peace during her pilgrimage, and desires and maintains the co-operation of men's wills in order to furnish the necessities of mortal life. It is also the sense in which we say that she causes earthly peace to bear upon Heavenly peace. For Heavenly peace is of a different kind altogether from earthly peace, and should be estimated exclusively from our design and equipment as rational creatures . . . This peace is correspondingly possessed by the Heavenly City in faith while on its pilgrimage, and by this same faith it lives righteously, also directing towards the attainment of that peace every good act which it performs either for God, or – since the city's life is inevitably a social one – for neighbour.[36]

In terms of its pessimistic psychology of man, grand philosophy of history and utter lack of worldly ambition, this is a singular political theory, if indeed it can be called a political theory at all. Augustine is at pains to portray Christianity as an apolitical religion outside the mainstream of intellectual developments in the West. Correspondingly his leading political ideas ignore many of the standard presumptions and preoccupations of the ancient world, the chief of these being the expectation that a religious community will seek to assert itself politically.[37] His language of the Two Cities, though it is in part a nod to this popular sentiment, utterly radicalizes the relationship between ethics and freedom. The political community is still an ethical community, just as it was for Plato, Aristotle and Cicero, but now ethics can no longer account for the true happiness of man.[38] This supreme end – freedom – is elevated by Augustine to a different plane altogether and, insofar as man is enjoined by his nature to pursue it,[39] this plane must assume the greatest significance for him: '"For our conversation is in heaven . . . [Phil. 3.20]" To cling therefore to earthly things is the death of the soul'.[40]

Such lofty language does away with the normal terms of political discussion. As Norman H. Baynes explains,

To Augustine forms of government are really irrelevant: the character of the State is determined by the character of the citizens who compose the State. The two great *civitates* of Augustine's vision are distinguished by two *loves*: "Two *loves* formed two cities" – love of self leading to contempt of God – love of God leading to contempt of self.[41]

From this perspective it is inevitable that all human endeavour should form a single piece: 'For these are the practices that pass from tutors and teachers, and from nuts and balls and birds, to governors and kings, and to money and estates and slaves. These very things pass on, as older years come in their turn, just as heavier punishments succeed the birch rod'.[42] There is, then, this depressing inevitability about the human condition, whichever aspect is being examined. As Professor Markus puts it,

> The complexity and poise of [Augustine's] final estimate of politics stems from his conviction that the quest for perfection and happiness through politics is doomed. The archetypal society, where alone true human fulfillment can be found, is the society of the angels and saints in heaven: not a *polis*.[43]

Notes

1 Tertullian, *To Scapula*, 2; translation from CCL 2, 1127–8, reproduced in *DECT*, pp. 226–8.
2 *Retract.*, 2, 43, 2 (author's translation).
3 Augustine (Ed. & tr. R. W. Dyson), *The City of God against the Pagans*, pp. xii–xiii.
4 Augustine first mentions his intention to write *De civitate Dei* at *De Gen. ad litt.*, XI, 15, 20. The latter work was written between 401 and 415; *De civitate Dei* was begun in 413.
5 *See De doctr. Christ.*, II, 40, 60 for a typical example of the way he goes about this. Cf. *De civ. Dei*, II, 16; *Confess.*, V, 3, 5; and *Serm.*, CXCVIII, 35.
6 H. St. L. B. Moss's estimation of the work is close to the mark: 'Viewed from the standpoint of his age, the *Civitas Dei* of Augustine is less a "philosophy of history" than a passionate assertion of Divine intervention in human affairs; less a prophetical formulation of the future limits of Church and State than the ecstatic vision of a philosopher-mystic, transcending the mournful realities of his time in the description of an ideal society, founded on the principal of true justice, whose gaze is fixed, not on the world of sense, but on the battlements of an eternal city not made with hands'. (H. St. L. B. Moss, *The Birth of the Middle Ages, 395–814* [London: Oxford University Press, 1957], p. 14).
7 *De civ. Dei*, XIV, 4.

8 *De civ. Dei*, V, 11: '. . . when man sinned, He did not permit him to go unpunished, but neither did He abandon him without mercy'.

9 This phrase comes from the popular hymn by J. G. Whittier: 'Dear Lord and Father of Mankind'.

10 William Shakespeare, *King Henry VIII*, act 3. As Peter Brown has pointed out, the Christian ethic, and in particular its concern for the poor, arrived into the ancient world as something of an innovation, though not without its precedent in the traditional Jewish ethic. *See* his *Poverty and Leadership in the Later Roman Empire* (Hanover, NH: University Press of New England, 2002), pp. 1–45, but in particular p. 6, where Brown explains how the Christian concern for the poor helped to challenge the strictly municipal vision of pagan society and usher in a new all-embracing conception.

11 Augustine follows St Paul in explaining why and how this happened. See *De sp. et litt.*, 48.

12 *En. in Ps.*, 57:1 (author's translation). Cf. *In Io. ev. tr.*, 49:12; *Confess.*, III, 7 & 8; *Solil.*, II, 34 & 35.

13 *See*, for instance, *De gr. Chr.*, I, 24, 25: 'Let them therefore read and under-stand, observe and acknowledge, that it is not by law and doctrine teaching from without, but by means of a secret, miraculous, and ineffable power working from within, that God causes revelations of truth to appear in the hearts of men as well as the good disposition of the will towards them'. (author's translation).

14 *Confess.*, V, 4, 7 (author's translation). Cf. *Confess.*, XI, 3, 5; *Serm.*, CCXCIIIA, 8; *Confess.*, X, 6, 8; *Confess.*, VII, 7, 6, 8; *Confess.*, X, 24, 35; *De Gen. ad litt.*, VII, 1, 1; *Serm.*, XXVIII(B), 2.

15 *De doctr. Christ.*, II, 37, 55 (author's translation).

16 Hence Augustine's thought at *De civ. Dei*, V, 17: 'From the point of view of this life of mortals, which, so to speak, is spent and ended in a few days, what does it matter under whose government a dying man lives, provided only that it does not compel him to do what is ungodly and wicked?' (author's translation).

17 *Ibid.*, XIV, 1 (author's translation).

18 At *Serm.*, XX(B), 8, Augustine gives four reasons why God might feel it necessary to test pilgrims: one, 'to test their mettle'; two, 'to scourge them'; three, 'to reveal their worth to those who may not already be aware of it'; four, 'to reveal them to themselves'.

19 *Confess.*, X, 28, 39 (author's translation). Cf. *En in Ps.*, CXIX, 17–20; *Serm.*, XLVII, 1; *Serm.*, XXIII(B), 12; *En. in Ps.*, CXLVI, 4–5.

20 *De civ. Dei*, I, 34: 'Nonetheless, it is thanks to God that you are still alive: to God Who, in sparing you, warns you to correct yourselves by repentance'.

21 *See* his study (tr. Sidney G. Sowers), *Salvation in History* (London: SCM

Press, 1967). Professor R. A. Markus thinks that the term 'sacred history' is more properly applied to Augustine. His reasoning is that '. . . Augustine's conception [of history] presupposes a clear distinction between "history" as what has happened ("the past") and "history" as the record of what has happened. In the phrase "sacred history", "history" is used in the second of these senses, and "sacred history" is defined by the special character of the record. This special character derives from the privileged status of the writers and of their interpretative judgement on the events recorded by them. This is the "prophetic" quality of inspiration in the biblical canon'. (R. A. Markus, *Saeculum: History and Society in the Theology of St. Augustine* [Cambridge: Cambridge University Press, 1988], p. 231). Professor Markus does not see a similar distinction in Cullmann's concept of 'salvation history', and so prefers his own when dealing with Augustine. Professor Markus is probably correct, indeed his comments are amply borne out by Augustine's illumination theory of truth (an apposite example occurring at *De civ. Dei*, VI, 6: 'O Marcus Varro, without doubt the most acute and learned of men: but only a man and not a god; and neither prompted by the Spirit of God to apprehend and announce things divine'. [author's translation]), but from a strictly political point of view, the term 'salvation history' might be preferred in this instance as a more straightforward rendering of what Augustine means.

22 *See*, for instance, *Serm.*, LXXII, 10; *Serm.*, CCXXXI, 5; CCXCVII, 9; CXIV(B), 14; *De Trin.*, XIII, 6–12.

23 *De civ. Dei*, II, 3. Cf. *En. in Ps.*, 80, 1; *Serm.*, CXIV(B), 14; *Serm.*, CCCXI, 8; Tertullian, *Apoligeticum*, 40.

24 Though it should be pointed out that Augustine never hesitated to praise the Romans when he felt that they had acted 'according to the lights of the Earthly City' (*De civ. Dei*, V, 19). For instance, at *ibid.*, V, 18, he holds the Romans' achievements up as an admonishment to the Christian to strive the more ardently to bring a similar glory upon the City of God.

25 *Ibid.*, III, 23; 24; 26; 27; 28; 29; 30. Cf. *ibid.*, XIX, 5.

26 For instance, at *ibid.*, XV, 4.

27 This metaphor owes much to Augustine. He uses it at *Confess.*, IX, 1, 1.

28 At *Ep.*, CLXXXIX, 4, Augustine gives examples of notable Christians who served as soldiers; at *De civ. Dei*, I, 21, he expounds the general law to govern the subject of Christian killing: '. . . he to whom authority is delegated, and who is but the sword in the hand of him who uses it, is not himself responsible for the death he deals'; at *Ep.* CXXXVIII, 2, 15, he cites the advice given by John the Baptist to the soldiers: 'Do violence to no man, neither accuse *any* falsely; and be content with your wages.' [Lk. 3.14]; and at *Contra Faustum*, XXII, 75, he gives his answer to perhaps the most

difficult dilemma facing the Christian soldier: '. . . a righteous man, even if serving under an ungodly king, may discharge the proper duty of his office in the state by fighting according to the command of his sovereign . . . [T]he soldier [in this position] is innocent because he is under a duty to obey . . .' (author's translation).

29 *Ep.*, CXXXVIII, 2 (author's translation), 10–15. Cf. *ibid.*, CLXXXV, 2, 8; *En. in Ps.*, LI, 6 & CXXIV, 7 & CXVIII[XXXI], 1; *De lib. arb.*, 1, 15, 31; *Serm.*, LXII, 5, 8–10 & 15 & CCCXXVI, 2.

30 *Serm.*, XXIII(B), 13: '. . . for there must be no respect . . . neither of the world nor of the age itself . . .' (author's translation)

31 *De civ. Dei*, XIX, 14: 'In the Earthly City, then, the whole use of temporal things is referred to the enjoyment of earthly peace, while In the Heavenly City it refers to the enjoyment of eternal peace.' (author's translation)

32 *See*, for instance, Augustine's comments on Christian dress and manners at *ibid.*, XIX, 19: 'The Heavenly City is not disturbed by the dress or manner of those who hold to the faith that arrives at God; but only if these things do not contravene the Divine precepts. It is in this sense that philosophers who become Christians are required to change their false doctrines, though not their dress or customary mode of life . . .' (author's translation)

33 At *ibid.*, V, 21, Augustine explains that God gives earthly kingdoms to '. . . the pious and impious alike, as it may please Him, Whose pleasure is never unjust . . . He, therefore, Who is the one true God, Who never withholds from the human race either His judgement or His aid, gave a kingdom to the Romans when it pleased Him, and indeed to the extent that it pleased Him to do so. In addition He gave kingdoms to the Assyrians and to the Persians . . . in the case of individual men He discriminated in the same way. He Who gave power to Marius also gave it to Gaius Caesar; He Who gave it to Augustus also gave it to Nero . . .' (author's translation). Cf. *De civ. Dei*, V, 19.

34 To speculate on the subject of Christian rule was a pleasure that was largely denied Augustine by his general outlook. Consequently, he has very little to say on it; a fact that has contributed a great deal to the misinterpretation of his leading political ideas. What he does say is absolutely characteristic, though, for it amounts to a series of warnings to the Christian ruler not to a) take things to himself and b) neglect to promote the worship of the one true God in his kingdom. *Ep.*, CLV, 3, 10–13 is typical of his attitude. Cf. *De civ. Dei*, V, 24–26.

35 *En. in Ps.*, IV, 8: 'And I believe this to be the bearing of that which some understand skillfully; I mean, what the Lord said on seeing Caesar's tribute money, "Render therefore unto Caesar the things which are Caesar's; and unto God the things that are God's." [Mt. 22.21] As if He had said, in just

the same way as Caesar exacts from you the impression of his image, so also does God: that the soul, illumined and impressed with the light of His countenance, must be rendered to Him.' (author's translation). Cf. *Serm.*, CCCLIX(B), 13.

36 *De civ. Dei*, XIX, 17 (author's translation).

37 M. Minucius Felix seems to admit this when he says, 'We distinguish nations and tribes: to God the whole world is a single household' (M. Minucius Felix, *Octavius.*, XXXIII).

38 *See*, for instance, his declaration at *De Gen. ad litt.*, IX, 9, 14.

39 See *Confess.*, X, 21, 31; *De civ. Dei*, XIV, 4.

40 *En. in Ps.*, CXIX, 25 (author's translation). Cf. Tertullian, *Apologeticum*, 41: 'nothing matters to us in this age but to escape from it with all speed'.

41 Baynes, *The Political Ideas of St. Augustine's* De civitate Dei, p. 16.

42 *Confess.*, I, 19, 30.

43 Markus, *Saeculum*, p. 103.

4

The reception and interpretation of Augustine's political ideas in history

POLITICAL AUGUSTINIANISM

It is now possible for us to appreciate just how far Augustine's doctrine of the Two Cities was from a manifesto for positive political action, let alone Christian empire. Yet within a little over half a century of his death, in AD 430, that is exactly how it was coming to be construed. The letter sent by Pope Gelasius I to the Byzantine Emperor Anastasius I in AD 494 has already been mentioned as a possible terminus for the medieval period.[1] This is because it represents the first concrete expression of an idea the reality of which was just beginning to be seen towards the end of Augustine's lifetime, as the Goths closed in on the walls of Hippo. These Germanic invaders were just one of a number of barbarian tribes that had begun to tear into the Empire from the beginning of the fourth century. By their sheer numbers and vigour they quickly broke up the machinery of centralized Roman rule, establishing their small kingdoms in its place. This confronted the Church with a new and unexpected prospect. Under the old empire she had mainly been concerned with maintaining her autonomy *vis-à-vis* the established authority and power of the Emperor. Now she found that with the barbarian invasions this position of established authority and power had transferred to her: in terms of her organization and style, she was now the most meaningful expression of the Roman imperial ideal. For their part the barbarians were happy to recognize in her a culture and learning far superior to their own, and soon the more enlightened among them began to desire to ornament their rule with the new treasures of Hellenic thought.

The concept of Latin Christendom and the ideas of Pope Gelasius I

Something that the Church was able to do in the meantime was to attempt to establish in theory the proper functions of the spiritual and secular authorities within Latin Christendom. For in this she might steal a march on the barbarians, as yet unschooled in the delicate history of Church and State relations.[2] It is this development that the letter of Pope Gelasius I exemplifies. Historians of ideas talk freely of the 'Gelasian' theory, or even just 'Gelasianism'. By this they mean Gelasius' suggestion that in any Christian civilization, two distinct and unequal powers prevail: the spiritual and the secular, or *regnum* and *sacerdotium* as they came officially to be known. They are distinct because they reflect the two chief categories of human need: the material and the spiritual. To minister to his purely material needs man has the kings and princes of the world; to minister to his purely spiritual needs he has the clergy. They are unequal because, by the nature of the case, spiritual needs must be considered more important than temporal needs. In Gelasius' own words:

> There are indeed, most august Emperor, two powers by which this world is chiefly ruled: the sacred authority of the Popes and the royal power. Of these the priestly power is much more important, because it has to render account for the kings of men themselves at the Divine tribunal. For you know, our very clement son, that although you have the chief place in dignity over the human race, yet you must submit yourself faithfully to those who have charge of Divine things, and look to them for the means of your salvation . . . For if in matters pertaining to the administration of public discipline, the bishops of the Church, knowing that the Empire has been conferred on you by Divine instrumentality, are themselves obedient to your laws, lest in purely material matters contrary opinions may seem to

be voiced, with what willingness, I ask you, should you obey those to whom is assigned the administration of Divine mysteries?[3]

We notice immediately how Gelasius' ideas seem to draw on a general Augustinian outlook; in fact it would not be too difficult to show that they all have their antecedent in something Augustine said. Yet there remains something about their arrangement here that is unfamiliar, un-Augustinian. This is the assumption of Christian rule and of the hopes and ambitions that naturally attach to such an outlook. Nothing could be more foreign to Augustine's mindset than this characteristically medieval optimism. We might recall how earlier we estimated the radicalism of Augustine's leading political ideas from the point of view of their foundation in a dogmatic scheme for the salvation of mankind. 'Perhaps', Dyson thinks,

it is better to call it an eschatological politics. [For] he does not so much abandon the traditional values of peace and justice as postpone the hope for their realization to the next world. The best that mortals can hope for in this world is a set of arrangements that is less bad than it might be. Any government is better than nothing, because without restraint there could only be chaos. But all government is defective because its mechanisms are the devices by which a fallen world is regulated. Even pagan governments can accomplish justice and peace of a kind. States presided over by Christian rulers can accomplish these things better than other States, at least partly by devoting their resources to the service of spiritual needs. But the virtues of the Christian State are not, strictly speaking, political virtues. They arise from the use that righteous individuals make of faulty instruments; but the instruments remain faulty, and not even Christian government can rise above imperfection.[4]

For us the outstanding feature of Dyson's analysis is his suggestion that it is individuals who are redeemed, not societies: that the advantage of Christian rule when it occurs is not that it perfects politics but that it turns it to the salvation of souls. Correspondingly the state is always a neutral concept for Augustine. Unlike Cicero, St Ambrose and the other Fathers, his definition of the state does not include justice and law in their normal configurations (on this point it is, then, surprisingly modern). But how can it, says Augustine, when no state can be sure that all its citizens worship the one true God? Elsewhere he buttresses this view with comments such as, 'What is a commonwealth but a multitude of men, bought together into some bond of agreement?';[5] 'A commonwealth is nothing else but a harmonious multitude of men';[6] and finally,

> [Thus] who is so blind that they cannot discern how great an ornament the human race is for the earth, including even those who do not themselves lead praiseworthy lives; and, by the same token, how effectively the commonwealth coerces even sinners into the order of earthly peace?[7]

These thoughts, the premisses to all Augustine's conclusions on man, society and the state, were never taken up with any great enthusiasm after his death, and throughout the medieval period they continued to be studiously ignored. For the fact is that for the whole of this time, Church and State remained embroiled in a dispute constructed from a quite different set of premisses. These premisses will be familiar as the three interrelated themes (or religious and political preoccupations) that began Chapter 2. Of these we may now say that they suggest a revealing fact: that Rome cast a long shadow over the medieval period: that long after she had ceased to be a meaningful political force, the language of her achievements continued to resonate in the minds of her barbarian conquerors. In James Viscount Bryce's opinion, the idea of Rome was imperishable

> . . . because it was universal; and when its power had ceased, it was remembered with awe and love by the races whose separate existence it had destroyed, because it had spared the weak while it smote

down the strong; because it had granted equal rights to all, and closed against none of its subjects the path of honorable ambition.[8]

The medieval political lens

Such awe and respect was not something that the Church had always enjoyed under the Roman Emperors. For schooled in the municipal character of the old Roman religion, they had often struggled to understand the privileged position that she sought for herself. Up until the ninth century, nearly all the friction between Church and State in the West was generated by misunderstandings of this sort. From Constantine to Charlemagne (AD 742–814), the dominant rulers sought to bring Church matters under their own personal authority while the Church stubbornly resisted such lay interference along the lines suggested by Gelasius. Indeed Gelasius' solution – a dualism of power, or clearly defined spheres of interest for the secular and spiritual authorities – might have met with more success had the disputants not persisted with the old imperial language. This language had grown up at a time when no clear distinction between the secular and spiritual was imagined. As we have already shown, the ancient did not view his life in terms of separate departments that might necessitate equally separate institutions to minister to them. To the contrary, his life *was* his city, and he saw no reason why it should not form him for all needed as a man. And notwithstanding the great violence done to this ideal by the cold efficiency of Roman imperial government, it was to leave its mark on the language of politics. In the main, it manifested itself in the inability of either Church or State to conceive their authority in anything other than absolute terms. This unconscious commitment to an ancient habit of mind would eventually drive them towards two quite incompatible theories of *world* government.[9] To the Church this would mean moving from the largely defensive posturing of her first thousand years to the aggressive policies of the Gregorian Reformation and, finally, on to the staggering papal plenitude of power. By the nature of the case the State's strategy would be reactionary in relation to this unprecedented chain of events. As time went on, it developed a noticeably conservative character. Imperialists could increasingly be found countering the irresistible logic of the Church's position with appeals to historical precedent and sympathetic biblical example.

That the Church's logic was irresistible was down to the fact that it had its ancestor in that commonplace of ancient thought: the presumed superiority of spirit over matter. Plato is the outstanding early example of the political potential in this idea and, though the Church might well have produced a similar effect out of her own early teachings,[10] the reality of her uncomfortable situation in the Empire and the other-worldly character of her mission conspired to make this an unrealistic project. All of this would change, however, with the Christianization of the Empire and then again with its dissolution at the hands of the barbarian invaders. But it would need a man of depth and authority to fashion a coherent political theory from the materials on offer: to set about transforming classical moral and political philosophy from the point of view of the Scriptures. Naturally the Church felt that in Augustine, and in his extended synthesis of Christianity and Neoplatonism, she had found such a man. For after all, with some careful editing, might not his doctrine of the Two Cites, though ostensibly teaching an austere realism, become the vehicle for a more enthusiastic message? Regrettably, the story of how Augustine came to be recruited for this unlikely cause cannot be told here; it has, besides, been told very well by others. It is enough that we have shown why the Church might have wanted to recruit him in the first place. What we need to turn to now is the question of how his political ideas appeared through the medieval lens? That is, which of them were brought into particular focus, and why? In addition, we should bear in mind how much depends on this. As we pointed out in the Introduction, Augustine's medieval interpreters effectively laid down the main lines for all subsequent misinterpretation of his political ideas. By rejecting his vision of the human condition, of the irredeemable character of institutions made with hands – both secular and spiritual – they fudged his carefully wrought distinction between the truths of reason and revelation, effectively turning political pessimism into prophetic utopianism.

Augustine: political pessimist or prophetic utopian?

A theme that will recur in our discussion of the reception and interpretation of Augustine's political ideas is their silence on certain key
points. It is our contention that this silence need not be confounding;
that Augustine can be made to speak of things that, for reasons of time
and inclination, he was never able to write down. Taking the case of
the medieval period, we might fairly presume that had he been able to
anticipate the future political pretensions of the Church, he would at
least have written in clarification of whether he was a political pessimist
or a prophetic utopian. To Henry Paolucci, at any rate, these were the
two outlooks that most adequately conveyed the distance of possible
opinions on his political ideas. As examples, he gave Friedrich Meinecke's
suggestion in his *Die idee der Staatsräson* that Augustine is the precursor
to Machiavelli and Étienne Gilson's assertion that he is in fact the chief
source of 'that ideal of a world society which is haunting the minds of
so many today'.[11]

That Paolucci chose his poles exceptionally well is shown by the question that many new students of Augustine's *De civitate Dei* ask: 'How can
such an optimistic philosophy of history account for such a pessimistic
set of social and political ideas?' How, in other words, can a dogmatic
belief in the wisdom and providence of a good and just God be reconciled with an unshakeable conviction in the futility and hopelessness of
human endeavour? In the previous chapter we noticed that, unlike Hegel
and Marx, Augustine's philosophy of history does not redeem politics;
that in fact it leaves it largely untouched, treating it as something natural
rather than conventional; so natural that it becomes one of the conditions
of life in a fallen world. Such talk invariably brings Hobbes to mind,
as well as Machiavelli. To both these men politics was a cynical game
forced upon men by their terror of the alternative,[12] and that Augustine
has plenty to say in support of this diagnosis is now clear. What is not
so clear, however, is what he has to say by way of a cure. In his opinion
men are everywhere sinning and openly flouting the laws of their cities
yet not disturbing God's eternal plan. In fact it is through their actions,
good and bad, that God works His plan. Sometimes it is possible for the

human mind to see this happening, as when criminals are sentenced to do productive work for the city whose laws they have contravened. But as Augustine readily concedes, these are rare instances, and, more usually God's Will is not clearly reflected in earthly arrangements.

Evidently, then, there is a troubling epistemological distance between Augustine's thinking on nature, morality and politics and this, his grand historical vision. How is it that men can freely disobey the various normative laws laid down for their benefit yet not disturb the higher, eternal law of God's sovereign Will? If the various normative laws are moral – that is to say, if they stand to reason – then what is the eternal law? Is it moral in any intelligible sense, or does it represent something else altogether? Indeed, does it have any positive existence at all, or does it merely express the conviction that God will mysteriously work all things to a good and just end? To ask these questions is to touch upon an interesting issue that we raised earlier: the difference between utopian and salvation histories. We said then that Augustine believed Adam had forfeited his right to a utopian history by disobeying God in the Garden of Eden, and that from that point onwards, salvation history began on the initiative of God's Grace and Mercy. We also made the point how disconcertingly independent salvation histories are of the normal strategies for human improvement, or, to put the matter from the other perspective, the distinguishing feature of any utopian history must surely be the way that it ennobles human activity and coordinates it in the pursuit of some final good. We might say that utopian histories are vindicated by the ordinary experiences of men: that they produce arrangements the fundamental goodness and justness of which appeal to the normal categories of human understanding. Not so the salvation histories or, at least, not so the salvation history of Augustine. We have already said something about the extraordinary generosity of Augustine's remarks on Divine sovereignty: that he seems to think that the goodness of God and of His actions comprehensively outreaches the limited terms of human understanding. Morality and the laws of nature; these things are truly good – time and time again Augustine is at pains to point this out.[13] Yet at the same time he always insists that, for all their suggestion of a foothold in the Divine scheme of things, they do not translate the sovereign Will of God. This insistence offers the greatest clue to where Augustine stands on the spectrum between political pessimism and prophetic utopianism. Its basis is his literal interpretation of the first three books of Genesis.

Augustine's interpretation of events in the Garden of Eden

At *De Genesi ad litteram*, VIII, 6, 12, Augustine interprets the name of the 'Tree of Good and Evil' to be a reference to the virtue by which the rational creation pleases God:

> It was proper that man, placed in a state of dependence upon the Lord God, should be given some prohibition, so that obedience would be the virtue by which he would please his Lord. I can truthfully say that this is the only virtue of every rational creature who lives life under God's rule, and that the fundamental and greatest vice is the overweening pride by which one wishes to have independence to his own ruin, and the name of the vice is disobedience. There would not, therefore, be any way for a man to realize and feel that he was subject to the Lord unless he was given some command.

This bold statement is the clue to Augustine's understanding of the Creation narrative as it unfolds across the first three books of Genesis. The rational creation – that is, man and the angels – is distinguished by its capacity to hear, to understand and to obey God's commands. The true gift and value of intellect, or reason, is that it places us in a position to choose to obey the commands of God's Will; this is a position that is denied the non-rational creation with will but not intellect.[14] This is the same point that Augustine chose to make in his *De libero arbitrio*, an early work begun in AD 388 – just a year after his baptism and the formative intellectual experiences of Cassiciacum:

> It is one thing to be rational, and another to be wise: for it is by reason that anyone is capable of receiving [and comprehending] a

command, but obedience is a matter of faith. Just as it is the nature
of reason to comprehend a command, it is wisdom which counsels
obedience. This is the same thing as to say that it is in the nature
of a rational creature to receive and comprehend commands, but
wisdom is a function of something else, namely, the will.[15]

Such a clear understanding of the use of intellect has important epistemological consequences, the essence of which we can sum up in the
following question: 'What sort of knowledge did Adam possess in
Paradise if his intellect was entirely inspired and directed by God?' The
answer to this question is also the definitive answer to the question of
whether Augustine was a political pessimist or a prophetic utopian. For
it is only by understanding what Augustine thought Adam gave up in
Paradise, that we can begin to appreciate what he might have thought
possible this side of it. If, for instance, Adam was able to share in the
first principles of God's Wisdom in Paradise, then there might be reason
to suspect that outside of it he was able to fashion a mode of life in
concert with the created order. This would support those who would
seek to find in Augustine's political ideas the justification for ambitious
ethical schemes, and thus a continuation of the trajectory of the Western
political tradition.

The type of knowledge that Adam possessed at any one time in
Paradise, as well as the nature of the Wisdom that he hoped to attain,
is best described in terms of the experience of a child growing up. From
the evidence of the first three books of Genesis it seems clear that Adam
knew nothing that God had not first told him, or allowed him to discover for himself; what is more, it was simply not in his created nature
to question the truth of what God was telling him or revealing to him.
Adam was like a child because he was ignorant of a great deal but not
conscious of this fact. He was happy in a way that it is not permitted for
men to be happy amidst the pressures of becoming their own sources of
truth.[16] His obedience of God's commands was absent of the impulse to
understand why they were right, and so, following the course that God
had established for him, he proved the rightness of His commands and

grew into the wisdom of His ways.[17] In technical language borrowed from legal philosophy, we would say that Adam was subject to a voluntarist conception of law: that his obedience did not refer to the content of the law but to its source: the Voice of God. Tellingly, Augustine stresses that when Adam's disobedience was discovered, God addressed only his ambition and pride with the words, 'Behold, the man is become as one of us, to know good and evil'.[18]

> God spoke these words not so much to heap opprobrium on Adam as to instill in the rest of mankind, for whom these words have been written down, a fear of being filled with the same pride. God said, 'Behold, the man is become as one of us, to know good and evil'. How are we to interpret this other than to say that it is an example presented for the purpose of inspiring us with fear? For in addition to [not becoming a god, as he had been promised] the man Adam did not even retain the condition in which he had been created.[19]

Adam had, in other words, secured nothing other than his descent into an inferior type of knowledge.

A consideration of Adam's epistemological status in Paradise allows us to reach certain conclusions regarding the nature of the society that he enjoyed there. From the evidence of his writings, Augustine seems genuinely to have thought that Adam and Eve would have gone on to found a numerous human race by conjugal union even if they had not sinned. It seems, then, that some sort of human society was always part of God's plan for Paradise:

> The vast number of angels in the Heavenly City cannot be adduced as proof that man and woman would not be joined in conjugal union if they were not to die. Indeed, the perfect number of saints to rise and join the angels was predestinated by the Lord when He said, 'For in the resurrection they neither marry, nor are given in marriage, but are as the angels of God in Heaven.' [Mt. 22.30] On this scheme, then, the earth was to be filled with men, and in view of the close

ties of relationship and the bond of unity so earnestly desired, it was to be populated by men from one common ancestor. For what other purpose, then, was a female helper like to the man sought unless it was to have the female sex assist in the sowing of the human race, as the fertility of the earth does in the sowing of crops?[20]

Working backwards from the epistemological condition of Paradise, this society would evidently have taken the form of a union of men and women, equal in respect of their shared access to the privileged knowledge of what to do in the actual present in order to bring about a complete reconciliation of interests and the manifestation of God's Will. In the attitude of its members to their Lord, this society would have resembled something of a dictatorship but, crucially, Augustine seems to think that it would have achieved what no human dictatorship can: true freedom through perfect submission and obedience – a state that has elsewhere been described by the term the 'Perfect Law of Liberty'.[21]

Law, human society and the requirements of freedom
To achieve true freedom through law has ever been the problem of political life, though it might be more accurate to say that it has ever been the problem that has made human life political. Everyone knows the opening lines to Jean-Jacques Rousseau's (1712–1778) *Du contrat social*: 'Man is born free, and everywhere he is in chains'.[22] And those more familiar with his work will know that he overcomes this dilemma by confounding freedom and chains in a kind of popular dictatorship, the dictatorship of the *Volonté Générale* 'General Will'. Rousseau's is certainly one way to combine 'liberty' and 'law'[23] – those two mutually antagonistic categories of the human mind. Another way is simply to seek an utter reconciliation between our personal will and the will of the law. We might fairly call it the freedom of the happy slave, for it consists in so delimiting our expectations that they come in time to match exactly the proscriptions of the law. This is the kind of solution that thinking men are apt to imagine on Christianity's behalf. T. H. Green (1836–1882) furnishes a typical example:

The law, merely as law or as an external command, is a source of bondage in a double sense. Presenting to man a command which yet it does not give him power to obey, it destroys the freedom of the life in which he does what he likes without recognizing any reason why he should not (the state of which St. Paul says 'I was alive without the law once') . . . Freedom (also called 'peace,' and 'reconciliation') comes when the spirit expressed in the law . . . becomes the principle of action in the man. To the man thus delivered, as St. Paul conceives him, we might almost apply phraseology like Kant's. 'He is free because conscious of himself as the author of the law which he obeys.' He is no longer a servant, but a son. He is conscious of union with God, Whose Will as an external law he before sought in vain to obey, but whose 'righteousness is fulfilled' in him now that he 'walks after the spirit.'[24]

But this solution, though it seems to give a very satisfactory philosophical phrasing of St Paul, is still some way from Augustine's thinking on the matter. To some extent we can anticipate this conclusion by noticing the way in which it grants man ownership of the 'spirit of the law'. We might remember how some time ago we gave Aquinas' definition of law in a similar context.[25] Now it seems that his definition would do very well here as a neat rendering of Green's thesis. To Aquinas, laws were always 'ordinances of reason'.[26] They were always ordinances of reason because whether or not Divinely inspired, they had to stand before the bar of human understanding before being passed into law. This power of veto is noticeably absent from Augustine's thought. He never imagines to put conditions on Divine inspiration or to qualify it in any way. When it comes to the sovereign Will of God, there are no 'slide-rules' or criteria of truth that can constrain it.[27] In fact, Augustine is quite certain that its content can have no bearing whatsoever on its goodness and justness, and this conviction stems from his literal reading of events in the Garden of Eden. For when Adam chose not to be part of a utopian history, he consigned all men to pay the price of his decision. The moment his eyes were opened in the Garden of Eden, God appeared to him in the mould of a dictator. In that instant, the freedom of perfect obedience in the Garden seemed a small and cruel thing compared to the great experiment in living that awaited him outside. To stay inside the Garden would have meant remaining in a state of naïve and loving submission to God, obeying commands whose first principles would always remain hidden from him. To leave it would have meant becoming the architect of his own destiny:

> The devil, then, would not have been able to tempt man to the manifest and open sin of doing what God had forbidden had man not already become conscious of his ability to will for himself. This is why Adam was delighted when it was said, 'ye shall be as gods.' [Gen. 3.5] But, of course, Adam and Eve would have more resembled gods if they had clung to their highest and truest source of inspiration in obedience. As it was, they became their own sources of inspiration in pride. This is so because created gods owe nothing to their nature [which is not in itself Divine], but become gods by their participation in the true God [cf. Ps. 81.12]. By striving after more, man is diminished; when once he has identified his capacity for self-sufficiency, he falls away from the One Who truly suffices him.[28]

And so Adam stepped out of the Garden of Eden to fashion a new world in his own fallen likeness, a world in which it is expedient to estimate everything from the point of view of selfishness, pride and greed, and yet also a world that is softened by a mysterious, still, small voice: mysterious because it is not at all clear where it comes from, and still because it expects to be obeyed.[29] We might on this evidence choose to call it a political world.

We have now arrived at Augustine's answer to those who question how the eternal law works its purpose through the various normative laws laid down for man's benefit. It is characteristically human to presume that at some fundamental level, all the laws of the universe form a single piece; that a clever man can begin at the bottom – with just a handful of dim intuitions, and from there work his way by sound reasoning to nearly the summit of wisdom.[30] In fact it is characteristically human to presume that the universe has laws at all, but this particular philosophical stone must be left unturned by us. To try to turn it here would be inappropriate, and it has, in any case, been well turned by others.[31] We must instead continue with the thought that, if we are willing to discount these presumptions, then the question how the various normative laws reconcile themselves to the eternal law ceases to be meaningful. It ceases to be meaningful because we are no longer talking about a difference of degree between the laws, but one of kind, and that leaves no hope for human understanding. The common morality of man anticipates nothing of the Divine goodness; neither, for that matter, does the peace and justice of earthly politics anticipate anything of the true peace and true justice of the City of God. The clearest proof, if proof be needed, is the nonsense that comes of trying to rationalize, or verify, the lights of conscience:

> If this faith is taken away from human affairs, who will not conclude that disorder and awful confusion must follow? For how can anyone love another out of mutual charity when loving itself is of the order of things unseen, and if we choose not to believe what we cannot see? In this way will the whole scheme of friendship perish insofar as it is premised in our belief in mutual love . . . [T]o this degree are human affairs thrown into disorder, if we choose not to believe in what we cannot see. In fact, they would in this case be altogether and utterly overthrown if we did not believe in the unseen good intentions of men towards one another . . . [I]f, then, we choose not to believe those things which we cannot see, the first victim will be human society which is sprung from a concord of men's wills.[32]

In his lectures on education, C. S. Lewis (1898–1963) gave a characteristically clear rendering of this Augustinian logic:

> There are progressions in which the last step is *sui generis* – incommensurable with the others – and in which to go the whole way is to undo all the labour of your previous journey. To reduce [morality] to a mere natural product is a step of that kind. Up to that point, the

kind of explanation which explains things away may give us something, though at a heavy cost. But you cannot go 'explaining away'
for ever: you will find that you have explained explanation itself
away. You cannot go on 'seeing through' things for ever. The whole
point of seeing through something is to see something through it. It
is good that the window should be transparent, because the street
or garden beyond is opaque. How if you saw through the garden
too? It is no use trying to 'see through' first principles. If you see
through everything, then everything is transparent. But a wholly
transparent world is an invisible world. To 'see through' all things
is the same as not to see.[33]

In order to see in this world a man must swallow his pride. He must
realize that the lights that illuminate his heart and mind are a Divine
gift.[34] And Augustine seems genuinely to think that if he will only start
to take this realization seriously, he will find himself pondering that most
profound of all profound mysteries: the Perfect Law of Liberty. As students of moral and political ideas, we are sensitive to how the desire to
achieve perfect freedom through law haunts our various endeavours as
individuals and citizens. It was of course no different in Augustine's day.
Perhaps, then, we can go so far as to say that it is this predicament that
has mainly shaped the Western political tradition; that there is something
of real and enduring value in Pascal's observation that, 'It is odd, when
one thinks of it, that there are people in the world who, having renounced
all the laws of God and nature, have themselves made laws which they
rigorously obey . . .'[35]

The Will of God, the will of man and the implications of a universal rationality

Considerations such as these give the clue to why Augustine thought the
commands of God's Sovereign Will appear so intolerable to men this side
of Paradise. The fact is that they aim at an end separated from the actual
present by an impossible distance of time.[36] This difference between eter-
nality and temporality is how Augustine believed the Creator/creature

relationship must appear from the metaphysical perspective (though he never intended that it should qualify the intrinsic goodness and justness of God's commands). It is the reason why God's commands do not, in one of Oswald Chambers' phrases, '. . . tell [a man] along the line of [his] natural senses what to expect'.[37] In Paradise none of this could matter while Adam remained obedient to the Perfect Law of Liberty; for then, looking to God for all his seeing, he shared in an eternity not of endless intervals of time – the way that eternity must appear from the temporal perspective – but of an actual present without end. To not have to worry about what the future may hold; to not have to apply forethought in order to secure tomorrow's necessities; to not be haunted by the fleeting and transient nature of pleasures:[38] these are among the advantages that we might associate with unquestioningly devolving all responsibility for the conduct of the actual present to God. But the point, of course, is that it was not for these advantages that Adam first obeyed God's commands. He obeyed them because he loved God with the whole of his heart and mind.[39] To conceive his situation before God in terms of advantages would have made no sense to him at all. It would have been illogical: for if it was true that he had known nothing else, what could it realistically be an advantage on? This is something of a truism, but to Augustine's mind it was of the first importance because it traces a watershed between two epistemologies. The one accepts knowledge on the word of God; the other looks to substantiate it with reference to something else.[40] The one imagines no intellectual meeting-place with God; the other that such a common understanding is possible. Augustine had a characteristic way of illustrating what he meant by this. He often talked of how we can know something in a positive or negative sense: that is, we can either know exactly what something is, and nothing more, or we can know what something is by setting it in relief against the experience of what it is not.[41] Accordingly,

He who loves the good without having known evil, that is to say, he who loves it in itself, before having had the chance to love it in relief against evil, is of all mankind most worthy of praise. But if

this were not a matter of singular merit it would not be attributed to
the Child of the race of Israel, Who, receiving the name Emmanuel,
'God with us' [Mt. 1.23; cf. Isa. 7.14], reconciled us to God . . .
Concerning Him the prophet said, 'For before the child shall know
to refuse the evil, and choose the good . . . [Isa. 7.16]'

But how does He reject or choose what He has not first known
unless it is that these two things, evil and good, are known in one
way by the knowledge of good and in another way by the experience of evil? . . . Hence, before the Child knew by experience a good
which He might lack, or, what is really the same thing, an evil which
He would feel in the loss of a good, He rejected evil to do good.
He has thus furnished us with a singular example of obedience; for
when we consider the matter we see that He did not come to do His
own will but the Will of Him by whom He was sent [cf. Jn 6.38].
In this He differed from him who chose to do his own will, not the
Will of his Creator. It is rightly said, then, that, 'For as by one man's
disobedience many were made sinners, so by the obedience of one
shall many be made righteous,' [Rom. 5.19] since, 'For as in Adam
all die, even so in Christ shall all be made alive.' [1 Cor. 15.22][42]

Augustine's point is that there is a categorical difference between the
proposition 'God is good' and the proposition 'good is God'. For if God
is good then goodness has a certain independence vis-à-vis God, and
therefore to understand goodness is to bring an aspect of God under
the legislation of the mind. But if good is God, then goodness is entirely
bound up in the mysterious movements of God's sovereign will; it has no
independence and cannot be reduced to some lowest common denominator – T. H. Green's 'spirit of the law', perhaps. It is commonplace to
observe that the human mind is so configured that it needs something of
this sort to stand apart as its ultimate source of reference; its criteria of
truth all demand some standard to which they can refer. Augustine seems
to see an explanation of this fact in the events of the Garden of Eden,
and consequently he is inclined to attribute all subsequent history to a

catastrophic change of mind initiated by an equally catastrophic change of heart. Yet unexpectedly, this does not make his outlook on temporal affairs especially idealistic. In his opinion salvation history is a fundamentally private matter: the narrative of discrete and uncoordinated events of individual salvation – each one miraculous, each one an instance of the private soul participating, through obedience, in the eternal purpose of God's sovereign Will.[43] Men fool themselves into thinking that their exertions intimate or realize an eternal plan. Or less logically still, they attempt to justify them by discerning in history a pattern of progress and development. Quite fantastic constructions of the mind have been thrown up by men determined not to face the precariousness of their existence alone. But whatever comfort they may take from inventing gods and philosophies and imagining that through them they can influence the general run of affairs, Augustine thinks that history, that is, temporal history – history viewed from the limited perspective of the actual present – will always be a matter of material causes, both within and without of man's control. If we were to call it a continuous collision of selfish wills set against the backdrop of a capricious and mysterious (natural) world we would not be far from Augustine's original meaning.

Here, then, are the foundations of that aspect of Augustine's political thinking which it is traditional to call pessimistic, or realistic: his vision of human history as a procession of the depressingly familiar, each episode just as bad as the last – and now underpinned by a damning epistemology. The human mind is not sufficient to create anything truly new; indeed, it is parasitic and must always discover some premiss from which to ratiocinate.[44] So that they do not devour each other in their hunger, men are tossed the laws of nature like scraps from the Divine table and, though the food is nourishing and good for their moral wellbeing, in its inexplicability it is harmful to their pride.[45]

We must now ask ourselves where this leaves those who would claim Augustine for prophetic utopianism? Despite what we have said, is there anything in his thinking to support a wider and less discriminating portfolio for salvation history? Or, what is effectively the same thing, are there any grounds for a positive Christian politics, some theory of world government to fill the void between the Two Cities and meet God halfway? On the evidence we have presented, the straightforward answer must be 'no', for although it is flattering to underestimate the significance that Augustine attaches to the watershed between temporality and eternity, he clearly believes there is no overcoming it. It may well be the case that God pilots the universe with exquisite control, but this fact can have no bearing on conditions within a time-bound world. It can have no bearing because even reason, man's one realistic hope of independence *vis-à-vis* God, is affected by it. Man, a part of the rational creation, has been designed to live in the enjoyment of loving obedience so that it is natural to him to live under law.[46] But it is not natural for God the Creator to live under law, for He is the source of the law and its inspiration. Consequently He does not pilot the universe according to principles or methods, that is, principles or methods the essence or spirit of which might be appropriated for use on earth. Augustine thinks that it is characteristic of fallen human nature to think that He might. For when Adam turned away from God, he did not turn away from law and its necessity; rather he became a 'law unto himself'. Augustine is not surprised, then, when men insist on presuming that the universe should submit to human categories of understanding: for the fact is that human categories of understanding are inextricably bound up with the metaphysics of temporality.[47] And therefore he is not surprised either when men insist on conceiving eternity in temporal terms, as intervals of time without end rather than one endless actual present. For the fact is that, although men may have escaped their duty of obedience to God, they have not escaped the limitations of their design and equipment. This gives uniformity to their efforts to establish a kind of paradise on earth as well as furnishing the theoretical basis of Christian realism.

These thoughts mark the limit of what Augustine was prepared to say about events in the Garden of Eden before the Fall. His general approach was to follow the narrative of the first three books of Genesis to the word; to interpret literally wherever possible; and only to fall back on allegory when literalism could reveal nothing sensible.[48] We notice in particular that it was because he treated the Garden of Eden as an episode in history, rather than a foundation myth, that he saw no more than a diagnostic potential in it.[49] It presented a unique event, the ending of one type of history and the beginning of another. Paradise is lost; it can have no bearing on earthly arrangements. Man is fallen; his salvation lies in an 'eternal city not made with hands'.[50] Thoughts such as these prevented Augustine from indulging the kind of political imagination that we have associated with the medieval mindset, and which was already gaining ground with certain writers before him.[51] As Dyson puts it:

> At the centre of Augustine's conception of political life lie two key ideas: the impairment of our relationship with God by sin, and the conviction that this impairment has consequences for every aspect of man's individual and collective life. It is in light of this conviction that Augustine so largely abandons the kind of political morality associated with Plato and Aristotle. It is also in light of it that he comprehensively dismisses the traditional moral and political claims of Rome.[52]

H.-X. Arquillière and political Augustinianism

It is now appropriate for us to examine the fate of Augustine's political ideas in the medieval period: that is, the use to which they were put by thinkers determined to reject the foundations of his Christian realism. Scholars of the period are in broad agreement that medieval thinkers exploited (consciously and unconsciously) a perceived ambiguity in Augustine's distinction between the truths of reason and revelation. Of these scholars the most significant for our purposes is H.-X. Arquillière, for it was he who was responsible for bringing the term 'political Augustinianism' to prominence. It is his analysis of the medieval intellectual climate that is going to be leaned on here. Our concern is to establish the main lines along which medieval thinkers misinterpreted Augustine's political ideas with a view to arguing that they set the pattern for all subsequent misinterpretations of them.

We have seen that, from the point of view of the history of ideas, the medieval period begins with the reversal in fortunes of the institutions of Church and State. The Church, hitherto dependent on the goodwill of the Roman Empire while at the same time remaining indifferent to its fortunes, finds itself in a position of authority and influence with the breaking up of the Empire by the barbarians. For their part the barbarians, politically represented by their small kingdoms (and in that sense very loosely rendered by the term 'State'), find themselves faced with an institution and an idea – the idea of Latin Christendom – whose splendour and scope they cannot but appreciate. Employing one of those regrettable generalizations of history, we might say that it is over the right to exploit the political potential in this idea that Church and State dispute in the medieval period. We can correspondingly characterize medieval political argument according to the following preoccupations:

1. The need to justify political activity in light of the doctrine of Original Sin: the question of the 'natural right of the State'.
2. The question of the state's position *vis-à-vis* the Church in light of the ontological superiority of spiritual over temporal matters.
3. The source, status and control of political power.

What should immediately strike us about these preoccupations is their distance from the ethical idealism of Hellenic thought. The philosophical individualism that Rome did so little to foster finds few opportunities for expression in the medieval period. It is replaced by a thinly disguised realism grounded in the importance of political power. This is a situation that could not easily have arisen while the Church remained true to the apolitical character of Scripture. As termini for the medieval period we might, then, choose dates that mark the time during which the papacy remained viable as a force for world government (AD 494–1493).[53]

We should now consider what aspects of Augustine's thought resonated with the medieval political milieu. Dyson suggests the following framework of six tightly interwoven themes:

1. The temporal and spiritual powers are separate spheres of authority, ordained to different purposes and employing different methods. But

the quality of the two powers is asymmetrical. It is asymmetrical because

2. spiritual power is intrinsically or metaphysically superior to temporal power, and,

3. unlike spiritual power, political power can achieve only what is negative and external, and is necessary at all only because human beings have become estranged from God. Political power has no positive moral good to contribute to our lives.

4. Ordinarily, inasmuch as the state is a divinely-ordained instrument of order and discipline, obedience is due as a matter of religious duty, even to wicked rulers; but spiritual matters must in the nature of the case take precedence over temporal ones in the event of conflict.

5. Christian rulers have a duty to rule well, to set a good example to those under them and to make their resources available for the advancement and defence of the Church. Their duties include the enactment and enforcement of laws against heretics and schismatics; but

6. those duties are owed by Christian rulers not because they are subject to the Church's command *qua* rulers, but because, *qua* Christians, they find themselves in a position that affords opportunities for service of a particular kind.[54]

These themes are certainly consistent with our enumeration of Augustine's political ideas. But in light of the dynamics of political argument in the medieval period they are clearly susceptible of a more enthusiastic interpretation. And the key to their susceptibility is the absence of any mention of God's Will. Disputants in the political struggles of the period did not typically concern themselves with this aspect of Augustine's thinking. Their priority was to establish a conceptual understanding of man, society and the state; to use this understanding as a basis for theories of world government; and, finally, not to trouble themselves with the question whether their plan might be coincidental with God's. This agenda caused them to pass over those aspects of Augustine's thought dealing with the ineffability of God, the metaphysical restrictions of temporality, and the limitations of man's fallen condition. Consequently they were able to be optimistic about the possibilities of politics in ways that he never could be. Probably the palmary example of this comes from Giles of Rome's (ca 1247–1316) *De ecclesiastica potestate*, one of the more forthright defences of the papal plenitude of power. It was written near the climax of the dispute between Pope Boniface VIII (1235–1303) and Philip the Fair of France (1268–1314) – probably, Dyson thinks, in 1302.[55] Giles had become the first Augustinian regent master at the University of Paris in 1285. From 1291 to 1294 he would be Prior General of the Augustinian Order of Hermits. In Part I, Chapter 5 of his work, Giles produces the following 'Augustinian' argument for the superiority of the Church in all matters spiritual and temporal. We will notice in particular how he argues from the spiritual government of the universe to the Church's government of the world without any intervening mention of God's Will:

> Therefore, if we wish to see which power stands under which power, we must pay attention to the government of the whole mechanism of the world. And we see in the government of the universe that the whole of corporeal substance is governed through the spiritual ... Hence Augustine, at *De Trinitate*, 3:4, says that 'certain more gross and inferior bodies are ruled in a certain order through the more subtle and the more potent; but all bodies through spirit, and the whole of creation by its Creator.' And what we see in the order and government of the universe we must picture to ourselves in the government of the commonwealth and in the government of the whole Christian people ... Therefore the most beautiful order of the universe is well reflected in the Church and among the faithful in that, just as inferior bodies are there ruled through superior and the whole of corporeal substance through spiritual and the spiritual itself by God, so also, in the Church, temporal and inferior Lords are ruled through superiors and all temporal and earthly power through the spiritual, and especially through the Supreme Pontiff; but the Supreme Pontiff will be subject to the judgement of God alone.[56]

There seems little doubt that Giles' argument in this case is plainly in the line of the Western political tradition as rejected by Augustine. His misinterpretation of Augustine takes an exemplary form and therefore lays down one of our 'main lines'. Giles took it for granted that the Christian God is a silent God who will no longer speak into the actual present as of old. He will no longer speak into the actual present because He has made His Will manifest in the rational order of the universe and the revealed truths of Scripture. Between these two revelations lies enough to form a man for all he might need in life. The key to God's Will correspondingly lies in interpreting and understanding, not listening and knowing. To attempt to view Augustine's political ideas through such a lens is evidently to distort them badly, for it is to take them into a tradition that they were consciously formulated to stand against. To remove the living reality of God's Will from Augustine's thought in this way is to force it to bear a false order and logic. This is the order and logic of a system.[57] A brief examination of H.-X. Arquillière's thesis will help us to see this.

Theories of world government and the Christian rationalization of political right

Arquillière begins his explanation of 'political Augustinianism' in a familiar place:

> [In this matter] Saint Augustine does not speak with a different voice to Saints Ambrose and John Chrysostom. He binds himself tightly to the tradition [of the natural right of the State], and, through those Fathers who precede him, to the New Testament which impregnates his thought . . . [As such, he believes that] the Christian is not freed from the obligations that license the citizen to obey those in rightful authority over him; and which being, in this present life, the government of temporal things . . . However, in distinction from his predecessors, he has been brought by the recriminations of the pagans to formulate an acerbic critique of the pagan state. He has applied his theological conceptions to the problem . . . He has applied his concept of justice to the state. He has scrutinized the

notion of the state. He has made appeal to Cicero and the Stoics. He has confronted their conceptions with the Christian idea of justice. We have seen, indeed, how high this idea exalts "free" justice: that which is born of Faith and Grace;[58] and Augustine seems to think that it is this idea of justice in particular that the Roman state – on account of the fact that it sets up cults to false gods – has set itself against. However, we have also ascertained by means of a most profound analysis, that behind these condemnable rites of idolatry, the grand doctor, in accordance with the tradition [of the Church], discerned the legitimate character of the ancient political constitutions: that is to say, their God-given rôle in maintaining order; and that in addition to this, he affirmed that even when their kings or emperors are apostates or pagans, they do not escape the designs of providence.[59]

Here, for Arquillière, is the germ of political Augustinianism. In theory the state can have nothing to do with true, Christian justice; indeed it is the archetypal fallen institution. However, by the logic of providence it is somehow implicated in what the Christian is enjoined to believe is God's good and just plan for the world. Ostensibly this conundrum is resolved by pointing towards its remedial function as a vehicle for human social life. But the fact remains that providence implies more than this. It is difficult for the human mind not to see in the very real goods of the state – goods such as peace, society, justice and so on – anticipations of a greater reality. It is in this elevating movement of the human mind that all the joys of purely intellectual speculation are found. Others before us have gone so far as to discern within it the basis of the Western criterion of truth.[60] For Arquillière, at any rate, it accurately traces the general process out of which a systematic Christian politics was developed:

Faced with the Roman state, the Church Fathers tended to affirm the primacy of spirituals in the life of faith. It was through this that the error was begun; for the primacy of the papacy had naturally to be implied in this idea. That said, the time of the papacy imposing itself on political society, as would occur with Nicholas I and Gregory VII, was still a long way off. But once it arrived, it would no longer suffice that the emperors allow Christianity to inspire their actions, like Constantine and Theodosius, and – for me the other concern – show themselves to be the defenders of the Faith. This would leave the notion of the state to be penetrated by the Christian idea. Moreover, the slow work of breaking up the well-established natural foundations of the state would work towards their dilution in a new conception of the Christian world until they were crystallized into something new and [effectively] issued in the Middle Ages. And of this gradual movement we have said that it is Gregory the Great who furnishes the clearest evidence of this transition from the thought of Augustine to that which we have called 'political Augustinianism'.[61]

Augustine plainly saw the state for what it was: a largely remedial device vindicated *ratione peccati*. And because of this he just as plainly saw what it could never be: a transformative force, rationalized according to the rôle it might play in the coordination of a new universal Christian society. The final good of any such society must be that it translates into temporal form, eternal principles of political right. Here, as we have seen, lies the crux of the matter. For to Augustine, the whole value and significance of the earth and its institutions, both secular and spiritual, is to bring a select group of men and women (pilgrims) to the point of realizing that their salvation consists in obedience to God's Voice in the actual present. This is the radical aspect of all Augustine's thinking on man, society and the state. It is also the radical aspect of his thinking on more strictly theological matters. As we will notice later, Augustine does not typically frame his understanding of Christian action in terms of ideologies and policies. This is because he thinks that it is impossible to legislate for what God will call individuals to do in the actual present, whether they are citizens, bishops or princes. The impulse to legislate for such things is explained for him in the narrative of the Fall; indeed, it is one of the most consistent features of fallen human nature:

For certain of our thoughts, though they pertain to future things, are anticipated with such plainness and certainty that they appear near to us [in time]. This we achieve by means of our memory . . . though memory, of course, belongs to the past rather than the future . . . We know, indeed we are certain, that this phenomenon plays out in our mind; it may be that it is produced by our mind. However, this is all that we can be certain of: for the more keenly we desire to investigate the matter the more profoundly does it outreach our words [and therefore also the thoughts which those words signify]. By this means our very intentions are confounded if we cannot arrive at clarity either by speech or by silent understanding. Given these considerations, that is, our infirmity of mind, do we not think it presumptuous to enquire whether the foreknowledge of God also corresponds to His memory and understanding? For after all, God is not obliged to contemplate each thing in a separate thought [and therefore the totality of things in a procession of thoughts], but sees all things in one unchanging thought which we call His eternal and ineffable vision [because it does not understand things according to their timely order of occurrence but in another way]. In our confusion and anguish we may well cry out to the living God: '*Such* knowledge *is* too wonderful for me; it is high, I cannot *attain* unto it.' [Ps. 139.6] For my own being intimates how wonderful and incomprehensible is Your knowledge – the knowledge by which You made me – when I cannot even understand myself whom You have made! And yet, 'while I was musing the fire burned,' [Ps. 39.3] in order that I might seek Your Face evermore. [cf. Ps. 105.4][62]

Let us now sum up what we have said in this section by making a few general remarks. Augustine's political ideas seem most apt to be misinterpreted when they are addressing the abiding preoccupation of the Western political tradition. This is the need to achieve the closest possible correspondence between principles of political right and some notion of eternal justice. In more recent times this need has expressed itself in the general movement to vindicate the principles of political right by the scientific criteria of truth – criteria that we associate with the methodological schools of empiricism and positivism. And yet Augustine says that no such correspondence is possible; that the desire for it is a dim recollection of the certainty that was given up by Adam in Paradise. From the point of view of ethics, Augustine seems to think after Plato that this desire asserts itself in the interactions of the moral and intellectual consciences – that is to say, in the dynamic arising from our preference for certain moral propositions (the propositions that we associate with the laws of nature) and our dissatisfaction with not being able to uncover their first principles (the dissatisfaction that describes so well Socrates' dialectical mode of enquiry). This is the same thing as to say that there is a clean epistemological break between Augustine's conception of salvation history and human history as it pursues its ordinary course through time. Human history, the history of earthly cities, touches salvation history in the most incidental and inconsequential ways. Occasionally, when a pilgrim is elevated to a position of secular prominence, the two histories come into a closer orbit, and Augustine seems genuinely to think that this arrangement works to the material benefit of those involved in ordinary human history. However, we have noticed how he insists there can be no closer correspondence than this. The goods of political life are as real and as enjoyable as anything is likely to be on this earth, but the point is that they are categorically different from the goods of the Pilgrim City and its final destination, the City of the Saints in Heaven. This is as extreme a political theory as we are likely to encounter, if indeed we can call it that, for it is difficult to fit it to any of the usual categories of political outlook. In terms of his pessimistic understanding of human psychology, Augustine is a realist; insofar as he locates ordinary morality in the mysterious workings of conscience, he is a conservative; yet by reason of his willingness to have all the world and its institutions serve the utility of a predestined band of pilgrims, he outreaches all the normal terms of political discourse. Here is a vision that is subversive of many aspects of the Western political tradition as we know it. Augustine exhibits an ability to live with thoughts that would cut at the roots of other's aspirations. Yet in an unexpected way, his Christian realism reveals him to be less committed than those who associate the ethical point of view with future certainties. Repeated conjunctions of cause and effect may have conditioned us to call certain states of affairs pleasurable or good. They may even furnish the final proof why we should refer our future conduct to their pursuit and perfection. But they cannot, on the face of it, tell us anything of our memory of a virtue that plainly was never in this world. If we aim at the rational good it is for a reason that we cannot easily give. The search for proof takes us to the root of what we call ethics: the question, what exactly should we do in each moment in order to secure our happiness? Corresponding reflections upon the human freedom to will may leave us with the unsatisfactory choice between pluralism and cognitivism. To Augustine it also appears that we are simply driven to pursue the rational good in this way, while his literal reading of Genesis offers a possible framework for understanding why it is that we are. However, if we are to make this use of him, we must continue with our discussion of the reception and interpretation of his political ideas in history. We have now seen how the medieval mind passed over his salvation history in order to better fit the contrasts of his mind to the hierocratic scheme of papal world government.[63] It was largely against this distorted Augustinianism that the intellectual movements of the Renaissance, as well as the political and religious innovations of the Reformation, would react.

AUGUSTINIAN POLITICAL THEOLOGY

The medieval mind, preoccupied with the political and religious implications of the idea of Latin Christendom, turned away from Augustine's theology of discipleship – away, in short, from his epistemology – and into the austere logic of his ontology. In a theoretical framework thus dominated by the categorical superiority of spirituals over temporals there was simply no room for the Hellenic philosophies of the individual. The awkward material conditions of medieval society contributed to this. Almost entire populations lived on the margins of existence and learning and culture flourished sporadically in little pockets: in the Church, in the new universities and in the palace courts. With little to draw him into the intellectual developments of his day the individual lived a life of relative isolation. There was no public press and books were expensive. There were no meaningful conceptions of national consciousness for him to identify with. There was no effective apparatus of government to call him to account and to which he might refer his hopes and anxieties. There was no political economy and international relations because there were no nation-states and, consequently, what passed for fiscal policy was impulsive and unsustainable. In a word, the method of medieval civilization was not the city-state, as in Greece, or the empire, as in Rome, but that system called 'feudalism'.[64] We might upon reflection regard it as the inevitable product of a time when all that so many had to give was their word and their strength.

The emergence of the individual in the West

We have given a sweeping portrayal of a difficult period in the development of the West, and we have done so in order to help explain why many of the leading concerns of medieval intellectuals unfold at a troubling level of abstraction. Medieval social and political ideas do not typically arise from, or refer to, the experiences of what we might call 'the ordinary man': the neutral, utility-maximizing 'agent' of ethical theory today. They do not because our ordinary man could have had little impact while there remained no significant way for him to influence his socio-political context. For large tracts of the medieval period he remained cut off, in theory and in fact, from the rarified atmosphere of intellectual discussion. And at the centre of that discussion was an idea of exemplary abstraction: the idea of Latin Christendom. If not completely divorced from the actual conditions of life at the start of the medieval period, this idea was certainly so towards the end. We know that *De civitate Dei* was Charlemagne's favourite book, and we can surmise that when he was crowned Holy Roman Emperor on Christmas Day AD 800 he could seriously have estimated his achievements in terms of it. Yet by the beginning of the fourteenth century, developments on the ground had conspired to create a socio-political context in which the ordinary man could leave his mark on the Western political tradition. These developments would reach their conclusion with the emergence of the nation-state as a viable political enterprise. At the height of the dispute between Philip the Fair of France and Pope Boniface VIII, the French Chancellor, Peter Flotte, would meet the Pope's claims to a plenitude of power with what had hitherto been the silent truth of the medieval period: 'Your power is in words; ours is real'.[65] This statement, which seems almost prophetic to us now, anticipates exactly the nature of the victory that the lay mind sought in the Renaissance and the Reformation. Such a statement could also only ever mean the gradual demise of the strategies that we have called political Augustinianism. In the new socio-political milieu of the Reformation it became particularly imperative to rescue Augustine's Two Cities from the constructions of medieval political argument, for increasing numbers of men were beginning to see life through Flotte's eyes. What they saw brought them close to the original Augustinian vision of the human condition as laid down in *De civitate Dei*. They saw plainly that this is a world that men have made with their own hands and according to the motives of their own hearts, that in the natural order of things religion serves political ends, and that it was upon just such an enlightened cynicism that the great pagan states of classical antiquity were built. As Giambattista Vico (1668–1744) would put it in the mid-eighteenth century,

> Within these human governments, even as the mighty current of a kingly river retains far out to sea the momentum of its flow and the sweetness of its waters, the age of the gods coursed on, for there persisted still that religious way of thinking according to which it was the gods who did whatever men themselves were doing.[66]

Of course none of these revelations would make religion redundant; they would simply return it to the position it had always occupied before the peculiar circumstances of the medieval period intervened and Christianity became, for a time, a serious force for world government. Machiavelli, more keenly aware than most of what was at stake, could already see good grounds for excluding 'ecclesiastical principalities' from his new science of politics:

> . . . such principalities are won by prowess or by fortune but kept without the help of either . . . these principalities alone are secure and happy. But as they are sustained by higher powers which the human mind cannot comprehend, I shall not argue about them . . .[67]

It is little wonder, then, that a general call for a return to a pristine, apostolic Christianity should go out at this time, and that thinking men should seek its inspiration in the thought of Augustine.[68] We must now turn to consider one of the more outstanding of these reactions to the strategies of political Augustinianism in the new Europe: the political theology of Martin Luther.

The theology of Martin Luther

At first sight Luther's theology bears some striking resemblances to Augustine's.[69] With Augustine he premisses his thought on a radically pessimistic psychology of man, and with Augustine he also insists that man's fallen nature extends even to his powers of reason, which now, totally adapted to his life of sin, cannot hope to fathom the Will of God in the manner of the Scholastics. However, in distinction from Augustine, he insists on seeing the pattern of salvation in the performance of God's Will considered in the abstract, as a concept. Such a disposition was bound to have its effect on a sincere and hard-thinking man, who, as H. Daniel-Rops suggests, was '. . . burdened with the tragic sense of sin in all its intensity'.[70]

Around 1505, Luther entered into a profound intellectual crisis that would drive him away from a career in the law and into an Augustinian monastery. The story has it that this crisis was precipitated by a walk he was forced to take alone in a gathering storm. A sudden mighty clap of thunder sent him into a paralysis of shock and awe at God's majesty. Fearing death in the moment, he implored God to spare him and promised to become a monk in return. The historian in us is predisposed

to suspect such decisive episodes, yet Daniel-Rops lets the story stand
and buttresses it with a succession of incidents that he thinks drove the
young Luther to an untimely preoccupation with death: 'A serious ill-
ness incurred during adolescence, the sudden death of a friend, a sword
wound acquired during a student's duel and which had bled for a long
time . . .'[71] Whatever the case may be, Luther entered the Augustinian
monastery at Erfurt decided to find peace of heart there. He studied the
works of Augustine in the hope of arriving at some remedy for his mel-
ancholy; he also followed the traditional monastic cure of prayer and
fasting, but nothing availed. Finally, some time in the year 1513, he saw
his way to a solution. Working in the tower room of the monastery at
Wittenberg on a new series of lectures on the Psalms, he found himself
staring at Psalm 30 – a celebration of God's Mercy, and in particular,
at v. 4: *in te Domine speravi non confundar in aeternum in iustitia tua
salva me* 'In You, O Lord, I have taken refuge; let me never be put to
shame; deliver me in Your righteousness'. In the autobiography that he
appended to the 1545 Wittenberg edition of his Latin works, he described
what happened next:

> Though I lived as a monk without reproach, I felt that I was a sin-
> ner before God with an extremely disturbed conscience. I could not
> believe that He was placated by my satisfaction. I did not love, yes,
> I hated the righteous God Who punishes sinners, and secretly, if
> not blasphemously, certainly murmuring greatly, I was angry with
> God, and said, 'As if, indeed, it is not enough, that miserable sin-
> ners, eternally lost through original sin, are crushed by every kind
> of calamity by the law of the Decalogue, without having God add
> pain to pain by the Gospel and also by the Gospel threatening us
> with His righteousness and wrath! . . .' Nevertheless, I beat impor-
> tunately upon St. Paul at that place, most ardently desiring to know
> what St. Paul wanted. At last, by the Mercy of God, meditating day
> and night, I gave heed to the context of the words, namely, 'In it the
> righteousness of God is revealed, as it is written,' 'He who through
> faith is righteous shall live'. There I began to understand that the

righteousness of God is that by which the righteous lives by a gift of God, namely by faith . . . Here I felt that I was altogether born again and had entered paradise itself through open gates.[72]

We are apt to be struck by two thoughts when reading this account. The first is how Luther seems to have brought himself to an intellectual crisis in all essential respects similar to Augustine's. Like Augustine he faced the impossibility of being able to engineer his own salvation, and like Augustine he turned away from a promising secular career to resolve the matter. The second suggests a significant dissimilarity. For, unlike Augustine, Luther evidently did not give up his conviction that salvation lies in somehow reconciling human intellectual and moral futility with the performance of God's Will.[73] This caused him to discover a solution to the problem that he had claimed could never be solved, and which, by contrast, had completely undone Augustine in the garden of his friend's villa at Milan. Viewing Luther and Augustine from the perspective of a shared intellectual crisis allows us to make further instructive comparisons. Augustine emerged from his crisis convinced that our only hope lies in being born again as new creations by the gift of God's mysteriously given Grace. Yet Luther emerged from his believing in a less capricious and laborious method: his justification *sola fide* 'by faith alone'. The contrast is exemplary. On the one hand we have Augustine – a man completely broken by his experience and uncertain how to take even the first step of his new life; on the other hand we have Luther – flushed with excitement like a man who has solved a complex mathematical equation and is already standing before the gates of Paradise. Both men believed that they had been born again, but to only one man did this mean that he must now begin retracing all the steps that he had walked apart from God in order to learn, instead, how to walk again with Him: 'So confession, my brothers, humbles us; humbled it justifies us; justified it exalts us'.[74] There is not a little irony in this. Luther's reaction, framed against the backdrop of growing popular resentment of papal excess, remained very much within the terms of the scholastic tradition that he had been so conscious to reject.

In comparing Luther to Augustine we must mention the more general grievances that contributed to his intellectual crisis, and which were to become immortalized in his *Ninety-Five Theses*.[75] These were primarily a response to the most flagrant expression of the Church's worldliness and power from the mid-fourteenth century: the selling of papal indulgences.[76] The theory behind this practice was logical. Christ's unique sacrifice had released a store of Divine merit far greater in quantity than that needed to save the whole of humanity. This left a significant surplus, and it was this surplus that the Church claimed to be able to dispense at her will, and for a fee, to those wishing to confess their sins but avoid doing penance. By Luther's time economic imperatives had created a more ambitious scheme. Indulgences were now sold on behalf of those already dead and presumed to be in purgatory. In addition the Church did little to discourage the belief that simple upfront payments could buy graded reliefs in the afterlife. Luther was not, of course, the only man to be angered by these practices, and this makes the trajectory of his thought very much the product of its time.[77] In a Europe inhabited by growing numbers of educated and free-thinking men, the Church could no longer claim a monopoly on truth. Nor could she use that monopoly to further her worldly aspirations without the support of the temporal powers. In fact a situation was coming to pass that bore a striking resemblance to the early days of Christianity – a resemblance that men like Luther were quick to recognize, and which spurred on their efforts to return an apostolic Church. In all aspects of learning and culture secular society had risen to meet the achievements of the Church, while in morals the Church had sunk to the depths of ordinary vice. The spell was broken. The tables had been turned: the time was ripe for the normal order of the world to be resumed. For after all, Christ had come into the world as a man in order to call men out of it, and this is information that we have treated as critical to the apolitical and other-worldly nature of early Christianity. Yet the medieval Church had conspired to make God a concept, and in so doing, had succeeded in remaining very much within the world.

From Luther's writings we can evince that he perceived the general momentum of events and became deeply troubled by them, that he saw in his own efforts at salvation the greater truth of man's fallibility and God's omniscience, but that he persisted in conceiving the general problem along the lines laid down by the Scholastics. That is to say, his crisis did not come out of the unique and unasked-for circumstances of his fallen heart as had Augustine's. We notice, for instance, that in the autobiographical fragment quoted above he states that the quality of his life as a monk was 'beyond reproach'; that this fact only heightened his anguish at not being able to satisfy the Law of God. And as Gerhard Ebeling has pointed out, the man Luther can only really be estimated from the point of view of his considerable scholarly activities.[78] He was a university professor who had mastered the philosophical and theological learning of his day, and he was actively engaged in teaching it to students. His intellectual crisis, though real enough, was correspondingly a crisis of belief rather than will: it referred to the thought that we can live an irreproachable life yet still be damned by a sin of shocking antiquity.

Luther's objection to Christianity has always been the objection of the thinking man. The British monk Pelagius (ca AD 354–418) was to provide one possible response in the fifth century. He would appeal to the commonsense understanding of justice by arguing that Adam's sin was a discrete event of no practical consequence to succeeding generations: we can choose to be good and by that means merit the favour of God.[79] Luther presents a more abstract alternative. He asks us to return to the same dogmas of Scripture that clearly preclude Pelagius' alternative (the dogmas of Christ's sacrifice on the Cross and atonement), and once there he asks us to ponder how these events undo the violence done by Adam to the life of virtue. It is a question that links Christian belief to the assumptions of the classical philosophies of the good life. The Scriptures tell us that we are impaired by an ancient crime, while the classical philosophies assume our capacity for goodness. Moreover it is the latter that seem to make the greater appeal to commonsense with their basis in the human freedom to will. To Socrates, for instance, virtue was knowledge: he did not have to question our ability or desire to choose the good life when once we had apprehended it.[80] His teaching correspondingly addressed itself, in the main, to the question of how indeed we might apprehend saving knowledge. The original Christianity would go on to transform this framework with its message that the Garden of Eden was never an ethical Paradise. In the narrative of Genesis, for instance, we find no support for the view that Adam forfeited his right to pursue the rational good with God's help. The scheme it suggests is, from the strictly moral and political point of view, closer to what we in the West would call a dictatorship. The nature of Adam's crime was to imagine that he would more closely resemble his Maker if he could understand His commands in theory, from first principles. It was, as Genesis suggests, a question of pride. Adam's punishment when God discovered his sin was his banishment from God's presence and inspiration. He was to walk the earth as a creature unformed, but believing the lie to be true: believing, that is, that he could form himself for all he needed in life. Ethics was, then, to use Augustine's view, Adam's reaction to the reality of having actually to live as a god, discriminating between good and evil. And this, too, is the sense in which Augustine thinks that the human freedom to will was not impaired with Adam's transgression; it is rather the pride that directs the will that is the continuing effect of the Fall. For it causes us to conceptualize our final good in ways that positively disqualify God from intervening in our affairs as He did in Paradise, and it is on this point that Augustine therefore invites us set the original Christianity in intellectual distinction from the more patterned later versions. Of these later versions Luther was certain that the outlook called scholasticism was a palmary example. The schoolmen's distinction between *fides informis* 'faith unformed' and *fides formata cum charitate* 'faith formed through love' was, in his mind, an incitement to pursue salvation after the pattern of the good life – that is, through good works. However, his experience of sin as well as his reading of Augustine and Paul had convinced him that this was not possible. But how, then, shall a man be saved in light of his damnation and the rigid constructions of Scripture? *Sola fides verbi Christi iustificat* 'Through faith in Christ unformed; or what is the same thing, through faith in Christ unqualified'.

The problem that Luther purported to have solved was constructed out of the medieval, scholastic assumption that the pattern of Christian salvation is broadly that of the classical doctrine of the good life. Luther was vexed by the thought that the Christian doctrines of Original Sin place an immovable obstacle in the way of this scheme. Yet his summary answer was always more likely to affirm this patterned view of Christianity than to remove the original problem, and it is in this sense that we earlier identified irony in his project. Daniel-Rops thought that his view was '. . . perfectly adapted to set an anguished soul at rest'.[81] Leighton Pullman would be rather less generous:

> The infirmities which cannot be avoided are confused with the sin which can be avoided, and the fundamental distinction between the mere feeling of an incitement to sin, and a deliberate consent of the will to that feeling, is destroyed. And the sinner is then consoled by the doctrine that when he believes, and so long as he believes, all his sins are as venial sins . . . What is this but an indulgence – an indulgence no longer purchased by money but by an emotion?[82]

And then, different again, is Augustine's opinion of this view. It is, as we have seen, informed by his understanding of Adam's wisdom in Paradise. He asks us to ponder how high a place belief should have in the Christian scheme of salvation, given certain well-known points of Scripture:

> And look: you have before you Christ as your end: you do not need to be seeking anymore. When once you have believed this, you have recognized it too; however, this is not to say that it is merely a matter of faith, but of faith and works. Each is necessary. For, as you heard the Apostle say, 'the devils also believe, and tremble;' [Jas 2.19] but their believing brings forth nothing. Faith on its own is not enough; it must be joined to works [and therefore to acts of will]: 'faith which worketh by love,' [Gal. 5.6] as the Apostle put it.[83]

We are inclined to see this more clearly, Augustine thinks, when we give up the attempt to understand Christian discipleship through the framework of the good life, or what he generally calls *culmen temporalis felicitatis* 'the summit of temporal happiness':

> For the Psalmist says that, once he had seen how abundantly the ungodly enjoyed the fleshly and earthly promises, his feet were almost gone and his steps had well nigh slipped. It was as if he had served God to no purpose: for he observed how those who held God in contempt actually increased in those rewards that he had expected to receive for his efforts. He also says that his attempts to understand this availed him little until he entered the sanctuary of God; for there he considered again the end of those to whom he had wrongly attributed happiness. Then, as he says, he understood how their rewards – the things in which they had exalted themselves – had cast them down; that they had been consumed for their iniquities and had perished [cf. Ps. 73.17–19] because the whole summit of temporal happiness had become for them like a dream from which the dreamer wakes and suddenly finds himself destitute of all the joys that he had imagined as he slept. And since they had, until this moment, appeared to themselves as great men, whether on this earth or in this Earthly City, he says, 'O Lord, in Thy city Thou shalt despise their image.' [cf Ps. 73.20][84]

The politics of Martin Luther

At just the point, then, when the moral bankruptcy of the Church had brought some to mourn the loss of a purer, apostolic Christianity, Luther helped them to lose sight of Christ Who had been that early Church. By preferring his conceptual understanding of God and never questioning his motivations as a leader,[85] Luther proceeded to build his new theology on un-Augustinian foundations.[86] This prevented him from reproducing Augustine's independence *vis-à-vis* politics at just the time when national governments were beginning to organize themselves apart from the Church. Hindered by the relatively rigid constructions of his theology, Luther was bound to be overtaken by events; in time he would be forced into some significant changes of mind.[87] He had before him a vision of a kind of pilgrim city, but it lacked the distinct epistemological basis of Augustine's. And it was a clear-headed realism that was required to make progress against the worldly ambitions of the new national heads of state. In J. W. Allen's opinion, Luther's inability to form a clear political theory could be traced directly to the ambiguity in his chief theological concepts:

> It seems quite evident that the thought of Luther was essentially unpolitical. If he can be said to have had any ideal of the State it was a theocratic ideal. But it would be wiser, I think, to say that he had none at all. Vaguely there floated before his mind a vision of a State ruled by the Word of God and by love and reason and natural law. Actually he acquiesced in the construction of such states and churches as the "Lutheran" Princes chose to build. For his profoundest feeling was that of his early teachers, the mystics, that in the long run only God's Will and God's Word counted or mattered.[88]

For Allen, then, Luther's historical and political significance could have been different to what it in fact was. As an Augustinian scholar he might have been more impressed by the West's return to its pre-medieval political trajectory, and gone on to find much in his master's thought to address the new situation. As it was he chose to release a number of wide and emotive concepts into the intellectual climate. The most important of these from our point of view was a kind of doctrine of the Two Cities, though, for the reasons we have already spoken of, Luther was never able to locate his pilgrim city in the new world order with any accuracy or consistency. He drew the line between spirituals and temporals clearly enough but, significantly, his understanding of what it would mean to be a new creation was too impractical to point towards any distinct earthly arrangements:

> We set forth two worlds, as it were, one of them heavenly and the other earthly. Into these we place these two kinds of righteousness, which are distinct and separated from each other. The righteousness of the Law is earthly and deals with earthly things; by it we perform

good works. But as the earth does not bring forth fruit unless it has
first been watered and made fruitful from above – for the earth cannot judge, renew, rule, and nourish the earth, so that it may do what
the Lord has commanded – so also by the righteousness of the Law
we do nothing even when we do much; we do not fulfill the Law
even when we fulfill it. Without any merit or work of our own, we
must first be justified by Christian righteousness, which has nothing
to do with the righteousness of the Law or with earthly and active
righteousness. But this righteousness is heavenly and passive. We
do not have it of ourselves; we received it from heaven. We do not
perform it; we accept it by faith, through which we ascend beyond
all laws and works. 'As, therefore, we have borne the image of the
earthly Adam,' as Paul says, 'let us bear the image of the Heavenly
One' [1 Cor. 15.49], Who is a New Man in a new world, where
there is no Law, no sin, no conscience, no death, but perfect joy,
righteousness, grace, peace, life, salvation, and glory.[89]

The problem that Luther saw in the coercive, secular powers of the
Church was not without its precedent in theory. As early as 1324 the
'accursed' Marsilius of Padua (ca 1275–1342) had published his *Defensor
pacis* 'The Defender of Peace', arguing that all coercive power was by
definition the prerogative of the temporal powers. He had in his sights the
papal plenitude of power, and in support of his views he would marshal
an impressive body of Scripture:[90]

I shall first show, that Christ himself came into the world not to
dominate men, nor to judge them by judgement in the third sense,
nor to wield temporal rule, but rather to be subject as regards the
status of the present life; and moreover, that he wanted to and did
exclude himself, his apostles and disciples, and their successors,
the bishops or priests, from all such coercive authority or worldly
rule, both by his example and by his words of counsel or command. I shall also show that the leading apostles, as Christ's true
imitators, did this same thing and taught their successors to do

likewise; and moreover, that both Christ and the apostles wanted to be and were continuously subject in property and in person to the coercive jurisdiction of secular rulers, and that they taught and commanded all others, to whom they preached or wrote the law of truth, to do likewise, under pain of eternal damnation. Then I shall write a chapter on the power or authority of the keys which Christ gave to the apostles and their successors in office, bishops and priests, so that it may be clear what is the nature, quality and extent of such power, both of the Roman bishop and of the others.[91]

It was never likely that such a thesis would avoid official condemnation in the time that Marsilius was writing. Three years later, in 1327, it was duly condemned as heretical by Pope John XXII (1249–1334). Luther might have put Marsilius' ideas to good use in the changed conditions of his time (he had almost certainly read his book in whole or in part), but he was not inclined to systematic statements of his political views. At any rate, he lacked a practical theory of Christian obedience to God in relation to which he could develop his views on the Christian's obligation to the state. As we have seen, his theology of discipleship solved a problem of mainly intellectual interest: but its practical result, once taken up by the masses in Germany, was to outstrip even his worst fears of misinterpretation and exploitation. He had formed his idea of justification by faith in Christ in order to reconcile his oppressive experience of sin with Paul's promise that we can be born again as new creations. We have characterized his dilemma at the time as exemplary of what happens when sincere men try to orientate the Christian teachings on salvation on the longstanding idea of the good life. But far from offering solace to souls similarly disturbed, Luther's triumphant idea was to go on to a career as the final vindication of licentiousness and pluralism. By divorcing good works from faith, Luther had effectively taught men not to be troubled by the events in the Garden of Eden, and of what those events might mean for their pilgrimages in this world. And once his ideas were abroad there was little that he could do to stop them being turned, one after the other, to the same conclusion: a man can be his own counsel on what constitutes righteous behaviour so long as he has faith, and believes! In fact so far did the moral condition of Germany sink with the dissemination of his ideas that he was driven to the following prediction in conversation with his friend, Philip Melanchthon (1497–1560):

> How many different masters will men be following in a hundred years' time? Confusion will then be at its height. No one will submit to government by anyone else's ideas or authority. Everyone will be trying to make himself his own Rabbi.[92]

Such, then, was the general tendency of Luther's ideas in the sphere of ethics. In the more formalized sphere of Church and State relations he was to have the more anticipated impact. The Earthly City, said Luther, is characterized by laws and works and a corresponding righteousness built upon merit. Its citizens are coerced into peaceful cohabitation according to the ancient scheme of right represented in the Decalogue. But this familiar meritocracy, with its exhibitions of goodness and sinfulness, runs up against a Christian doctrine of damnation that Luther evidently shared our difficulty in accepting. By what standard, then, are we to judge Christian righteousness, if not by the scheme of right employed in the Earthly City? Had Luther responded to this question he might have produced a very different theology and politics. As it was, he who chose to address the matter at the most abstract level, using Augustine's doctrine of the Two Cities to describe a heavenly city of 'passive' pilgrims. These sojourners inhabit earthly states and discharge all the normal obligations of the citizen. However, they are positively disqualified from referring any failings or successes in this arena to their final end as Christians. The righteousness that they exhibit as pilgrims is, as it was for Augustine, an unmerited gift of Grace. This scheme is tolerably close to Augustine's at many points; some would say that it replicates his ambiguity about the exact temporal location of the Pilgrim City, but we have argued that any apparent ambiguities in Augustine's political ideas can be overcome by relating them to his own experiences of confession and Grace. For those experiences tell of an intellectually distinct understanding of Christian obedience, developed in light of the assumptions of classical moral and political philosophy, and for that reason Pauline. Augustine thus has answers for the questions Christianity repeatedly encounters in a world committed to the ethical perspective. 'Just look at this evangelical society', said Melanchthon, 'see how many adulterers, drunkards and gamblers it contains, see how many vicious and ignoble folk there are! Take a peep into our homes. Are they any more chaste than those you regard as pagan?'[93] A Christian ethic premised upon an intellectualist conception of law cannot easily counter this barb, for since the fall of the Roman Empire the Church has not consistently been able to claim the first place in morals. To Augustine, however, this is not the issue. His understanding of Christian obedience is unqualified: his understanding of God's Will is voluntarist. His Christian realism attempts, on the level of theory, to promote those aspects of morality and government that he considers foundational to the end of peace. It is, then, markedly open to non-Christian contributions:

Is this not then happiness, to have sons safe, daughters beautiful, garners full, cattle abundant, no downfall, I say not of a wall, but not even of a hedge, no tumult and clamour in the streets, but quiet, peace, abundance, a fullness of everything in homes as well as in cities? Is this not then happiness? or [perhaps you think] the righteous should shun it? Or is it rather that you do not find the houses of the righteous to be abounding in these things, this happiness? Did not Abraham's house abound with gold, silver, children, servants, cattle? [cf. Gen. 12.5; 13.2–6] . . . What do we say? is this not happiness? Nonetheless, it remains on the left hand. What is on the left hand? Things temporal, mortal, bodily. Now I do not wish you to shun these things, but only to not think that they belong on the right hand . . . For what should they have set on the right hand? God, eternity, the years of God which do not pass away [cf. Ps. 102.27] . . . Let us use the left hand in this time bound age; let us hope for the eternity of the right hand.[94]

In stark contrast to this, Augustine's doctrine of the Two Cities became, in Luther's hands, a limiting premiss. The inadequacies of the left hand, the Earthly City, by turns justified his indifference to politics as well as his acquiescence in it. As recently as the Second World War, Lutheran arguments were used by German theologians to rationalize cooperation, passive or otherwise, with the Nazi government.[95] Politics for Luther was, on the face of it, a sordid business: conducted by the 'sword' and therefore persistently at odds with Christian concepts such as peace, fraternity, love and justice. When it suited his purpose he preached that political coercion is completely superfluous for the Christian; in fact his main justification of Christian political activity came to be that it expresses a pastoral concern for the ordinary plight of men. Yet at the same time he did not sufficiently explain how the pilgrim city, his right hand, inwardly transforms conventional morality while outwardly conforming to it. Nor did he sufficiently explain the obverse: how earthly citizens may outwardly conform to conventional morality while inwardly justifying damnation. The categorical difference that Augustine preached between the left and right hands did not, it seems, have the same appeal to Luther as the alternative that we earlier called the 'thinking man's Christianity': the idea of the spirit expressed in the law becoming the principle of action in the man. His vision of an ideal Christian society on earth correspondingly contained elements of relativism that, to Augustine, would have undermined the economy of salvation laid down in the Gospels. Luther's slogan that every reformed man is his own priest, that a community of Christians manifests God's Will in its unregulated actions, extended his passive righteousness even to God: '. . . the righteous person does nothing . . . his works do not make him righteous . . . [rather] his righteousness creates works'.[96] And a passive and silent god is a surprising result for a theology that began as a protest against the presumptuousness of Rome, though it does to some extent explain the whimsicality of Luther's later politics. Where God is silent others must speak, and lead, on His behalf. Perhaps, in fact, this statement accurately characterizes the whole tendency that we have called Augustinian political theology.

Belief in a silent god nerves the Christian to extraordinary efforts on behalf of him, the more so when his religious identification places him in awkward relation to the coercive powers. To some extent his responses can be anticipated from the resources he has to hand. On the one hand, he has Augustine's distinction between two citizenships, which, to him, must appear as an expression of the ancient Greek dualism between mind and matter, religion and politics. We have already remarked on the fact that before the birth of philosophy in the West, these categories were united in a single conception. And on the other hand, he has his predilection for what we might fairly call the natural-law style of moral and political argument: the assumption that an ethical or ideological perspective is consistent with the designs of Providence. We have seen that Augustine traced this assumption to Adam's original belief that God conceives His future decisions in terms of unchanging first principles so that He is therefore bound by the same epistemological constructions that bind man:

> God's Grace is something apart by itself, so too is the nature of man. If we examine the matter we see that a man is born and grows; as he grows he learns the things of men. What does he know, then, but earth, of earth? He speaks the things of men, knows the things of men, learns the things of men. Carnal, he judges carnally; indeed, he even supposes carnally. Look: he is man from the ground upwards! Let the Grace of God come and enlighten his darkness . . . let it take the mind of man, and turn it to its own light [Ps. 18.28] . . .[97]

What response to a suspicious world is the Christian then inclined to make out of these materials? Generally, he will seek to argue for distinct but coordinate powers for Church and State. He will justify his scheme on the principles of a) the natural division of human need into the spiritual and material, and b) the final good of man. He will, in other words, arrive at a certainty about the matter that may or may not seek a superior status for the Church. But certainty in such matters is usually achieved at the expense of realism. The historian of ideas is bound to be struck by the fact that the biblical category of sin could never have been intended to establish an ethic. Adam and Eve were offered no rational explanation why they should not eat the fruit of the tree of good and evil. God might just as well have forbidden them to do anything He pleased and not altered the biblical category of sin at all. As Augustine characteristically puts it, God will do what He will, for '. . . there is no difficulty to impede Him, and no law of nature to forbid Him, from doing so'.[98] The idea that corresponding categories like righteousness and justice can be usefully applied to distinguish the Pilgrim City from the reprobate on earth is, so Augustine tells us, the fruit of something else: 'This whole life of human affairs is a confusion; it does not belong to God. In this confusion, in this Babylon, Sion is held captive . . .'[99] It is one of the hallmarks of his thought to insist that the predestined and the eternally damned are mixed together on earth, in the Church: 'In that ineffable foreknowledge of God, many who seem to be without are in reality within, and many who seem to be within yet really are without'.[100] In Luther, on the other hand, we encounter for the first time, as Oliver O'Donovan explains, '. . . that characteristic figure of the modern West, the self-reflecting soul who, burdened with a sense of inward space, stands at a quizzical distance from the roles assigned him in society'.[101] The irony in this is brought home to us as we reflect upon the scholastic, Aristotelian ancestry of Luther's passive god. When, according to Cornford, for example,

> . . . Greek philosophy deified the speculative intellect, it made the supreme effort to work clear of all that was vague and mythical in religion, only to find that the intellect had become a deity and followed the elder Gods of emotional faith to the seventh heaven. In the system of Aristotle . . . God is sublimated to the topmost pinnacle of abstraction, and conceived as Form without Matter – a pure Thought, cut off from all active or creative energy, for the Ultimate End can have no other end beyond itself . . . God cannot [therefore] love the world, or send forth his *Logos* into it; but the world is expected to love him, and all its life is to be caused by desire for this monastic and self-hypnotized abstraction. It may be doubted whether this passion has ever been genuinely felt even by the most intellectual of mystics, much less by the rest of creation. It

is only by calling it 'God,' and persuading ourselves that it is alive, and active, and blessed – all which is manifestly mythical – that we can induce the faintest feeling of attraction towards it.[102]

We must now introduce the next period in the history of the West in which Augustine's political ideas were distorted by agendas other than his own. The period that we have called Augustinian political theory begins, approximately, with the Enlightenment of the West. We have seen that a kind of enlightenment had preceded Luther's attacks on the traditional hierarchy of Latin Christendom – a renaissance of the pre-medieval free inquiry;[103] however, the endeavour and audacity of what would unfold two centuries later would be something else. According to Luther, every baptized Christian was his own priest; in the eighteenth century it seemed that every educated man had become his own philosopher.[104] Developments in commerce, in government and in education and culture had conspired to raise the ordinary man to a position of account in the world.[105] Now the institutions, processes and beliefs that had long repressed the natural enthusiasm of the mind were lifted. Up rushed a madness of ideas as men discovered that they had been labouring under a thousand misapprehensions. Dogma, myth and superstition were challenged and everywhere men imagined themselves in Athens. But what, precisely, was the essence of their euphoria? Perhaps W. E. H. Lecky gives the clue:

> He who has realized, on the one hand, his power of acting according to his will, and, on the other hand, the power of his will to emancipate itself from the empire of pain and pleasure, and to modify and control the current of the emotions, has probably touched the limits of his freedom.[106]

AUGUSTINIAN POLITICAL THEORY

It is at this point, then, that we break off our historical narrative, for the period of Augustinian political theory begins with the general realization that the human will operates, under its own power, in an objective and determinate world of cause and effect. The beginning of Augustinian political theory is, so far as we are concerned, conterminous with Francis Bacon's (1561–1626) '. . . just and legitimate familiarity betwixt the mind and things'.[107] Intuitions that were suppressed during the medieval period grow bolder in the sympathetic climate. Religion and myth are returned to their sociological basis, appearing as disingenuous reactions to the caprice of the actual present. It is worth remembering that as early as the sixth century BC, Xenophanes (ca BC 570– 475) was able to suggest the following deconstruction of them:

> Homer and Hesiod have attributed to the gods everything that is a shame and reproach among men, stealing and committing adultery and deceiving each other. But mortals consider that the gods are born, and that they have clothes and speech and bodies like their own. The Ethiopians say that their gods are snub-nosed and black, the Thracians that theirs have light blue eyes and red hair. But if cattle and horses or lions had hands, or were able to draw with their hands and do the works that men can do, horses would draw the forms of the gods like horses, and cattle like cattle, and they would make their bodies such as they each had themselves.[108]

It is among thoughts such as these that we sense the mood most sympathetic to the Augustinian economy of salvation. Religion and myth are directed against God insofar as they distract men from the hopelessness of their situation in the Earthly City. The laws of nature and the echoes of eternity and perfection that are shed abroad in men's hearts allow them to fashion a life on earth in imitation of the imagined Heavenly City. But at the same time these gifts of God furnish the troubling insight that no creation of human hands can ever measure up to the Divine standards, and, by that means, be the key to the transformation of human nature:

> . . . could there be any less fruitful scenario than mankind, imagin-
> ing itself in the control of [gods] which it has made? For a man can
> more easily dishonour his design as a rational creature by worship-
> ping the works of his own hands as gods than can those same works
> become gods through his worship of them. It can sooner happen
> that 'Man *that* is in honour, and understandeth not' may become
> 'like the beasts *that* perish,' [Ps. 49.20] than that a work of his hands
> should be preferred to his own design, made in God's image. It is
> entirely deservedly, then, that man is lost to Him Who made him,
> when he places above himself that which he himself has made.[109]

The universalism of Augustine's Christianity is, therefore, his belief in
the ability of every man to question the creations of human hands in
much the same manner as the Enlightenment thinkers.[110] Deconstruction
of the human condition in this way is not, then, for him what it was for
a man like Rousseau.[111] For the only institution that truth threatens is
pride and the whole system of living built upon it: 'Behold where He is:
it is wherever truth is known'.[112] The noble ignorance that a man like
Rousseau preaches might, for a time, buy us a kind of happiness; but
Augustine's suggestion is that it is preached out of a fear that there is no
viable alternative. The man brought low by a realistic assessment of the
human condition is, in his mind, raised up and close to recognizing God.
His subsequent passage through life, though it may not be as a pilgrim,
will at least be as an exile, and this exile status that offers secular insights
and advantages is open, so Augustine thinks, to any thinking man who
chooses not to have the truth reflect well upon him.

> Attribute to the truth whatever you have gained from the truth, and
> what you have gained you will not lose. All your rottenness will be
> changed to flourishing; all your diseases will be healed; all in you
> that flows and fades will be restored, and made anew, and bound
> around you [cf. Ps. 103.3–5].

Even those aspects of you that once dragged you down to their depths will now stand fast with you; and they will serve you as you abide with God Who abides always [cf. Heb. 1.11; 1 Pet. 1.23].[113]

The Augustinian political theory of Jean Bethke Elshtain

It is probably in the attempt to reconcile this call to the exile with the other, more conventional, aspects of his political ideas that the fascination of Augustine for the modern political theorist lies. With no apparent damage to its overall consistency, his thinking is able to accommodate a carefully directed attack on the heart of the Western political tradition – that is, on the epistemological foundations of its concept of political right – and a gracious affirmation of all that is good about the sociable life of man. Jean Bethke Elshtain is one of the contemporary political theorists to be drawn in by this unusual scenario. In her book *Augustine and the Limits of Politics*,[114] she attempts to argue Augustine's relevance to Western political theory today. It is a sincere book written, in part, out of her own experience of trying to make her way in the world with Augustine, but also out of the conviction that Augustine is peculiarly well placed to speak into a world exhausted by its repeated attempts to achieve perfection through politics and now painfully coming to terms with the insufficiencies of the human self.[115] However, for our purposes, it also qualifies as a typical work of Augustinian political theory, for it harbours an un-Augustinian agenda. In her concern to show that Augustinian insights into the human condition can furnish the basis for a new, positive politics grounded in the acceptance and celebration of human fallibility, she is guilty of distorting his political ideas. It is often a very subtle distortion, and we should keep in mind the work that Elshtain has done to defend Augustine against his modern critics,[116] but it is a distortion nonetheless and, as far as we are concerned, an exemplary one. We have consistently highlighted the fact that Augustine did not diagnose the human condition with a view to finding a cure; he wanted men to lose all hope in a city built with human hands. Elshtain's work on Augustine's political ideas is conversely inspired by the hope that he might yet address the needs of the pilgrim in a hostile post-Enlightenment world. The coercive aspect of human government that he ascribes to our love of self is not, for her, as significant as the language of love that he reserves for relations in the Heavenly City. This causes her to pass over the secular advantages of his Christian realism and base her defence of him in the potential of his language of heavenly love. Her project is exemplary of the tendency that we have called Augustinian political theory because it misinterprets his belief in the irredeemable character of earthly arrangements for indifference. She is correspondingly apt to conclude that Augustine's political ideas are vulnerable to the dominant perspectives of modern political theory.

What does Elshtain's hope in fact manifest itself as? The answer can be found in the following passage from her book:

> . . . Augustine offers us not merely a condemnation of [our] appetite for unbridled *cupiditas* in the form of the *libido dominandi*, he gives us the great gift of an alternative way of thinking and being in the world, a way that is in many vital respects available to those who are not doctrinally Augustine's brothers and sisters. In the twentieth century, justification and rationalization of violence as the *modus operandi* of social change introduces an element of remorseless moral absolutism into politics. The delectation of mounds of bodies stacked up as our handiwork, the riveting possibility of salutary bloodletting, grips the imagination. The result is a pile of garbage and a pile of bodies. The fact of death becomes the primary political statement. Inflamed militants march to the Grim Reaper's habituating drumbeat. The cadence is nigh irresistible to many. Augustine would have us resist – in the name of love.[117]

This is really a very clear manifesto for Elshtain's position. The statement that Augustine 'would have us resist' speaks of ideological certainty; if this is indeed the case, it is difficult for us to reconcile it to his conviction that the institutions of the Earthly City are remedial in relation to a fixed human nature. From the historical point of view, Augustine's achievement as a political thinker was to establish a metaphysical watershed between Christian salvation history and ordinary human history, to use that watershed as the final vindication of all that is manifestly good in the Western political tradition (as opposed to using the presumed correspondence between principles of political right and eternal justice), and to analyse as far as he was able the mechanism of life in this world. By basing her perspective in a more enthusiastic interpretation of his achievements, Elshtain may be drawing on her Lutheran roots.[118] At any rate, she is positioning herself to solve a problem that could never have constructed itself in Augustine's mature mind.

How, then, does Elshtain see a solution to the problem of political life in Augustine's understanding of love? She does so by reading a great deal into his use of love as a diagnostic tool. We have seen that, for Augustine, the certain way to discover the true character of a people was to investigate the object of their deepest affection. He based his refutation of Cicero's definition of justice on this principle. In addition his standard definition of the Two Cities drew on a distinction based in love: 'These two cities are constructed from two loves: Jerusalem is made from the love of God; Babylon is made from the love of things secular. It follows, then, that one need only question another's love to discover their citizenship'.[119] Yet to Elshtain, Augustine's understanding of love is capable of bearing a less discriminating interpretation:

> No single man can create a commonwealth. There is no ur-Founder, no great bringer of order. It begins in ties of fellowship, in households, clans, and tribes, in earthly love and its many discontents. And it begins in an ontology of peace not war [she means here to refer to the ancient glorification of war].[120]

This more general scheme suggests a substantive existence for love even though it seems mainly to have had a functional significance for Augustine – the orientation of the whole towards something.[121] Notwithstanding this, Elshtain persists with her positive reading because she believes that Augustine's teaching on the sociable nature of man is really an aspect of his teaching on the love of God for us. This means she feels that she can produce an intellectually respectable ethic from the unpromising materials of Augustine's political ideas:

> Even in our good works we are dislocated creatures, torn by discord, but striving to attain some measure of *Concordia*. But love abides. And the more we try to emulate God's love, the stronger will be our hope; the more decent our lives with and among one another.[122]

This is not, however, a scheme that Augustine could ever have recommended. He would have contended that it is impossible for man to emulate God's love when it is made manifest in His arbitrary Will spoken into the actual present. God's love is His judgement, and the goodness of God's judgement is only seldom expressed as a concord of earthly affairs. Luther saw this, and it troubled him so much that he intuited an entire theology into denying it.

Elshtain's motives in pursuing her interpretation of Augustine are entirely laudable. She has given advanced thought to the Western political tradition and its contemporary forms, she has become disturbed by what she has seen of it in the culture around her, but, unfortunately, she has misunderstood what Augustine's life as a pilgrim consisted in. The thought with which she prefaces her book, that it has been written 'one *peregrinus* to, and with, another',[123] is a sentimentalization of Augustine's experience. For his pilgrimage was not an earnest intellectual exploration of what it should mean to be a man living between two cities. It was something that Elshtain might find it difficult to like: a perfect subjection and obedience to the Will of God – the Perfect Law of Liberty.

> While we are pilgrims our righteousness consists in this – that we press forward to that perfect and full righteousness in which there shall be perfect and full charity in God's sight; and that now we hold to our course by perfectly and rightly keeping under our body and bringing it into subjection [cf. 1 Cor. 9.27].[124]

The temptation to style Augustine after the classical pilgrim is, however, very real. Augustine could greatly respect a man like Pelagius, whom he called *vir sanctus* 'venerable man',[125] but he could not, after his own experiences, put the same value on the pursuit of the rational good. The final good is ultimately what God commands. Men participate in it by their obedience. The traditional virtues refer to Adam's Original Sin and the consequent need to base human life on the principle of peace. The Christian pilgrim enjoys the certainty of right action and a kind of perfection while he obeys God. In these moments he is elevated above the wanderer, the tireless seeker after truth, sailing like the hero of Virgil's (BC 70–19) *Aeneid* towards ever-receding shores.[126] By the same token he does not stand comparison to the longstanding image of the participant in truth: the man in whom dislocated elements of faith and reason, love and knowledge, have become united in a single conception.[127] This vision of the pilgrim may disappoint many of our expectations, but it may be that it is more resilient to the claims of modern moral and political theory:

> From whence does the soul, whose pilgrimage has become long [cf. Lk. 15.13], understand that if she thirsts for You, if her tears are now made her bread while it is said to her each day, 'Where is your God?' [cf. Ps. 42.3–4] – if she seeks of You one thing, and desires it – she may go on to dwell in Your house all the days of her life? [cf. Ps. 27.4] And what is her life except Yourself? And what are Your days except Your eternality, just as are Your years, which have no end because You are ever the same? [cf. Ps. 102.27; Heb. 1.12] From these considerations may that soul, which can do so, understand how far above all times are You, the Eternal. For Your house, which is not on pilgrimage, even though it is not coeternal with You, yet unceasingly and unfailingly clings to You and by that means remains above the vicissitudes of time.[128]

Notes

1 *See* Ch. 1, n. 16.
2 It is acceptable to use 'Church/State' language in the medieval context if we remember that these two terms really signify two aspects of the single conception of Latin Christendom. *See* R. W. Dyson, *Normative Theories*

of Society and Government in Five Medieval Thinkers: St. Augustine, John of Salisbury, Giles of Rome, St. Thomas Aquinas, and Marsilius of Padua (Lewiston: Edwin Mellen Press, 2003), pp. 69–70.

3 CS, p. 11. We should point out that in the Eastern half of the empire, comparatively unmolested by barbarians, Gelasius' ideal was very nearly realized. In form and outlook the Byzantine Empire largely continued the trajectory of the great pagan states of antiquity, its Emperors assuming supreme authority over both State and Church. Since Professor Ullmann, this unique mode of rule has been described by the term 'caesaropapism'. For further information *see* J. M. Hussey, *The Byzantine World* (London: Hutchinson University Library, 1967), p. 84; and Sir Ernest Barker, *Social and Political Thought in Byzantium* (Oxford: Clarendon Press, 1957), pp. 23–77.

4 Dyson, *St. Augustine of Hippo*, p. 185.

5 *Ep.*, CXXXVIII, 2 (author's translation).

6 *Ibid.*, CLV, 3 (author's translation).

7 *De Gen. ad litt.*, IX, 9 (author's translation).

8 James Viscount Bryce, 'Rome's legacy to the middle ages', in David Thompson (Ed.), *The Idea of Rome from Antiquity to the Renaissance* (Albuquerque: University of New Mexico Press, 1971), p. 145.

9 Professor Walter Ullmann's 'ascending' and descending' theses of government furnish a helpful framework for thinking on this subject, though their simplifying tendencies should not be forgotten. *See* his *Law & Politics in the Middle Ages: An Introduction to the Sources of Medieval Political Thought* (London: Sources of History, 1975), p. 32.

10 *See* the texts and discussions in Sykes, *Power and Christian Theology*, pp. 27–54.

11 *See* Introduction, n. 59.

12 *See* Thomas Hobbes (Ed. Edwin Curley), *Leviathan* (Indianapolis: Hackett Publishing Company, 1994), XIII, 9. Cf. Thucydides, I, 2–8; and Niccolò Machiavelli (Ed. George Bull), *The Prince* (Harmondsworth: Penguin, 1970), p. 96.

13 For instance at *De civ. Dei*, XII, 5.

14 See *De Gen. ad litt.*, VI, 12, 21: 'The pre-eminence of man consists in this, that God made him to His own image by giving him an intellect by which he surpasses the beasts . . .' Cf. *In Io. ev. tr.*, VIII, 6; *Contra adv. L. et P.*, I, 19; *De cont.*, IV, 11.

15 *De lib. arb.*, III, 24 (author's translation). Cf. *De pecc. mer. et rem.*, II, 35, 21: 'They therefore served God, because that dutiful obedience was committed to them by which God can alone be worshipped'. (author's translation).

16 Cf. *De mend.*, XV, 29: '. . . "Take therefore no thought for the morrow;"

[Mt. 6.34] and, "Take no thought for your life, what ye shall eat, or what ye shall drink; nor yet for your body, what ye shall put on." [Mt. 6.25] . . . it is sufficiently clear that these commands are to be understood in the following sense: that we ought to do nothing out of necessity, that is, out of a love of obtaining temporal things or [its obverse] the fear of want'. (author's translation).

17 See *De Mag.*, XIV, 46: 'By His grace I shall love Him the more ardently I advance in learning'. (author's translation).

18 Gen. 3.22.

19 *De Gen. ad litt.*, XI, 39, 53 (author's translation).

20 *Ibid.*, IX, 9, 15 (author's translation).

21 This phrase is taken from the title of a book by the Rev'd R. R. Williams. The book is his *The Perfect Law of Liberty: An Interpretation of Psalm 119* (London: A. R. Mowbray & Co., 1952).

22 Jean-Jacques Rousseau, *Du contrat social, ou principes du droit politique* (Paris: Éditions Garnier Frères, 1962), p. 236.

23 'To find a form of association that defends and protects with the whole force of the community, the person and the property of each associate; and in which each associate, though unified with all, nevertheless obeys himself, while also remaining just as free as before. Such is the fundamental problem which the *Contrat Social* gives the answer to'. *Ibid.*, p. 243 (author's translation).

24 T. H. Green, 'On the different senses of "freedom" as applied to will and to the moral progress of man', in *Lectures on the Principles of Political Obligation* (London: Longmans, Green & Co., 1907), pp. 4–5.

25 *See* above, Ch. 2.

26 Two excellent introductions to Thomas's specifically political ideas are R. W. Dyson (Ed.), *Thomas Aquinas: Political Writings* (Cambridge: Cambridge University Press, 2002) and Paul E. Sigmund (Ed.), *St. Thomas Aquinas on Politics and Ethics* (New York: W. W. Norton & Company, 1988).

27 See *Confess.*, III, 9, 17; *Confess.*, X, 29, 40.

28 *De civ. Dei*, XIV, 13 (author's translation).

29 See *Confess.*, IX, 2, 4.

30 As a young new convert Augustine remained similarly convinced for some time. He even conceived a substantial work called the *De libris Disciplinarum*, designed on the plan of an encyclopaedia of secular learning and arranged to show that all knowledge finds its consummation in God – 'To move passionately from things corporeal to things incorporeal, which progress is made almost with fixed steps that lead or are led' (*Retract.*, I, 6 [author's translation]).

31 Preeminently by David Hume, of course. In his *A Treatise of Human Nature*, Hume argued that the inductive mode of reasoning is based upon an outrageous assumption, and that men are compelled to believe it by an inexplicable habit of mind. The best short account of his ideas can be found in the abstract that he published in support of his work. *See* David Hume, 'An abstract of a book lately published, entitled, *A Treatise of Human Nature, Etc.*', in David Hume (Ed. D. G. C. Macnabb), *A Treatise of Human Nature, Book One* (London: Collins, 1962), p. 348, appendix A. There is an excellent analysis of Hume's argument in Karl Popper's *Objective Knowledge, An Evolutionary Approach* (Oxford: Oxford University Press, 1972), pp. 3–4.

32 *De fide r. quae n. v.*, II, 4 (author's translation). *See* also, *In Io. ev. tr.*, VIII, 2: 'Observe this whole world, ordered, as it were, in a single human commonwealth. Observe its administrations, its degrees of power, its conditions of citizenship, its laws and manners and arts! All of this has been brought about through the soul, yet this power of the soul is not visible'. (author's translation).

33 C. S. Lewis, *The Abolition of Man* (New York: HarperCollins, 2002), p. 81. C. S. Lewis gave his best and most accessible defense of natural law in a short broadcast talk, which first aired in 1941. It can be found reprinted, with some alterations, as 'Right and wrong: a clue to the meaning of the universe', in *Broadcast Talks* (London: Geoffrey Bles, The Centenary Press, 1942), pp. 9–37. For more on what he sees as the destructive power of reason, *see* another short paper, 'Meditation in a toolshed', in *Compelling Reason* (London: HarperCollins, 1996), pp. 53–8.

34 See *Serm.*, CCCVI(E), 5.

35 Blaise Pascal, *Pensées*, VI, 393.

36 *Serm.*, XXVIII(B), 10. Julian of Norwich (ca 1342–1416) had a good way of putting the difficulty: 'Things which God's foreknowledge saw before creation, and which He so rightly and worthily brings to their proper end in time, break upon us suddenly and take us by surprise. And because of this blindness and lack of foresight we say they are chances and hazards'. (Julian of Norwich [tr. Clifton Wolters], *Revelations of Divine Love* [Harmondsworth: Penguin, 1978], p. 80).

37 Oswald Chambers, *Not Knowing Whither* (London: Edinburgh, Marshall, Morgan & Scott, 1957), p. 11.

38 For instance, *Confess.*, X, 28, 39.

39 See *Ibid.*, X, 22, 32; *Serm.*, XXII(A), 3.

40 Cf. Ernst Cassirer's assessment of Aquinas' position in his *The Myth of the State*, p. 111.

41 He explains this at *De Gen. ad litt.*, VIII, 16, 34. Cf. *Confess.*, VIII, 3, 6–8;

En. in Ps., I, 6. *See* also *De civ. Dei*, XI, 18, for a discussion along more strictly aesthetic lines.

42 *Ibid.*, VIII, 14, 32 (author's translation).

43 This scheme can be made to correspond with Markus' views. In his *Saeculum*, he argues against imposing the traditional historicism of salvation histories upon Augustine. Instead, he recommends an approach that begins with accepting that history of any sort is recorded history: that it consists in a human interpretation of events. This links it to the question of knowledge. From this position Markus then argues that Augustine's mature conception of history – the conception that informed his *De civitate Dei* – was based in a distinction between secular and sacred historical knowledge. This conception allowed him to claim that the biblical interpretation of history was sacred because the authors had been gifted a Divine, prophetic perspective on events. It was this gifted perspective and not a more generally accessible pattern in history that allowed them to produce their unique interpretation of events. In Markus' words: 'Sacred history is simply what is written in the scriptural canon. It is history written under divine inspiration and endowed with divine authority, presenting, under this inspiration, its secular material within a perspective which transcends that of the secular historian . . . [Consequently] until the end of the world, all history is homogeneous . . . it cannot be mapped out in terms of a pattern drawn from sacred history . . . it can no longer contain decisive turning-points . . . Every moment may have its unique and mysterious significance in the ultimate divine *tableau* of men's doings and sufferings; but it is the significance to which God's revelation does not supply the facts'. (pp. 16–21).

44 *See*, for instance, *De nat. boni*, XXVII: 'However, "from Him" does not mean the same thing as "of Him". What is of Him may be said also to be from Him; but not everything that is from Him may properly be said to be of Him . . . man [for instance] cannot make something of nothing. But God, of Whom are all things, from Whom are all things, and in Whom are all things, had no need of any prior material to assist His omnipotence'. (author's translation). *See* also Massimiliano Finazzer Flory, 'Introduzione', in Giovanni Reale & Carlo Sini, *Agostino e La Scrittura dell'Interiorità* (Milano: Edizioni San Paolo, 2006), pp. 7–8.

45 *See* C. S. Lewis, *The Abolition of Man*, pp. 43–4.

46 See *De civ. Dei*, XIII, 20.

47 See *Serm.*, CCCLX(B), 3.

48 For instance, see how Augustine justifies the method of his *De Genesi contra Manichaeos* at *De Gen. ad litt.*, VIII, 2, 5. And for another point of view see *De civ. Dei*, XIII, 21.

49 As he explains it at *ibid.*, VIII, 1, 2: 'The narrative in these books is not

written in a literary style proper to allegory, as in the Canticle of Canticles, but from beginning to end in a style proper to history, as in the Books of Kings and the other works of that type'.

50 The expression is Moss's, *see* Ch. 3, n. 6, above. Cf. *En. in Ps.*, CXLVI, 5.

51 The chief of these was Eusebius in the fourth century, for whom the conversion of Constantine prefigured the real possibility of an enduring Christian polity. *See* his *Oration in Honour of Constantine on the Thirtieth Anniversary of his Reign*, in DECT, pp. 231–4.

52 Dyson, *Normative Theories of Society and Government*, p. 66.

53 It is customary and proper to remark that such termini are by the nature of the case arbitrary; however, if this qualification is borne in mind then they need not be in any fundamental sense misleading. In this instance our termini are the letter sent by Pope Gelasius I to the Byzantine Emperor Anastasius I and the Bull *Inter caetera Divinae* of Pope Alexander VI (1431–1503), composed upon the discovery of America. The full text of the latter with commentary can be found at *CS*, pp. 153–9.

54 Dyson, *St. Augustine of Hippo*, pp. 169–70.

55 R. W. Dyson (Ed.), *Giles of Rome's on Ecclesiastical Power: A Medieval Theory of World Government* (New York: Columbia University Press, 2004), p. xx.

56 *Ibid.*, pp. 25–9.

57 What is here implied about the systematic nature of medieval political argument is amply illustrated by the short treatise *Quaestio de potestate papae*, or *Rex pacificus*, as it is known from its incipit. It is an anonymous rejection of papal claims to power, produced at some time between 1296 and 1303, that is, during the dispute between Philip the Fair of France and Pope Boniface VIII. In particular, the opening section giving arguments for the proposition of papal power over spirituals and temporals gives a clear insight into the medieval cast of mind. The only complete critical edition and translation in English is that produced by R. W. Dyson: *Quaestio de potestate papae (Rex pacificus)/An Enquiry into the Power of the Pope* (New York: Edwin Mellen Press, 1999).

58 As Arquillière explains elsewhere, 'Here we truly have the central idea, the essence of all the developments, often disparate, that make up the twenty-six books of *De civitate Dei*. It leads to faith, it is the sign of redemption, the opening of Grace, the cause of all the supernatural virtues and the cause of wellbeing. At bottom, this idea is none other than the evangelical justice which Saint Paul turned into a theology applicable to the complications of the lives of the first Christians. Saint Augustine is the first to apply it to the constitution of the State'. (Arquillière, *L'Augustinisme politique*, p. 71 [author's translation]).

59 Arquillière, *L'Augustinisme politique*, pp. 117–19 (author's translation). Cf. A. J. Carlyle's observation that 'It must . . . be recognised that St. Augustine is compelled to abstract the quality of justice from the definition of the State, not by any course of reflection upon the nature of the State, but by his theological conception of justice, a conception which might be regarded as true upon his premises, but which can only be understood as related to those premisses. We cannot express a judgement upon the very interesting question whether St. Augustine's definition of the State exercised any great influence upon the course of political speculation. We have not found that this part of his work is often cited; indeed, we have not come across any instance of this in the earlier Middle Ages at all. But it is hardly possible to escape the conclusion that, however indirectly, this attitude of St. Augustine towards the conception of justice in society is related to that conception of the unrestricted authority of the ruler, which, as we have seen, takes shape about this period, and was drawn out so sharply by St. Gregory the Great'. (*HMPTW*, Vol. I, pp. 168–9).

60 Herbert Spencer's thoughts on this have already been quoted: see Ch. 2, n. 6 above; but Socrates (BC 469–399) is the outstanding example. In the dialogue *Euthyphro*, he is recorded as asking Euthyphro, a self-proclaimed expert on religious matters, what the meaning of 'piety' is. Euthyphro answers by giving him an example of piety, but Socrates immediately points out that what he really wants to know is '. . . the general idea which makes all pious things to be pious'. For he wants '. . . a standard to which I may look, and by which I may measure actions, whether yours or those of any one else, and then I shall be able to say that such and such an action is pious, such another impious'. (Plato [tr. Benjamin Jowett], *The Four Socratic Dialogues of Plato* [Oxford: Clarendon Press, 1903], pp. 16–17).

61 Arquillière, *L'Augustinisme politique*, p. 120 (author's translation).

62 *De Trin.*, XV, 7, 13 (author's translation).

63 As H. A. L. Fisher commented, 'At the beginning of the thirteenth century the fabric of Christian belief in the West still retained the mould which it had received from the mind of St. Augustine. The City of God stood out sharply against the city of man, eternity against time, perfection against sin'. (H. A. L. Fisher, *A History of Europe* [London: Edward Arnold & Co., 1949], p. 281).

64 Feudalism was by no means a uniform or ideal social order. In medieval Europe it exhibited many variations and forms. This is made clear by Professor F. L. Ganshof in his *Feudalism* (London: Longman, 1964), still the best short introduction to the subject.

65 Flotte's statement is recorded by C. Raymond Beazley, in his *A Notebook of Mediaeval History* (Oxford: Clarendon Press, 1917), p. 159. It was the

prototype for other such legendary snubs to papal authority as King Henry VIII's (1491–1547) 'Act of Supremacy' (1534) and his daughter Elizabeth I's (1533–1603) blatant refusal to acknowledge her excommunication and deposition by Pope Pius V (1570).

66 Giambattista Vico (tr. Thomas Goddard Bergin & Max Harold Fisch), *Scienza Nuova* (Ithaca, London: Cornell University Press, 1984), p. 234.

67 Niccolò Machiavelli (tr. George Bull), *The Prince* (Harmondsworth: Penguin, 1970), pp. 73–4.

68 Two strands of late medieval thought in particular reacted against the presumptions of Thomism and the Scholastic method and, in so doing, prepared the ground for Lutheranism. They were the *Devotio Moderna*, and the *Via Moderna*. The former was a primarily mystical movement premissed on a passive acceptance of the utter futility of human effort towards God and developed by the Brethren of the Common Life in Germany and the Netherlands towards the end of the fourteenth century. The latter was an intellectual reaction against the Thomistic regard for reason in discerning the Will of God. William of Ockham (ca 1285–1347) was its outstanding early exponent.

69 In the preface to his *Heidelberg Disputation* (1518), an important exposition of his developed early theology, Luther cites his most influential sources as being '. . . St. Paul, the especially chosen vessel and instrument of Christ, and also . . . St. Augustine, His most trustworthy interpreter'. (Timothy F. Lull [Ed.], *Martin Luther's Basic Theological Writings* [Minneapolis: Fortress Press, 2005], p. 48).

70 H. Daniel-Rops (tr. Audrey Butler), *The Protestant Reformation* (London: J. M. Dent & Sons, 1961), p. 285. Daniel-Rops' account of Luther's intellectual crisis is very full and includes synopses of some of the more prominent scholarly opinions on it. *See* pp. 284–90.

71 *Ibid.*, p. 282.

72 Jaroslav Pelikan and Helmut T. Lehman (Eds.), *Luther's Works: American Edition* (Philadelphia: Fortress Press, 1957–75), pp. 336–8, in Lull (Ed.), *Martin Luther's Basic Theological Writings*, pp. 8–9.

73 *See*, for instance, his *Disputation against Scholastic Theology* (1517), articles 10, 29, 34, 57, 58, 59, 63, 66, 67, 68, 82, 83, 84 & 89, in *ibid.*, pp. 34–8.

74 *Serm.*, XXIII(A), 4 (author's translation).

75 The story has it that Luther nailed these 95 theses to the door of the Castle Church at Wittenberg, but historians have long doubted whether this actually happened. An English translation can be found at Lull (Ed.), *Martin Luther's Basic Theological Writings*, pp. 40–7.

76 The sale of indulgences had been given a theological basis as early as 1343 in the Bull *Unigenitas*.

77 *See* Quentin Skinner's comments on the tradition of anti-clerical humanist satire that had begun to gain ground with the publication of Sebastian Brant's (ca 1457–1521) *Ship of Fools* in 1494 (Quentin Skinner, *The Foundations of Modern Political Thought*, Vol. II [Cambridge: Cambridge University Press, 2005], pp. 27–34).

78 *See* Gerhard Ebeling, *Luther: An Introduction to His Thought* (London: Fontana, 1975), p. 15.

79 In his first work against the Pelagians, *De peccatorum meritis et remissione*, Augustine characterized their position thus: 'There are some persons who, presuming so much upon the free determination of the human will, suppose that it need not sin, and that indeed we require no divine assistance [to will to do good] but inherit this capacity in our very nature'. (II, 2, 2 [author's translation]).

80 As Ernest Barker points out, this assumption was not exclusive to Socrates in his time: 'To the Sophists, therefore, as to Socrates, real goodness depended upon and consisted in a special knowledge; nor can we say that the identification of goodness with knowledge is, in itself, a peculiarly Socratic doctrine. On the contrary, the Sophists, professing as they did to teach goodness, were committed as deeply as Socrates to the proposition that "goodness is knowledge". If it were not, it would not be teachable; and if it were not teachable, the *raison d'être* of their profession was gone'. (Ernest Barker, *Greek Political Theory: Plato and His Predecessors* [London: Methuen, 1960], p. 101).

81 Daniel-Rops (tr. Audrey Butler), *The Protestant Reformation*, p. 288.

82 Leighton Pullman, *Religion since the Reformation* (Oxford: Clarendon Press, 1924), p. 7.

83 *Serm.*, XVI(A), 11 (author's translation).

84 *De civ. Dei*, X, 25 (author's translation). This whole passage refers to Psalm 73.

85 *See*, for instance, the way in which Luther conceives his position as Doctor in his *Lectures on Galatians* (1535): 'This calls for a wise and faithful father who can moderate the Law in such a way that it stays within its limits. For if I were to . . .' (Lull [Ed.], *Martin Luther's Basic Theological Writings*, p. 20).

86 For instance, in proof 26 of the *Heidelberg Disputation*, Luther explains that in practice – that is, in the everyday life of the Christian – Christ is a principle not a Person: 'For through faith Christ is in us, indeed, one with us. Christ is just and has fulfilled all the commands of God, wherefore we also fulfill everything through Him since He was made ours through faith'. (*ibid.*, p. 60).

87 *See* J. W. Allen, *A History of Political Thought in the Sixteenth Century* (London: Methuen, 1957), pp. 18–30.

88 *Ibid.*, pp. 28.

89 Martin Luther, *Lectures on Galations* (1535), in Lull (Ed.), *Martin Luther's Basic Theological Writings*, p. 21.

90 An excellent summary of the scriptural evidence in support of this view can be found at Sykes, *Power and Christian Theology*, pp. 54–60.

91 Marsilius of Padua (tr. & intr. Alan Gewirth), *Defensor Pacis* (Toronto: Toronto University Press, 1980), pp. 114–15.

92 Daniel-Rops (tr. Audrey Butler), *The Protestant Reformation*, p. 353.

93 *Ibid.*, p. 352.

94 *En. in Ps.*, CXLIII, 18 (author's translation). Cf. *Ep.*, CXXXVII, 5, 20 & CXXXVIII, 2, 11; 2, 17.

95 See the documents and commentary in J. Noakes & G. Pridham (Eds.), *Nazism 1919–1945*, Vol. 2 (Exeter: Exeter University Press, 2000), pp. 388–95. But note especially their word of caution: 'The response of the churches to the regime was . . . complex and ambiguous. It varied among individual priests and pastors and individual bishops . . .' (p. 388).

96 Martin Luther, *Heidelberg Disputation* (1518), in Lull (Ed.), *Martin Luther's Basic Theological Writings*, p. 59. Cf. *De perf. iust. hom.*, VIII, 17: 'Now from this body of death not every one is liberated who ends the present life, but only he who in this life has received Grace, and given proof of not receiving it in vain by spending his days in good works'.

97 *In Io. ev. tr.*, XIV, 6 (author's translation). Cf. *En. in Ps.*, LXVII, 13.

98 *De civ. Dei*, XXI, 8.

99 *En. in Ps.*, CXXV, 3 (author's translation).

100 *De bapt.*, V, 27, 38 (author's translation). Cf. *ibid.*, V, 28, 39; *ep.*, CCVIII, 2; *En. in Ps.*, XXXIX, 10; *Contra Faustum*, XIII, 16; *De cath. rud.*, XIX, 31; *Confess.*, XIII, 14, 15.

101 Oliver O'Donovan, *The Desire of the Nations: Rediscovering the Roots of Political Theology* (Cambridge: Cambridge University Press, 1999), p. 209.

102 Cornford, *From Religion to Philosophy*, p. 261.

103 *See* Walter Ullmann, 'The medieval origins of the Renaissance', in André Chastel *et al.*, *The Renaissance: Essays in Interpretation* (London, Methuen, 1982), pp. 33–83.

104 Bronowski and Mazlish cite Leonardo da Vinci (1452–1519) as the outstanding example of the Renaissance spirit that anticipated the enlightenment of Europe, '. . . to an age still dominated by the traditional categories of Aristotle and Aquinas, [Leonardo] brought the right mind. When almost all thinking was still guided by universal and *a priori* plans of nature, he

made a single profound discovery. He discovered that nature speaks to us in detail, and that only through the detail can we find her grand design'. (Bronowski & Mazlish, *The Western Intellectual Tradition*, p. 37).

105 The nature of his new account in the world lay in his indispensability. As Gerhard Ritter explains, this first manifested itself on the battlefield where, in particular, the English middle-class crossbowmen and archers began to wield a decisive influence. Later, '. . . the urban middle-class with its great fund of money took its place as a very self-conscious third estate alongside of the clergy and the nobility. It challenged the clergy's monopoly in education and the nobility's in the bearing of arms. The more money proved itself indispensable to monarchical governments as a means of power, the greater became the influence of the middle class and especially the capitalists'. (Gerhard Ritter, 'Origins of the modern state', in Heinz Lubasz [Ed.], *The Development of the Modern State* [London: Collier-Macmillan, 1964], p. 21).

106 W. E. H. Lecky, *History of the Rise and Spirit of Rationalism in Europe* (London: Longmans Green & Co., 1910), p. xi.

107 Joseph Devey (Ed.), *The Physical and Metaphysical Works of Lord Bacon* (London: George Bell & Sons, 1901), p. 1.

108 Xenophanes, fragments 11, 14, 16 & 15, in Kirk and Raven, *The Presocratic Philosophers*, pp. 168–9. Cf. Apuleius, *Asclepius.*, 23.

109 *De civ. Dei*, VIII, 23 (author's translation). Cf. *En. in Ps.*, XCV, 14: 'Woe to those who have hope in this age; woe to them that cling to what they brought forth through hope in this age'. (author's translation).

110 *See*, for instance, *De Trin.*, XIV, 15, 21: 'And [the mind] remembers the Lord its God [cf. Deut. 8.14] . . . it is reminded that it may be turned to God [Ps. 22.27], as though to that light by which it was in some way touched, even when turned away from Him. This explains why it is that even the ungodly think of eternity, and rightly blame and rightly praise many things in the morals of men'. (author's translation). Cf. *De sp. et litt.*, XXVII, 48; *En. in Ps.*, LVII, 1; *De serm. Dom. in m.*, II, 1, 1.

111 For Rousseau, the gains to be had from the new philosophical investigation in the eighteenth century, the 'arts and sciences', were ultimately negative. The dim intuitions of the human heart could still be a powerful force for good in the hands of simple, rustic folk – the more so as they were disinclined to seek out their source. But if the arts and sciences could not construct something positive to go in their place, then they should leave well alone: 'Almighty God! Thou Who holdest in Thy hand the minds of men, deliver us from the fatal arts and sciences of our forefathers; give us back ignorance, innocence and poverty, which alone can make us happy and are precious in Thy sight'. (Jean-Jacques Rousseau, 'Discourse on the

arts and sciences', in G. D. H. Cole [tr.], *The Social Contract and Discourses* [London: Toronto, J. M. Dent & Sons, 1930], p. 152). Rousseau had some cause to doubt the final good of philosophy's contribution to society, for, as Berlin put it, 'The conflict of the rival explanations (or models) of social and individual life had, by the late eighteenth century, grown to be a scandal. If one examines what answers were offered, let us say, between the death of Newton and the birth of Darwin, to a central political question – why anyone should obey anyone else – the babel of voices is appalling, perhaps the most confused in recorded history'. (Isaiah Berlin, 'Does political theory still exist?', in Peter Laslett & W. G. Runciman [Eds.], *Philosophy, Politics, and Society* [Oxford: Basil Blackwell, 1972], p. 21).

112 *Confess.*, IV, 12, 18.

113 *Confess.*, IV, 11, 16 (author's translation). Cf. *De civ. Dei*, X, 28: 'He does not, however, destroy and bring to naught His own gift in them, but only what they arrogate to themselves, and do not attribute to Him'.

114 Jean Bethke Elshtain, *Augustine and the Limits of Politics* (Notre Dame, Indiana: University of Notre Dame Press, 1995).

115 This is what she seems to say in the conclusion to her article, 'Augustine', in Peter Scott & William Cavanagh (Eds.), *The Blackwell Companion to Political Theology* (Oxford: Blackwell, 2004), pp. 35–47: 'The teleology of historic progress is no longer believable, although a version of it is still touted by voluptuaries of techno-progress or genetic engineering that may yet "perfect" the human race. The presumably solid underpinnings of the self gave way in the twentieth century under the onslaught of Nietzsche and Freud'. (pp. 46–7).

116 *See* in particular, Elshtain, *Augustine and the Limits of Politics*, pp. 1–18; and also her comment on p. 118 '. . . This man who desired "not only a devout reader, but also an open-minded critic," gets too few of each, or both, in our harsh and cynical time. But he perdures'.

117 *Ibid.*, pp. 114–15.

118 See *ibid.*, p. xi: 'As I struggled with belief and unbelief, faith and skepticism, abandoning (so I then thought) my Lutheran beliefs and identity, I found I could not bid Augustine adieu'.

119 *En. in Ps.*, LXIV, 2 (author's translation).

120 Elshtain, *Augustine and the Limits of Politics*, p. 97.

121 *See* in particular Augustine's discussion of this at *In Io. ev. tr.*, VII, 8.

122 Elshtain, *Augustine and the Limits of Politics*, p. 89.

123 *Ibid.*, p. xiii.

124 *De perf. iust. hom.*, VIII, 18 (author's translation).

125 At *De pecc. mer. et rem.*, III, 1, 1.

126 Garry Wills, *Saint Augustine* (New York: Penguin, 1999) p. xii.

127 *See* Brown, *Augustine of Hippo*, pp. 367–77.
128 *Confess.*, XII, 11, 13 (author's translation).

5

Augustine's early life and education

We have now concluded our account of the reception and interpretation of Augustine's political ideas in history. In this short chapter we must prepare the ground for the second part of our book by giving the facts of Augustine's life up until his nineteenth year – the year that it is customary to celebrate as his conversion to philosophy. Such intellectual landmarks are never immune to qualification and tend inevitably to grow in retrospect, but there seems little reason to doubt the significance of this one. For from his nineteenth year, Augustine underwent a profound change in outlook and intellectual equipment. Prompted by his reading of Cicero's *Hortensius,* he began to become increasingly attuned to a deep disquiet in his heart, and to refer more and more of his hopes and achievements to stilling it. It is, however, important that we emphasize that this was a purely intellectual event, common enough to men of Augustine's sensibility and circumstances; the kind of event that very seldom issues in much more than a change of mind, and whose public expression is the preference for a new type of literature. It is only in exceptional cases that conversions to philosophy have their effects beyond the library, and then, strictly speaking, they become something else.

THE MATERIAL AND CULTURAL
CIRCUMSTANCES OF AUGUSTINE'S BIRTH

In what way could the material and cultural circumstances of Augustine's birth be said to have contributed to his subsequent outlook? His father, Patricius (died ca AD 370), was a respectable free-born citizen of Thagaste (the present-day Souk Ahras, in Algeria) in Proconsular Africa. He was of the decurion class and therefore expected to be involved in the administration of the town's affairs.[1] However, in Roman North Africa of the mid-fourth century, the kudos of this position had come to be outweighed by very real disadvantages. Africa at that time was being crushed under the weight of unbearable taxes imposed from Rome, and Patricius and others with him on the municipal council would have been charged with paying and raising them.[2] There is evidence that these men were prepared to go to some lengths to avoid being implicated in what was a difficult and thankless task.[3] Augustine indicates that Patricius was certainly not one to shirk his duties; to the contrary, he was proud of his birth and set great store by his rank and privileges, but he must have found it increasingly difficult to be part of a class effectively under siege from above and below: that is, forced by the powers that be to extract inflationary taxes from an impoverished and resentful peasantry.[4] In one of his letters Augustine mentions that his inherited share of the family property was equal to approximately one-twentieth of the land that he held in trust as Bishop of Hippo.[5] In today's terms, this would be a sizeable estate, but the truth at the time was that Patricius was not alone able to raise the monies to send his talented son to university at Carthage. In the end this was achieved with the financial help of a rich patron, Romanianus (quite possibly a family relation). However, short of referring him to some class stereotype, there is not much more of fact that we can say for Patricius. He is probably the most notorious victim of what Peter Brown has called Augustine's 'significant silences'.[6]

AUGUSTINE'S FATHER, PATRICIUS

Patricius' rôle in the *Confessiones* strikes us as symbolic; at any rate, his testimonial lacks the customary warmth and romance. Augustine seems content to allow him to stand as the archetypal citizen of the Earthly City: the father wholly unconcerned with his son's spiritual development but intoxicated by his prospects of worldly success.[7] Nearly all of Augustine's remarks on his father seem designed to point a moral at the expense of the Earthly City; however, if we read through this rhetoric we can form a picture of Patricius which, though limited, is probably not far from the truth. He was evidently true to the civic identity of his class: an old-fashioned Roman, grave in his responsibilities and settled in his outlook. This probably meant that he was liable to be made fun of by Augustine and his friends. It seems that he suffered the fate of many average fathers who have brilliant sons. On the one hand, the limitations of his outlook prevented him from taking anything but a superficial interest in his son's achievements; on the other hand, his bourgeois ambitions[8] heightened his son's sensitivities to the Earthly City's priorities. We will have more to say on this later.

From another point of view, Patricius' faults were not high in the catalogue of sins by the standard of the day. Augustine mentions that he was unfaithful to Monica's (AD 331–387) bed on a handful of occasions[9] and liable to be an overzealous disciplinarian.[10] In addition, the *Confessiones* contain small but significant testaments to his generosity as a father[11] and overall respectfulness as a husband.[12]

AUGUSTINE'S MOTHER, MONICA

Augustine gives us a great deal of information about his mother, Monica (or Monnica, as her name is often spelt in the manuscripts). Catholics today are apt to regard her as one of the outstanding examples of Christian womanhood, such was her reputation for faith, courage, charity and love. E.-H. Vollet observed that, 'After the name of Mary, hers is the name that Catholic woman invoke with most emotion'.[13] Agostino Trapè calls her '. . . an exceptional woman. Given by nature a brilliant intelligence, a strong character, and a profound sensibility'.[14]

It seems to have been Monica's sincerest wish to establish a Christian household and to educate her children and husband in the faith. She would work at this task assiduously, sometimes against the instincts of her pagan husband. Her three children would eventually turn out as confessing Christians and her husband would be baptized on his deathbed. Her children were Augustine (almost certainly the eldest), his brother Navigius (whom some scholars have as the eldest) and a sister who remains unnamed (though one tradition names her as Perpetua).[15]

Monica's faith was relentless and unquestioning. She endured the humiliations and violent temper of her husband[16] and encouraged others to acquiesce in the settled order of things,[17] yet we should not automatically attribute her *modus vivendi* to a rustic simplicity of mind. It is quite possible that she was the first realist whom Augustine encountered; at any rate, her method of managing her husband made a powerful impression upon him. In his *Confessiones* he describes how she would exhort her colleagues in life to abandon the romantic notion of making headway against the vanity and anger of their husbands. Instead, they should reign in their ambitions and use a woman's cunning to make progress wherever it was possible. She used to joke that they should look upon their marriage contracts as binding them in slavery to their husbands, for by this means they might operate more mindfully in the heat of the moment and not set off an inferno by fighting pride with pride.[18]

AUGUSTINE'S EDUCATION UP TO HIS NINETEENTH YEAR

Augustine underwent the typical early education of the Roman boy.[19] It was exclusively matched to the conditions of public success in the ancient world and aimed to turn out orators – men who could swing public opinion. And in the absence of science and statistics, oratory could very well furnish the respected standard of right action. As Rome's most celebrated teacher, Quintilian (AD 35–96), put it,

> If we constantly have occasion to speak of justice, fortitude, temperance, and other similar topics, so that a cause can scarcely be found in which some such discussion does not occur, and if all such subjects are to be illustrated by invention and elocution, can it be doubted that, wherever power of intellect and copiousness of language are required, the art of the orator is to be there pre-eminently exerted?[20]

In addition we should remember that this was an intellectually conservative age; wisdom was conceived to be a finite quantity – won and preserved for all time in the great writings of antiquity and assumed to be of infinite future applicability. The task of the Roman educator was correspondingly to empty this store of wisdom into the mind of the Roman boy. As Brown describes it, '. . . the aim was to measure up to the timeless perfection of an ancient classic'.[21] It was an education that few could take to easily, and that fewer still could properly appreciate until coming of age. It was also, then, an education that relied heavily on the rod. Augustine has his own description of this hardship:

> Therefore I was sent to school that I might learn my letters, the utility of which I could not see in my wretchedness. Notwithstanding this, I was beaten whenever I was slow to learn. This method was praised by the majority; at any rate, it had been laid down before us by many as the miserable path which we were to follow. In this way both toil and sorrow were multiplied for the sons of Adam [cf. Gen. 3.16] . . . A little one, but with no little feeling, I prayed to You that I would not be beaten at school . . . we sinned by writing, reading, and thinking over our lessons less than was required of us. However, Lord, this was not because we lacked memory or intelligence – for You decreed that we should have these things in sufficient measure for our years – it was rather that we loved to

play. Yet this love of play was punished in us by men who played just as much themselves, but called their contests 'business' rather than games.[22]

From the beatings of his first school at Thagaste, Augustine would graduate to the less painful and more sophisticated environment of the university town of Madauros. He was then about 11 years old and already an outstanding prospect.[23] He was also beginning to grow into the wisdom of what he was doing. This would, in retrospect, become a precious time of untroubled boyish learning. For after just five years his charmed world would fall apart: Patricius had no more money to continue his education. He must return immediately to Thagaste and there await the time when enough money could be found to send him on to university at Carthage. This was evidently a complicated year for Augustine – a year in which he desperately needed to be taken in hand by a father sharing his sensibilities. What actually happened was a disaster. Both his parents, now very much in awe of their son and investing heavily in his future, neglected to focus on the mundane but urgent aspects of his life:

> These were not those hopes of the age to come which I knew my mother herself to have, but those hopes for my learning, which, as I knew, both parents wanted too much: he, because he almost never thought of You but only of vain things for me; she, because she thought that the usual studies would be no obstacle to me attaining You, and perhaps even of some help.[24]

It was a perilous situation: Augustine, now clearly the intellectual superior of his parents, was correspondingly given a moral license out of all proportion to his emotional maturity. 'Meanwhile, the lines of liberty at play were loosened over me beyond any just severity and the result was dissolution and various punishments'.[25] As a result Augustine suffered a double punishment. Betrayed by his parents in his hour of need and alarmed to be so discomposed by passions beyond his control, he more ardently sought comfort in the pattern of the world.

> During the idleness of that sixteenth-year . . . the briars of lust grew wantonly over my head, and there was no hand to root them out. Moreover, when my father saw me at the baths, he noted how I was becoming a man and putting on the rebellious clothing of that estate. Seeing this, he was able to start taking pride in his grandchildren, and even found joy in telling it to my mother.[26]

Finally, in AD 371, the money for Carthage was found with the help of Romanianus.

Augustine's description of his arrival at Carthage is famous: 'I came to Carthage, where a cauldron of shameful loves seethed and sounded about me on every side'.[27] It is also, on the face of it, unremarkable. There must be many undergraduates who have gone up to university with similar thoughts in mind. In actual fact Augustine would turn out to be better behaved than most. Within a year he had taken a mistress, entering into a respectable relationship with her. She bore him a son, Adeodatus, in AD 372, and he tells us that he dearly and faithfully loved her for 15 years.[28] She would eventually be given up in Milan, where Augustine's career demanded an advantageous marriage. We are apt to condemn Augustine for this, and indeed his short description of the episode is full of regret and guilt.[29] But overall it seems that Augustine was a good student, though still consciously referring his activities to the heartache caused by his parents. He was also liable to exaggerate his misdeeds in order to stay in with the fashionable crowd.[30]

It is at Carthage that the interesting question of Augustine's residual Christianity comes up. We have noted that he grew up in a Christian home maintained by a devout mother, imbibing the sort of faith that children are renowned for. Augustine says that he used to pray not to be beaten at school, something for which he was mocked by his elders.[31] Evidently, though, the Christianity of his upbringing had made some sort of claim on his heart:

> We discovered, Lord, certain men who prayed to You, and we learned from them. We imagined You, as far as we were able, as

some sort of mighty One Who, though not appearing before our senses, could nonetheless hear us and help us.[32]

This strikes us as a delightful picture of a small mind making terms with someone beyond its reckoning. Augustine would later come to regard it as an example not of innocence but of the advantages of the child's outlook: an unencumbered faith, fragile and unable to last long in the tarnishing atmosphere of the world. By the time of his arrival at Carthage, he had, by his own admission, become the arrogant and gifted young scholar. He would soon be the leading student in the school of rhetoric,[33] impressing his teachers with his ability to master the most complicated scientific treatises alone.[34]

He was training for a career in the law and had already cultivated the appropriate, sophisticated outlook. Then, quite by chance, he came across a now extinct work by Cicero: the *Hortensius* – apparently an exhortation to philosophy. He had picked it up with mercenary intentions, wanting to copy its eloquence for the law courts, but something in the substance of what Cicero was saying struck him deeply. In his description of the event there are, perhaps, echoes of the boy Augustine at Madauros before his world fell apart.[35] For before him was the great orator, Cicero, extolling the virtues of wisdom for wisdom's sake. This must have seemed like a vindication of everything that he had felt as he first learned to love his work. It called forth the emotions of his sixteenth year. He saw himself plainly: an ardour for the things of the world competing with its obverse, the shame of having become so much his father's son.[36]

This book changed my affections: it turned my prayers to You, Lord, and by that means gave an altogether different purpose to my life. At once my vain hopes lost their value to me, and in their place I desired unchanging wisdom. I desired it with an incredible warmth of heart; and so I began to rise up, in order better to return to You [cf. Lk. 15.18] . . . I did not, then, use this book to sharpen my tongue, for it had not impressed me by its style but rather by the substance of what it spoke.[37]

In this short sketch we have attributed great significance to the trauma of Augustine's adjustment to the Earthly City. He was to discover, more acutely than most, how we are all born to the burden of paying a price we do not owe. It is a price set by the unique and unasked-for circumstances of our birth. We generally form ourselves in reaction against these circumstances and by that means perpetuate the trauma for the next generation.[38] These depressing cycles of initiation and citizenship describe the pattern of the world – what Augustine called *vitae humanae procellosam societatem* 'the stormy society of human life'. Augustine would later come to appreciate that these cycles are, on these terms, irresistible. The freedom of the human will indicates that no one is without the means to resist, while the human mind has shown that it is capable of conceiving better states of affairs, but neither of these can replace lost innocence. And Augustine seems genuinely to have thought that only innocence could break the mechanism of the Earthly City, yet not even newborn babies possess it: '. . . it is not the infant's will that is harmless, but the weakness of infant limbs'.[39] It is this lack of innocence – pride – that prompts our first compliance, and soon we are too compromised to resist. The virtue that children possess over adults is properly speaking a characteristic of their estate rather than their nature. They are humble insofar as their limited development holds them in unquestioning obedience to their parents. For Augustine, then, the outstanding characteristics of life are a tragic irony and a depressing inertia. The advances that we associate with progress and development are resigned, by him, to the realm of the conventional rather than the foundational:

> I lay on the threshold of the world's customs and contrivances, a wretched boy: for this was the stage and arena where I feared more to commit a barbarism than I guarded myself against envying those who did not. I say these things in confession to You, my God, because these were the very things that earned me praise from men – and to earn such praise was, for me, at that time, to lead a life of honour . . . Is this the outlook of boyish innocence? It is not, O Lord, it is not: I pray leave to say it, my God. For this same outlook

is acquired from tutors and teachers, and from nuts and balls and birds it passes to governors and kings. In time it comes to bear upon money and estates and slaves. This outlook persists, then, so that as we grow older more severe punishments succeed the birch rod. It was therefore the symbol of humility that You recommended in the child's estate when You said, 'for of such is the Kingdom of Heaven.' [Mt. 19.14][40]

Notes

1 Anthony Rich's definition of a *decurio* is 'A senator in any of the municipal towns or colonies, who held a corresponding rank, and discharged similar functions in his town to what the senators did at Rome'. He cites as an ancient authority on the matter, Cicero, *Oratio pro Sestio*, IV, 10. (*A Dictionary of Roman and Greek Antiquities* [London: Longmans, Green, and Co., 1901], p. 234).

2 This was in accordance with standard Roman procedure: those that paid the taxes were invariably required to administer them too. In practice, this gave them considerable freedom to put the costs onto those beneath them. *See* W. H. C. Frend, *The Donatist Church: A Movement of Protest in North Africa* (Oxford: Clarendon Press, 1952), p. 63 for more on this.

3 The *Codex Theodosianus* contains a number of decrees concerned with African *Decuriones* attempting to escape their duties.

4 Augustine described him as an '. . . inconsiderable burgher of Thagaste'. (*Confess.*, II, 3, 5). And elsewhere he described himself as '. . . a poor man, born of poor parents'. (*Serm.*, CCCLVI, 13). As Brown points out in his *Poverty and Leadership in the Later Roman Empire*, 'Impoverishment was what most ancient persons feared most for themselves. And with good reason. Impoverishment could come at any time, from any number of misfortunes . . .' (p. 15).

5 See *Ep.*, CXXVI, 7. He later endowed it to the Church of Thagaste on being elected bishop.

6 Brown, *Augustine of Hippo*, p. 18.

7 At *Confess.*, II, 3, 6, Augustine describes it as '. . . that intoxication, wherein this world, from the unseen wine of its own perverse will, tending down towards lower things, forgets You, its Creator, and loves Your creatures more than Yourself'.

8 It is Dyson who uses the term 'bourgeois' to describe the aspirations of Patricius' outlook (Dyson, *St. Augustine of Hippo*, p. 1).

9 See *Confess.*, IX, 9, 19.

10 *Ibid.*

11 See *ibid.*, II, 3, 5.

12 See *ibid.*, IX, 9, 19.

13 F.-C Dreyfus (Ed.), *La Grande Encyclopédie: Inventaire Raisonné, des Sciences, des Lettres et des Arts* (Paris: H. Lamirault et Cie, Éditeurs, 1886–1902), p. 663b.

14 Trapè, *Agostino: l'uomo, il pastore, il mistico*, p. 29.

15 Navigius is mentioned in the *Confessiones* as being present at Monica's death (*Confess.*, IX, 11, 27). He travelled to Cassiciacum with Augustine and took his part in a number of the dialogues there: *Contra Acad.*, I, 2, 5–14; *De b. vita*, I, 6–7 & 2, 14; and *De ord.*, I, 2, 5. Possidius mentions him having two daughters who were both consecrated (*Vita*, 26, 1). Augustine mentions his sister in a letter. Evidently she became the abbess of a community of women at Hippo (*Ep.*, CCXI, 4); and Possidius explains how this came about (*Vita*, 26, 1).

16 *See* the evidence of this at *Confess.*, IX, 9, 19.

17 Augustine is surely drawing on his mother's example while making this recommendation to his congregation: 'And any good wife calls her husband her lord and master; indeed, it is not only that she calls him so, but that she really thinks so: she means it, she accepts it in her heart, she professes it with her lips, she even regards her nuptial contract as the deed of her purchase'. (*Serm.*, XXXVII, 7 [author's translation]).

18 See *Confess.*, IX, 9, 19–22.

19 *See* Brown, *Augustine of Hippo*, pp. 23–8, for a short account of Augustine's early education. For a more general survey of the essentials of the Roman education, *see* Laurie, *Historical Survey of Pre-Christian Education*, (London: Longmans, Green, 1907) pp. 301–411.

20 Quintilian (tr. John Selby Watson), *Institutio Oratoria*, (New York: Bobbs-Merrill, 1965), Preface, p. 12. *See* also Laurie's comment that '. . . in all things – even in the study of Greek – there was a Roman practical aim, while in all subjects, save literature and what bore directly on the full understanding of the poets, the Roman was superficial and utilitarian. Might we not say, superficial *because* utilitarian?' (Laurie, *Historical Survey of Pre-Christian Education*, p. 340).

21 Brown, *Augustine of Hippo*, p. 37.

22 *Confess.*, I, 9, 14–15 (author's translation).

23 The standard practice was for Roman boys to graduate from the primary *ludus publicus* to the secondary school of the *grammaticus* when they were 11 or 12.

24 *Confess.*, II, 3, 8 (author's translation).

25 *Ibid.*, II, 3, 8.

26 *Ibid.*, II, 3, 6 (author's translation).

27 *Ibid.*, III, 1, 1.

28 See *ibid.*, IV, 2, 2.

29 See *ibid.*, VI, 15, 25.

30 See *ibid.*, II, 3, 7: '. . . I surged forward in such blindness that I was ashamed to be remiss in shamelessness in the midst of my comrades. For I heard them boast of their shameless acts, and hold them up the more debased they were . . . But lest I be put to scorn, I made myself out to be more depraved than I was'. (author's translation) cf. *ibid.*, III, 3, 5–6.

31 *Ibid.*, I, 9, 14.

32 *Ibid.* (author's translation).

33 *Ibid.*, III, 3, 6.

34 *Ibid.*, IV, 16.

35 The boy whom Augustine describes in the following terms: 'I delighted in truth, inasmuch as it appeared to me in my little pursuits, and in my thoughts about these things. I did not want to make mistakes; I was endowed with a vigorous memory; I was well instructed in speech; I was refined by friendship. In addition, I shunned sadness, dejection, and ignorance'. (*ibid.*, I, 20, 31 [author's translation]).

36 See *ibid.*, III, 1, 1: '. . . by a more hidden want I hated myself for wanting little'.

37 *Ibid.*, III, 4, 7 (author's translation).

38 *See*, for instance, *De pecc. mer. et rem.*, II, 9, 11: 'It follows that every son who is born into this old and infirm nature [of his father] will of necessity partake of its effects. If he is then to be born again, he must first be renewed by the Spirit in order to have his sin remitted. This change must take place in him: even if he were born to a father renewed by Spirit it would avail him not'. (author's translation).

39 *Confess.*, I, 7, 11. Cf. *ibid.*, I, 7, 12: 'But "if I was conceived in iniquity," [cf. Ps. 116.16] and if my mother nourished me within her womb in sins where, I beseech You, O Lord my God, where or when was your servant innocent?'

40 *Ibid.*, I, 19, 30 (author's translation).

6

The Earthly City

Leo Tolstoy's (1828–1910) *War and Peace* contains an episode of intellectual conversion not unlike Augustine's. Its subject is Prince Andrei Bolkonsky, fallen in the field at Austerlitz:

> Above him there was now only the sky – the lofty sky, not clear yet still immeasurably lofty, with grey clouds creeping softly across it. 'How quiet, peaceful and solemn! Quite different from when I was running,' thought Prince Andrei. 'Quite different from us running and shouting and fighting. Not at all like the gunner and the Frenchman dragging the mop from one another with frightened, frantic faces. How differently do these clouds float across that lofty limitless sky! How was it I did not see that sky before? And how happy I am to have found it at last! Yes, all is vanity, all is delusion except these infinite heavens. There is nothing, nothing but that. But even it does not exist, there is nothing but peace and stillness. Thanks be to God! . . .'[1]

Some time after having been removed to a French dressing station for treatment, Prince Andrei finally encounters his hero Napoleon in the flesh:

> Although five minutes previously Prince Andrei had been able to say a few words to the soldiers who were carrying him, now with his eyes fixed steadily on Napoleon he was silent . . . So trivial seemed

159

to him at that moment all the interests that engrossed Napoleon, so petty did his hero with his paltry vanity and delight in victory appear, compared to that lofty, righteous and kindly sky which he had seen and comprehended, that he could not answer him.[2]

The setting is dramatic but the events are not unusual. Tolstoy wrote *War and Peace* with the purpose of celebrating life – life understood in its most general sense. He shared Rousseau's vague conviction that the arts and sciences had more potential to do ill than good, and he regarded war as the grandest human conceit, incapable of redirecting history though it purported to. Napoleon was his example. Life, however, was something that it was open to any man to experience, whether peasant or prince. He had only to question his motives for lording it over men and history, and then give himself up to the obverse: a wide and unquestioning faith in the goodness of the human spirit and its consanguinity with nature. It is our suggestion that this process – the rejection of the world – was approximately Augustine's reaction to reading Cicero's *Hortensius*. It took him back to the 'humility found in the child's estate', to a time when, not yet compromised by his dealings with his fellow citizens, he could imagine a different city:

How did all this help me, my God, my true life [cf. Jn 11.25; 14.6]? To what purpose was my ability to declaim praised above that of my schoolmates? Is this not all just smoke and wind? Was there really no other subject on which to exercise my tongue [than to speak the words of Juno]? Your praises, Lord – Your praises as we find them in Your Scriptures – would have carried the palm of my heart, and shielded it from empty trifles, the shameful prey of flying creatures.[3]

Likewise Tolstoy has Prince Andrei return to such a place:

The quiet home life and peaceful happiness of Bald Hills passed before [Prince Andrei's] imagination. He was enjoying that happiness when that little Napoleon suddenly appeared with his indifferent, narrow look of satisfaction at the misery of others, and was followed by doubts and torments, and only the heavens promised peace.[4]

From our point of view, Tolstoy is useful because he illustrates the generic character of these episodes. They occur whenever the mind of a thoughtful man is arrested by the incongruity of human nature and the lights of conscience, war and peace. They are fortified through the memory by a kind of myth of innocence. They invite the subject to envisage a golden age in his past that might conceivably be recreated in the future. In Augustine's words,

> . . . what delighted me in the [Hortensius] was that its argument impelled me to catch hold of, not some or other school or sect, but wisdom itself, whatsoever it might be [here Augustine is expressing the general, limited and purely intellectual nature of his experience]. It stirred me up: I was enkindled and set afire to love, to seek, and to attain wisdom. In fact only this caused me thought, that Christ's name was not in it. For this name, O Lord, this name of my Saviour, Your Son, had my conscientious heart taken in with my mother's milk; it had somehow retained it, and all this according to Your mercy [cf. Ps. 25.7]. I subsequently found that whatever lacked this name, no matter how learned or polished or truthful it seemed, could not completely hold me. Bearing these things in mind, I decided to turn to the Scriptures and seek my wisdom there.[5]

Augustine's disappointment upon turning to the Scriptures is well known. It is a disappointment that he thinks would be shared by any who try to find in them the clue to a salvation conceived along human lines. That is to say, by any who have been flattered by the classical assumption that man participates, by his very nature, in that which elevates and saves. As improving literature they are anachronistic; even in Augustine's time the morality exhibited in the Old Testament was questionable. What is

more, they do not seem capable of furnishing satisfying explanations of
the genesis of the earth and the psychology of the human condition. In
short, the Scriptures address few of the standard preoccupations of salvation literature. Their predominant other-worldliness can be offensive
to the man who has already seen his way to an intellectually respectable
good life on earth:

> And behold, I [now] see something within them that was neither dis-
> cerned by the proud nor revealed to the children [cf. Jas 4.6; 1 Pet.
> 5.5]. It was lowly on approach, but became lofty as one advanced
> in it; and all its aspects were veiled over in mysteries. No one in my
> state could have entered into it; I could not even bend my neck for its
> passageways. When I first turned to the Scriptures, my expectations
> were such that I was only able to compare them to the dignity of
> Tully's writings. Thus I found them wanting: in my swollen condi-
> tion I disdained their humble style, and my sharp gaze could not
> pick out their depths. In truth, my expectations were wholly out of
> line with the nature of its wisdom, which was such that one had
> first to become humble like a child in order to grow up in it. But I
> disdained to be a little child and, swollen with pride, I considered
> myself a great fellow [cf. Mt. 7.27].[6]

THE MYTH OF INNOCENCE

The idea we have called the myth of innocence has both political and
philosophical repercussions. From the former point of view it describes
a charmed state of being on the cusp of full earthly citizenship; from the
latter it suggests the possibility of human moral and intellectual transformation. However it is in psychology that we find a striking example
of its application. The psychoanalytic school founded by Sigmund Freud
(1856–1939) is based upon the belief that psychological formation consists in a pristine child negotiating the imperfect and artificial impositions
of family and society:

With irresistible might it will be impressed on you by what processes of development, of repression, and of sublimation and reaction there arises out of the child, with its peculiar gifts and tendencies, the so-called normal man, the bearer and partly the victim of our painfully acquired civilization.[7]

Psychoanalysis correspondingly promises enlightenment, freedom and happiness by means of an engineered descent through the layers of repression and compromise to the pristine child beneath. At the time of his intellectual conversion Augustine was similarly invested in the idea that he might, by his own powers, remove his archeology of personal and imposed ambition. Later, after his conversion to God, he would identify the weakness of this scheme which raises sentiment above reality:

The food in dreams is very like the food we eat when we are awake; however, we are not fed by it: we merely sleep. But those fantasies could not in any way anticipate You as You appear to me now in the reality of Your spoken voice. They could not because they were corporeal fantasies, false bodies, conceived in the mind and therefore less certain than any real body seen by the eyes, whether in the heavens or on the earth. These real bodies we see in common with the beasts of the field and the birds of the air, and they are more certain than those we conjure up in imagination. Again, we can be more certain of the impressions these real bodies make in our minds than of the vaster and unlimited forms which they anticipate in our imaginations; for these latter do not exist at all. On such empty phantasms was I fed – and yet I was not really fed at all.[8]

By this scheme there is no obstacle to our being raised up to meet God in a place of intellectual parity. Sin is conventional rather than foundational, and our freedom to choose the good is the proof of it. Scripture's insistence that sin is a permanent part of our being is, on the face of it, ideological. In addition, the thought that sin could have anything other than an ethical meaning strikes us as unfair; at any rate, it seems only right that our efforts to be good should be taken into consideration. This was evidently the trajectory of Augustine's thinking at the time. He would later establish it in opposition to the key Christian theme of death and resurrection, and to the truth that causes men to be '. . . cast down and broken by You, my God . . .'[9] As he would put it, the Christian insistence that we must be born again as new creations is not merely dogma: it is an intellectually distinct answer to the alternatives premised upon the myth of innocence. As we have seen, his purely metaphysical speculations amplify St Paul's warnings about perverting the natural order of illumination. When St Paul preached to the Athenian people, many of whom were philosophers, he voiced the paradox that the supreme being of their imagination – the 'Unknown God' – could be counted among those gods and temples built by human hands.[10] Likewise many of Augustine's writings contain warnings that Christian death and resurrection means more than a change of mind, or library. It means more than these things because its purpose is not to take us back to a vision of our unencumbered selves. The damage done by Adam was foundational. We have become our own sources of inspiration though we were designed to be inspired by God. We have built a world in likeness of our own image, and we have compounded our dilemma by using that likeness to account for the Unknown God. It is in fact our propensity to see the question of salvation in terms of the dualism of good and evil that is ideological. The condition of being fallen is only partly accounted for by those transgressions against the conscience that occur after birth, once we are old enough to be liable for our choices. If it were wholly accounted for, we would be hard pressed to see any sense in the traditional Christian insistence upon Grace. It may be that there are men who have lived irreproachably after the lights of conscience; it is those same lights that tell us that infants cannot be held culpable for any wrongdoing. But the proposition invoiced in these thoughts – that the corruption of human nature, if it is to be believed in at all, must refer to some substantial disfigurement of us – is the dogma of the fallen mind, not the Christian Scriptures. That Adam's Original Sin initiated something that fact and science may disprove is, according to Augustine, a fundamental misrepresentation of what our happiness once consisted in:

> Now a man makes, so to speak, a good tree when he receives the Grace of God . . . He makes a bad tree when he makes himself bad. That is to say, when he falls away from Him Who is the unchanging good. It is in this declension from Him [in this new awareness of himself] that the origin of his evil will lies. Now this decline does not initiate some other corrupt nature; it merely corrupts that which has already been created good. As such, when once this evil will has been healed [and man chooses once again to do God's Will and not his own] no vestige of evil remains: for although his nature no doubt received an injury [while he walked apart from God] it was never in itself evil.[11]

MANICHAEISM

Buoyed by the myth of innocence and dangerously in love with life, Augustine fell in with one of the stranger religions to make an appearance in the West. Manichaeism was a syncretic religion made up of elements from the ancient Babylonian, or Persian, religion, as well as Christianity and Buddhism. The chief appeal of Manichaeism lay in its claim to have rationalized these elements in an intellectually satisfying system. It therefore offers us a considerable insight into the moral and religious expectations of educated men at this time in the West's history. What, in essence, was the appeal of the religion that Mani (ca AD 216–276) founded in his native Persia, in AD 242? It combined the mystic's love of symbolism and ceremony with the ascetic's preference for a way of life. But arguably more appealing still, at least more appealing to men like Augustine, it had the explanatory power of a pseudo-science. The problem that it purported to solve – the coexistence of good and evil in the world – was a scientific problem, but the solution that it gave was a fantastic cosmogony, positing a material existence for both. In this way it cloaked itself in the legitimacy of a real dilemma in order to better take men far from the truth. Like the great pseudo-sciences of our own times, it tended to produce fanatics. As Karl Popper (1902–1994) would put it,

> I found that those of my friends who were admirers of Marx, Freud, and Adler, were impressed by a number of points common to these theories, and especially by their apparent *explanatory power*. These theories appeared to be able to explain practically everything that happened within the fields to which they referred. The study of them seemed to have the effect of an intellectual conversion or revelation, opening your eyes to a new truth hidden from those not yet initiated. Once your eyes were thus opened you saw confirming instances everywhere: the world was full of *verifications* of the theory. Whatever happened always confirmed it. Thus its truth appeared manifest; and unbelievers were clearly people who did not want to see the manifest truth; who refused to see it, either because it was against their class interest, or because of the repressions which were still 'un-analysed' and crying aloud for treatment.[12]

We should, however, remember that in a time before the compartmentalization of knowledge and the specializations of modern academia men like Augustine could expect to be able to monopolize truth in a single, all-embracing theory. Such aspirations are rare today; indeed the last serious attempt to do something similar was probably the *Encyclopédie*, planned and prosecuted in the eighteenth century by the French *philosophes*. We should also point out that Augustine's support of Manichaeism never became fanatical. In his opinion he was far too vain to give himself up to a cause so completely. Its greatest hold on him turned out to be its flattering explanation of good and evil, designed to set anxious and censorious minds at rest.

> Even at Rome [that is, when he was in his twenty-ninth year] . . . I still thought that sin must refer to something in us – to some sort of different nature. It offended my pride to think that it might be we

who sin [by an act of will]; and this thought that I might ultimately
be beyond responsibility for my evil gave me joy. This joy consisted
in understanding my sin as an abstract thing: not as disobeying You.
Therefore I did not offer my soul to You in confession, for healing
[cf. Ps. 41.4]. I loved to excuse myself, accusing I know not what
other being that was with me but independent of me. But in truth,
my own impiety had divided me against myself, so that it was the
whole of me who sinned and not some independent capacity within
me [cf. Mt. 12.26].[13]

At any rate, this desire to explain his psychology on the principle of two
natures outlasted all his purely intellectual interests in the religion. These
had begun to wane early on; they would be given up completely once
Faustus of Milevis, the great Manichaean teacher, had failed to answer
his more pressing, scientific questions.[14] Augustine's own assessment of
his time as a Manichee is characteristically unsentimental:

For the . . . period of nine years, from the nineteenth year of my
age to the twenty-eighth, we were seduced and we seduced others,
deceived and deceiving by various desires, both openly by the so-
called liberal arts and secretly in the name of a false religion, proud
in the one, superstitious in the other, and everywhere vain.[15]

SKEPTICISM

Augustine's attitude to sin deserves more of our attention. A preoccupation with his perceived failings emerges as one of the main themes of his
Confessiones. Many of his modern commentators would say that this
preoccupation is obsessive; some that it is neurotic. Looked at objectively,
Augustine seems to have had no special reason to censure himself. He was
not a notable tearaway as a boy: his most notorious crime seems to have
been the pointless theft of some pears from a neighbour's tree.[16] And we
have already seen how his student days at Carthage were unremarkable

for wantonness. It seems, then, that we cannot account for Augustine's introspection out of the particular cases of his youth. His attitude to sin must respond to a more general phenomenon. His guilt, if we may call it that, predates his will. That is to say, the tendency that he addresses in the opening books of his *Confessiones* is in fact exhibited in all decisions taken apart from God's Will. In the last book of his *Confessiones*, a sustained exegesis of Genesis and perhaps, then, the most autobiographical book of all, Augustine emphatically separates the category of sin from its ethical meaning and by that means extracts his final diagnosis of the Earthly City.[17] In our present state – that is, cut off from God's illumination – Augustine thinks that we should be a *misera inquietudine defluentium spirituum* 'restless misery of obsolete spirits'.[18] Some of us already are, and certainly all of us have the critical faculties to become so. However, many more – the majority – choose to seek comfort in the self-deceptions that Augustine broadly associates with the romantic, or idealist, outlook. These are not restless or depressed; they are not exiles, for they have assumed the confidence of Adam, seeing everything through the spirit of man rather than the spirit of God. Their sin, if we can call it that, is the extent to which they have perverted the natural order of love: '. . . [T]hey desire to enjoy Your creation rather than You'.[19] By the same token, they cannot ratiocinate from things seen to things unseen through any natural capacity, for the difference between good and evil is the presence of the spirit of God. 'At one time we have been moved to do good, after our heart conceived this out of Your Spirit, whereas at a former time, having forsaken You, we were moved to do evil'.[20]

In the opening books of the *Confessiones* it appears that Augustine is diagnosing himself mainly in terms of this 'exile' category of citizenship. Needless to say it was a citizenship that he bore reluctantly at the time, and his resistance to it would grow the more that it obstructed his efforts to find happiness in the pattern of the world. What is more, he is consistently determined to show that it was not his possession through any peculiar merit of his own. If it was implanted in him by a human agent, that agent may have been his mother; at any rate, it is onto her that he deflects our admiration and respect. For he would much rather we envisage him in the words of his famous prayer: an average sinner frustrated by an unrelenting Grace: 'Give me chastity and continence, but not yet!'[21] But it seems that Grace was working on fallow ground. Augustine is the first to admit that he possessed qualities of intellect and character that might drive him to oblivion or be put to use in the service of the Lord. On the one hand, a stark moral and intellectual honesty prevented him from sentimentalizing his own experiences, while, on the other hand, the way in which this fitted him for scholarship was evident from an early age.[22]

It was probably to be expected, then, that Augustine would eventually bring himself through Manichaeism and into a brief association with the skeptical philosophy of the Academics: 'The thought arose in me that those philosophers whom they call the Academics were wiser than the rest. They were of the opinion that all things are doubtful, and they decreed that no truth can be comprehended by man'.[23] Augustine was at Rome during this time, unable to break completely with his Manichean friends even though he was now certain that their philosophy had nothing to offer him. He suggests that his problem was that he was '. . . hat[ing] the truth for the sake of that very thing which [he was] lov[ing] instead of the truth'.[24] This was his desire to locate something of the Divine within him, and by that means avoid the total dependence of man upon God taught in the Scriptures.[25] It competed with the nobler aspects of his character and issued in a distressing ambivalence. Augustine's association with the Academics would be brief and relatively unimportant, though not without a symbolic significance. Years later, as he was facing God in the garden of the villa at Milan, he would admit the following to Him: 'I thought that the reason I deferred from day to day to reject worldly hopes and to follow You alone was because there seemed nothing certain by which I could direct my course'.[26] Evidently, however, this noble attitude had been an indulgence based in pride:

> Where are you, my tongue? You said that you would not relinquish your burden of vanity for the sake of an uncertain truth. Look now, it [the unsavoury truth of your heart] is certain, and yet that

burden still weighs you down – and this when there are men who
have neither worn themselves out in search of truth, nor meditated
for ten years and more on such things, and yet won wings for their
readier shoulders.[27]

NEOPLATONISM

From the Skepticism of Rome Augustine would move to Milan '. . . and
to Ambrose, its bishop, a man famed throughout the world as one of
its very best men, and Your devout worshipper'.[28] When we consider
Ambrose's qualities and sensitivities, and also his rôle in Augustine's life,
it is tempting to regard him as the father that the boy Augustine never
had. As Romans they could nominally meet as equals: Augustine was
now 30 years old and the newly elected Professor of Rhetoric at Milan,
a public position of considerable prominence given the propensity of the
imperial court to reside there in the later fourth century. However, the
reality was that they inhabited different worlds. Ambrose acted in defiance of the Earthly City and its pretensions while Augustine owed his
success to them – a fact that was disturbing him greatly. The opportunity to listen to Ambrose's sermons and come into his circle of influence
would press the contradictions of his life to breaking point. But just how
far had Augustine come in his attempt to make terms with the Christian
Scriptures? He tells us that he was still influenced by a residual material-
ism from his Manichean days:

> . . . and it seemed to me most irreverent to believe that You take the
> form of our flesh, and are therefore defined by the same lines that
> define our bodily form. I wished to think upon my God, yet I could
> not conceive of Him other than as a great corporeal mass. This
> was because I remained convinced that there was no other form, or
> existence, than bodily form and substance.[29]

On the other hand, he was no longer encumbered by the prospect of formulating a faith that he might believe with a clear intellectual conscience. His experiences as a Manichee and an Academic had caused him to recast his initial conception of salvation. The doctrines of the Manichees had been refuted by science and the Academics could not explain the languages of perfection and the human desire to live virtuously. In both cases his hope of apprehending saving knowledge had suffered. Neoplatonism would renew his hope for a time. Its dualist metaphysic was a major advance on the Manichaean, and in addition its idealism sought accurately to articulate the unquiet in the human heart. Most of all it suggested a form of pilgrimage that might have occupied him for the rest of his life. However, this would turn out to be the extent of its usefulness to him, for the matter that had come to trouble him most was not one that it was equipped to address:

> That new will by which I was prompted to praise You freely, O God, the only sure delight, and also to find my joy in You, was not yet able to overcome that prior will, grown intransigent with age [and habit]. Thus did my two wills, the one old, the other new [cf. Eph. 4.22; 24], the first carnal, and the second spiritual [cf. Rom. 7.14], contend with one another; and by their conflict they broke up my soul.[30]

This battle of wills, sprung from the same nature and therefore not to be explained away by any dualism, was the mould in which Augustine's salvation began to appear to him under the influence of Ambrose.[31] The unquiet in his heart was now such that it would not be stilled by any change of mind, not least one vindicated by the prideful myth of innocence. The unquiet heart must, instead, be changed for a new heart altogether.

> And this was, so to speak, the proper mean – the middle region – of my wellbeing: to remain in Your image [as a rational creature], and to serve You by subduing my body [cf. Gen. 1.26–27]. But when I would rise up against You in my pride, and run against the Lord,

'*even* on *His* neck,' with, 'the thick bosses of [my] bucklers,' [Job 15.26] even these lowest things were set above me, and, as they pressed down on me, I could find no space to breathe . . . This state grew out of my wound, for You humble the proud man, just as one who has been wounded [cf. Ps. 89.10]. By this wound, by my swelling, I was separated me from You; and my bloated face closed up my eyes.[32]

Augustine had now put himself beyond the reach of any form of Platonism or Neoplatonism. Salvation was no longer a question of measuring up to an ideal standard.[33] Plato had proved a great deal about the riches and poverty of reason; his technical language furnished new idioms for the expression of faith in an unseen God, but his philosophy could not account for the unqualified love of God. In the end, it was only St Paul who could do this. His characterization of the paradox of the human freedom to will, especially at Rom. 7.7–25, furnished Augustine with an intellectually distinct answer to the question of why the voluntarist law of God's Will should satisfy the requirements of freedom in a time-bound world. According to Paul, men are born into a freedom that is expressed in their capacity to choose in the actual present, yet this freedom is bondage if no meaningful choice is possible. It is in this that the paradox lies: for no meaningful choice is possible that does not refer either side of the actual present. Only God's spoken commands are sufficient in the actual present in this way because their authority is content-independent. The sinfulness of human nature is correspondingly expressed for St Paul in the fact that thinking men will only countenance obedience to content-dependent commands. This is the chief sense in which they have chosen to become like gods, knowing good and evil. It is also the chief sense in which we should interpret his resignation to sin – expressed at Rom. 7.15–20 – as a statement of metaphysical fact. For if meaningful choice in a time-bound world is the first requirement of freedom, then law, or morality, is its denial. By replacing God's Will with forethought, we are compelled to do two things when we were only designed to do one. Forsaking the uncomplicated freedom of childhood – that time when unquestioning obedience made a carefree existence possible – we grow into the pride of becoming our own sources of truth. This is what our hearts desire because they are fallen, but at the same time it issues in the following paradox: you cannot be truly free under a law of your own creation.[34] To mistake the essence of freedom for the pride of having authored the laws that you obey is, as St Paul would have put it, to betray your sinful nature. Only a fallen man would choose this kind of wisdom in preference to the freedom of perfect obedience in the actual present – to the freedom from having to author the laws that you obey.

> Those who live according to the sinful nature have their minds set on what that nature desires; but those who live in accordance with the Spirit have their minds set on what the Spirit desires. The mind of sinful man is death, but the mind controlled by the Spirit is life and peace; the sinful mind is hostile to God. It does not submit to God's law, nor can it do so. Those controlled by the sinful nature cannot please God.[35]

At the age of 30 and on the cusp of Christianity, Augustine had identified the root of classical moral and political philosophy and corroborated it with evidence from his own heart. In terms of non-religious Western thought, he had concluded that the apostolic Christianity of St Paul was an accurate expression of the requirements of freedom laid down in our design and equipment; that at any rate, it was a more accurate expression than the wisdom of classical antiquity, which favoured presumption over the ordinary experiences of men:

Where [in the books of the Platonists] was that charity which builds upon the foundation of humility, which is Christ Jesus [cf. 1 Cor. 8.1 and 3.11]? When would those books teach it to me? In fact I believe it was for this reason that You decided to have me fall upon those books first, before Your Scriptures. You wished my memory to be impressed with how I was affected by them, so that, later on, when I was made civilized by Your books, and my wounds had been tended by Your healing fingers, I might be able to discern for myself what great difference lies between presumption and contrition: that is, between those who see their destination but do not see the way to it, and those who see the way not only to beholding our blessed fatherland but also to residing in it . . . Most avidly, then, and indeed most fruitfully, did I take up the writings of Your Apostle Paul.[36]

Notes

1 Leo Tolstoy (tr. Rosemary Edmonds), *War and Peace* (Harmondsworth: Penguin, 1974), p. 326.
2 Tolstoy, *War and Peace*, p. 340.
3 *Confess.*, I, 17, 27 (author's translation).
4 *Ibid.*, p. 341.
5 *Ibid.*, III, 4, 8 (author's translation).
6 *Ibid.*, III, 5, 9 (author's translation).
7 Sigmund Freud, 'The origin and development of psychoanalysis', *American Journal of Psychology*, Vol. XXI, No. 2 (1910), pp. 181–218.
8 *Confess.*, III, 6, 10 (author's translation). Cf. *Serm.*, CCCLX(B), 3.
9 *Ibid.*, IV, 1, 1.
10 *See* Acts 17.16–34.
11 *De gr. Chr.*, I, 19, 20 (author's translation).
12 Karl R. Popper, *Conjectures and Refutations: The Growth of Scientific Knowledge* (London: Routledge & Kegan Paul, 1969), pp. 34–5.
13 *Confess.*, V, 10, 18 (author's translation).
14 For the details of this event see *Confess.*, V, 3; 6 & 7.
15 *Ibid.*, IV, 1, 1.
16 For the details of this see *ibid.*, II, 4–10.
17 Our suggestion here is somewhat contentious. As James J. O'Donnell argues, 'What are the last four books doing there? The latest catalogue of efforts to answer that question is two decades old and books and articles addressing it in one form or another continue to appear. Some of the ideas they propose have merit, but none has been presented in a way to compel, or even very strongly to encourage, assent. One prevailing weakness of many of these efforts has been the assumption that there lies somewhere unnoticed about the *Confessions* a neglected key to unlock all mysteries. But for a text as multilayered and subtle as the *Confessions*, any attempt to find a single key is pointless. Augustine himself says that he meant to stir our souls not test our ingenuity as lock-picks'. (James J. O'Donnell, *Augustine: Confessions* (Oxford: Clarendon Press, 1992, p. xxiii). *See* also Max Zepf's comment that '. . . The entire work is divided into two parts which seem to

have nothing whatsoever to do with each other. The Biography of the first ten books is suddenly resolved into a dry exposition of the first three chapters of Genesis. Who has not been compelled to shake his head and ask what purpose Augustine could have had in mind when he thus brought together such various materials?' (Max Zepf, *Augustine's Confessions; Heidelburger Abhandburgen Zur Philosophie und ihrer Geschichte*, hrsg. V. C. Hoffman and H. Rickert, 1924, quoted in the *Lutheran Church Quarterly*, Vol. XXI, No. 3, July 1948, p. 214. This Quotation from John C. Cooper, 'Why did Augustine write books XI – XIII of the *Confessions?*', AS, Vol. 2 (1971), p. 37. Cooper's article is more sympathetic to our view. He privileges content over structure, and this leads him to conclude that the *Confessiones* are indeed a unity. However, because he views them as a 'spiritual history' (p. 38), a kind of 'theological autobiography', he finds their master key in the theme of a journey towards intellectually satisfying belief (*see* especially pp. 41–2).

18 See *Confess.*, XIII, 8, 9.

19 *Ibid.*, XIII, 31, 46.

20 *Ibid.*, XIII, 38, 53.

21 *Ibid.*, VIII, 7, 17.

22 See *ibid.*, I, 20, 31.

23 *Ibid.*, V, 10, 18.

24 *Ibid.*, X, 23, 34.

25 See *De nat. boni*, XXVII.

26 *Confess.*, VIII, 7, 18.

27 *Ibid.*, VIII, 7, 18 (author's translation).

28 *Ibid.*, V, 13, 23.

29 *Ibid.*, V, 10, 19 (author's translation).

30 *Ibid.*, VIII, 5, 10 (author's translation).

31 *See*, for instance, Augustine's remark at *ibid.*, VI, 4, 6, that '. . . I often heard Ambrose speaking in his sermons to the people as though he most earnestly commended it as a rule that "the letter killeth, but the spirit giveth life."' [2 Cor. 3.6] (author's translation).

32 *Ibid.*, VII, 7, 11 (author's translation).

33 See *Ench.*, LXIV: '. . . although every crime is a sin, every sin is not a crime . . . [for] as the Apostle John says, 'If we say that we have no sin, we deceive ourselves, and the truth is not in us.' [1 Jn 1.8] (author's translation).

34 The conviction that you can is the suppressed premiss to the 'social contract' style of moral and political argument. It has had its advocates in all the major intellectual periods. In the classical period, Plato gave it its first, tentative expression in his dialogue, *Crito*. Throughout the medieval period in the Christian West, the sovereignty of the community was a persistent sentiment

that achieved its most outstanding expression in John of Salisbury's (ca 1115–1180) defence of tyrannicide in his *Policraticus*. Towards the end of the Renaissance, Thomas Hobbes wrote his *Leviathan*; then came three works stretching into the Enlightenment. The first of these was John Locke's (1632–1704) *Two Treatises on Government*; the second was David Hume's *Of the Original Contract*; and the third was Jean-Jacques Rousseau's *du Contrat Social*. In the nineteenth century, Herbert Spencer flirted with the style in his *The Man versus the State*. Most recently, John Rawls has written influentially in the style: his *A Theory of Justice* is widely considered the outstanding work in political theory in the twentieth century.

35 Rom. 8.5–8.
36 *Confess.*, VII, 20, 26 (author's translation).

7

The Heavenly City

The climax of Fyodor Dostoyevsky's (1821–1881) *Crime and Punishment* is a lesson in the moral and political significance of confession. This act was intensely political for Dostoyevsky: a declaration of citizenship. For confession places us, for a moment, in right relation to the things of value in the world, and it does this by disclosing the parasitic character of the human condition. We cannot of ourselves create anything good *ex nihilo* though it flatters us to imagine we can. What must pass for this ability is our talent for self-deception. We are liable to ascribe perfection and virtue to our own efforts, and by the same token we are capable of going to great lengths to avoid reproof. The natural human tendency is therefore away from confession and towards self-vindication. In *Crime and Punishment* Dostoyevsky has his hero Raskolnikoff exhibit this in an exemplary way. Forced by pride to commit a terrible crime, Raskolnikoff diminishes his guilt by blaming a hostile and unfair world. He sets himself apart from it, coming to live by a private morality oriented on the unsolicited circumstances of his birth and the unfulfilled prospects of his imagination. He becomes the antithesis to Augustine's exile and is soon dangerously out of alignment with the lights of conscience and the normal mechanism of shame and improvement. He becomes immune to any form of reproach and superior to all who try to help him. Finally, however, his redemption begins with an act of will – it is not an act of belief because Raskolnikoff cannot envisage the change that it will bring about. In his mind it may be that it appears as a final act of defiance. At any

177

rate, it is the beginning of a lengthy and difficult process of regeneration:

> The market-place was now full of people. This fact displeased Raskolnikoff greatly; nevertheless he went to that part of it where the crowd was thickest. He would have bought solitude at any price, but he felt that he could not enjoy it for a single moment. Having got to the centre of the place, the young man suddenly recalled Sonia's words: 'Go to some public place, bow to the crowd, kiss the earth you have soiled by your sin, and say in a loud voice, in the presence of everyone: "I am a murderer."' At the recollection of this he trembled in every limb. The anguish of the last few days had hardened his heart to such an extent, that he felt satisfied to find himself yet open to feelings of another kind, and gave himself entirely up to this one. Sincere sorrow overpowered him, his eyes filled with tears. He knelt in the very middle of the place, bowed earthwards, and joyfully kissed the miry ground. After having risen, he knelt down once more.
>
> 'There's a fellow who has got a tile loose!' observed a lad standing by . . .
>
> 'He is a pilgrim bound for Jerusalem, lads; he is taking leave of his children and his native land; he is wishing everybody goodbye, even St. Petersburg and the ground of the capital,' added a respectable man, slightly the worse for drink.[1]

Augustine's *Confessiones* begin with a more general confession addressed directly to God. It is a confession of the nature of the distance between man and God understood in characteristically metaphysical terms. Augustine is articulating the single fact that, for him, makes the human condition fallen and hopeless apart from Grace. We were born outside the Garden of Eden and cannot know God in the way that Adam did, yet we carry a kind of memory of the difference it made to know God, and by this means we can call to Him across an impossible distance of space and time. On the one hand this is Augustine's confession on behalf of all men; on the other hand, it is also his personal confession. We have seen how when he first encountered the Scriptures he was dismayed at their rude tone and inability to address the classical conception of salvation. Later, he would come to regret this reaction and realize that it was in fact the classical conception of salvation that was unable to address the proper requirements of freedom. The early, formative events of Augustine's life are therefore bound up in his leading ideas to an unusual extent. This is especially the case with his leading political ideas. His doctrine of the Two Cities introduces late antiquity to a new category of citizenship: the Christian pilgrim, in this world but not of it, confessing his heart to God in the actual present and receiving instructions from Him. If this is Augustine's innovation in political thought, we must then regard his *Confessiones* as exemplary of it. They begin with a confession peculiar to their author but spoken on behalf of all men, and they end with four chapters amplifying that confession in discussions of memory, time and eternity, form and matter, and the creation of the world *ex nihilo*. The opening confession thus prefigures a substantially new approach to the Christianization of classical moral and political philosophy. It transfers the burden of proof from Christianity to philosophy. Philosophy must now account for the lights of conscience more than Christianity must prove our sinfulness; indeed sinfulness and the ethical perspectives attached to it are abandoned by Augustine in favour of what he calls *unam conspirationem societatis infidelium* 'the single conspiracy of the society of the unfaithful':[2]

Great are You, O Lord, and greatly to be praised: great is Your power, and Your wisdom is unsearchable [cf. Ps. 48.1; 96.4; 145.3; 147.5]. And man, this part of Your creation, wishes to praise You – man who bears about with him his mortality, the witness both to his sinfulness and to the fact that You resist the proud [cf. Jas 4.6; 1 Pet. 5.5]. Yet notwithstanding these things, man, this part of Your creation, wishes to praise You. You arouse him to take delight in praising You; for You have made us for Yourself, and our hearts are correspondingly unquiet until they rest in You. Lord, teach me to know and to understand which comes first: to call upon You or to praise You, or, by the same token, to know You or to call upon You [cf. Ps. 119.34; 73; 144]? But how does one call upon You without first knowing You? Otherwise, one might call upon another instead of You? Or is it rather that You must be called upon in order to be known? Yet, 'How then shall they call on Him in whom they have not believed? And how shall they believe in Him of whom they have not heard? And how shall they hear without a preacher?' [Rom. 10.14] And, 'they shall praise the Lord that seek Him' [Ps. 22.26]. For they that seek Him find Him, and finding Him they praise Him [cf. Mt. 7.8; Lk. 11.10]. Lord, let me seek You by calling upon You, and call upon You by believing in You; for You have been preached to us. Lord, that faith which You have given to me calls upon You; that faith which You have breathed into me by the incarnation of Your Son and through the ministry of Your preachers.[3]

IN THE GARDEN AT MILAN

It was AD 386 and Augustine had now been in Milan for two years as Imperial Professor of Rhetoric. He had outreached Manichaeism, Skepticism and Neoplatonism, and was now committed in theory to a Pauline theology of man. He enjoyed the company of like-minded friends, men like Alypius and Nebridius, who were both childhood friends from Africa:

> With increasing anxiety I went about my daily affairs, and each day I sighed to You. I frequented Your Church whenever it was possible for me to escape my onerous tasks, under whose burden I groaned. Alypius had now joined me, having been relieved of his legal duties after his third term as assessor . . . By reason of our friendship, Nebridius had agreed to teach under Verecundus . . .[4]

On the face of it, Augustine might have continued very well in this way, securing his income through teaching and devoting his spare time to theological reflection. His intellectual conscience had already reached an advanced stage of satisfaction:

> Surely, 'all men are vain in whom there is not the knowledge of God: and who by these good things that are seen could not understand, could not find, Him Who is.' [Wis. 13.1] I was no longer in that vanity, having passed beyond it. By the testimony of the whole creation I had found You, our Creator, and Your Word, Who is God with You, and Who is One God with You, through Whom You created all things. [cf. Jn 1.1–3][5]

However, his searching had precipitated a profound unhappiness that was never going to be ended by a choice of lifestyle. To Augustine it appeared as though he approached the question of his salvation like a drowsy man:

> Thus by the burdens of this world I was sweetly weighed down, just as a man often is in sleep. Thoughts werein I meditated upon You were like the efforts of those who want to arouse themselves but, still overcome by deep drowsiness, sink back again.[6]

Had he not read St Paul so seriously he might conceivably have spared himself the agony of this choice between the familiar path of worldly success and the totally unknown path of God's judgement:

> Thus it was by my own experiences that I gained insight into what I had read, how, 'the flesh lusteth against the spirit, and the spirit against the flesh' [Gal. 5.17]. I was the agent in both states, but more so in that which I approved of than in that which I disapproved of. This was because, in large part, I now suffered the latter state against my will rather than chose it voluntarily. However, it had, of course, been by my persistent free acts that this rebellious state had hardened into habit – I had, as it were, willingly set this trajectory which I now willed against.[7]

This conceptualization of Christianity was strikingly different to the schemes of salvation of pagan antiquity. We have seen that Augustine did at one time conceive his Christianity along their lines, believing that his salvation would become his ability to interpret a saving truth into the diverse circumstances of his life.[8] Under the influence of St Paul, however, his theoretical knowledge of Christian doctrine would come to count for increasingly little. The decision that he was facing seemed daily to become more political than intellectual: a matter of choosing whom to love, and by that means securing a new citizenship:

> Your affections are your steps: your will the way. By loving you ascend, by neglect you descend. Even though you are standing on the earth you are in Heaven if you love God. For the heart is not exalted in the way that the body is exalted: for the latter to be exalted a change of place must occur: for the former, a change of will.[9]

As Baynes would put it, '. . . because Augustine himself had experienced what it was to be unable to *will* the right, *will* is the paramount factor in human life. The last word is not with the *mind*, but with the emotions – with what one *loves*'.[10]

One afternoon, while Augustine was 'twisting and turning in his chain',[11] a high-ranking African called Ponticianus sought him out at the villa he was renting in Milan.[12] Alypius was with Augustine but Nebridius was away on business. Ponticianus was already a Christian, and probably intrigued to meet this African, a former Manichee and now a catechumen. He happened to see a book lying on a gaming table;

> . . . he took it up, and, opening it, was surprised to find that it was by the Apostle Paul. He had presumed that it was another of those books that I had been wearing myself out in teaching . . . When I told him how I had spent myself on the Apostle's writings, a discussion arose in which he narrated the story of Anthony, an Egyptian monk . . . From this subject his conversation turned to the companies within the monasteries, and also to their manner of

life . . . [Then it came about that he told us how one of his friends discovered, by chance, a book on the life of St Anthony.[13]] Then, having read some of it, and suddenly filled with holy love, he was by sober shame made angry with himself [cf. Ps. 4.4]. He immediately turned his eyes upon his friend [who had accompanied him that day] and exclaimed: 'Tell me, I implore you, to what end we labour so? What are we seeking for by all of this? To what purpose do we serve in office? What greater hope can we have at the Palace than to become friends of the Emperor? And what is there in that position that is not fragile and subject to whim? By what dangers would we contend with only to arrive, as it were, at this greater danger? And when would we arrive there? But see how, if I wish to become God's friend, so to speak, I can do it here and now.' [cf. Jas 2.23] He spoke these words, and in upheaval during this birth of his new life, he turned back upon those pages. As he read on, he was changed within himself.[14]

As Ponticianus narrated this story, it became impossible for Augustine not to refer it to his own drowsing attitude:

You took me from behind my own back, where I had placed myself because I did not wish to look upon myself. You stood me face to face with myself, so that I might see how foul I was . . .[15]

Then, during that great struggle in my inner house, which I had violently initiated against my soul, in the closet of my heart . . . I turned upon Alypius and cried out to him: 'What is the matter with us? . . . The unlearned rise up and storm Heaven [cf. Mt. 11.12]. We, on the other hand, lack heart: our learning does not suffice, and so we wallow in flesh and blood.' [cf. Gal. 1.16; Mt. 16.17; 1 Cor. 15.50][16]

Augustine was now facing the political decision that he had avoided for so long. A life that he could not envisage appeared before him – a new citizenship – and competed with the old:

I groaned in spirit [cf. Jn 11.33]: for I was most indignant that I
could not bring myself to enter into Your Will and Covenant, my
God – in fact my very bones cried out to me to enter into Your
Covenant, and by their praise they lifted me up to the skies. It is
not by ships or chariots that we enter therein; indeed, we need not
go so far as I had done by removing myself from the house to the
garden, where we sat: for not only to set out, but even to reach that
place was nothing other than to will it. But to will it bravely and
sincerely, that is, not to keep anything back or to try to anticipate
the event . . .[17]

Augustine was still a young man, young enough to choose a new life, yet
he was facing how fundamental is the hold of the Earthly City on its citizens. None of us choose our parents, none of us choose even to be born:
the beginning of our lives is in the nature of the case unfair. Augustine
thinks that God correspondingly calls each of us to return to the scene
of some injustice, picked out by us during childhood and thereafter held,
jealously and unconsciously, as the vindication of a set of rights *vis-à-vis*
God. In Augustine's case, God required him to return to the scene of His
apparent silence at the moment when his father betrayed him and his
life fell apart:

Dare I say that You, my God, remained silent while I departed farther
from You? Did You really remain silent to me at that time? Whose
words was my mother, Your faithful servant, made to sing in my
ears if not Yours? . . . These words appeared to me as nothing but a
woman's warning, which I should scorn to heed. Of course they were
really Your warnings and I did not know it. I thought that only she
spoke, whereas in truth You spoke to me through her [Isa. 42.14].
In this way, in her person, You were held in contempt by me, her
son, 'the son of Thine handmaid [Ps. 116.16]' and Your servant.[18]

It may even be that the apparent silence of God was the spur to his
whole effort to confect an intellectually respectable Christianity. At any

rate, it probably accounts for his recurring magnanimity towards God, especially during his Manichaean period:

> I was carried away outside myself by the voices of my error, and under the weight of my pride I sank down into the depths. You did not give to my hearing joy and gladness, nor did my bones rejoice, for they had not yet been humbled.[19]

> Because some sort of reverence forced me to believe that a good God would create no evil nature . . . my mind . . . was struck back again, for the Catholic faith was not such as I thought it to be.[20]

This magnanimity would issue, for a time, in the not uncommon conviction that mind is the '. . . highest and the incommunicable good'.[21] However, by the time that Augustine was visited by Ponticianus, what remained of his earthly citizenship was largely the prejudice of the unknown. His old life no longer appeared to him as something valuable in itself; if he were to choose it, and he might yet, it would be for its familiarity and consistency:

> . . . in that state when eternity delights us from above and the pleasures found in temporal goods hold us from below, there is only one soul at work. It wavers between this or that course, dividing its will between them [at one time loving one, at another time loving the other]. So long as this continues, that is, so long as eternity is delighted in because of its truth and temporality is preferred because it is familiar and out of habit, the soul is torn apart and badly hurt.[22]

> Trifles of trifles and vanities of vanities, they still detained me [cf. Eccl. 1.2; 12.8]. Like old mistresses they plucked at my fleshly garment, softly whispering, 'Do you really dismiss us?' and, 'From that moment we shall be gone from you for eternity' and again, 'From that moment these things will be forbidden to you for eternity' . . . But now by far less than half did I hear them . . . Yet they still

detained me: a powerful habit kept entreating me, 'Do you think you can continue without them?' I thus hesitated to drag myself away from them and step over to that place whither I had been called.[23]

A great deal has been written about what happened next.[24] We are fortunate only to have to interpret it from the political point of view. In Augustine's mature opinion, 'This was the sum of it: not to will what I willed and to will what You willed'.[25]

> . . . out of what deep and hidden place was my free will summoned in a moment, so that I might bend my neck to Your mild yoke and my shoulders to Your light burden [cf. Mt. 11.30; Ps. 18.16], O Christ Jesus, 'my strength, and my redeemer' [Ps. 19.14]? . . . My soul was now unencumbered by the gnawing demand to cultivate the favour of others; to strive for material gain; and to scratch lust's itchy sore. I now talked endlessly to You, my brightness, my wealth, my wellbeing, my Lord God.[26]

From this moment forth, Augustine was committed to living in the Pilgrim City. He had given up the responsibility of conducting himself in the actual present, the responsibility called pride, and he would now be directed by God in all things in a supernatural way:[27]

> Nor do I say any good thing to men except what You have first heard from me; nor do You hear any such thing from me but what You have first spoken to me.[28]

> Steadfastly believe in God, and, as far as you are able, commit yourself entirely to Him. Do not will to be your own man, under your own sway; rather, profess yourself to be the servant of that most clement and profitable Lord. For He will not hesitate to lift you up to Himself, and he will not allow anything to come to pass except what will profit you, though this may not always be clear to you at the time.[29]

'UN PUNTO DI ARRIVO E UN
PUNTO DI PARTENZA'

'A point of arrival and a point of departure' – these were the words chosen by Agostino Trapè to describe the significance of Augustine's conversion.[30] Augustine had had the change of heart that he had envisaged and shirked; now he would have to learn to live under his new citizenship: 'What cries did I send up to You, my God, when I read the psalms of David, those canticles of faith, those songs of devotion, which exclude a boastful mind, I who was but an uncouth beginner in Your faithful love . . .'[31] The Roman jurist Ulpian (died AD 228) once observed that 'Nothing is so natural as that an agreement should be dissolved by the same method as that by which it was made'.[32] On the evidence, there seems to have been something of this method in Augustine's daily dealings with God. The old life, the old man, had habit on his side; in order to be born again a new man Augustine would have to unpick a lifetime's routine of thought and action. He would have to keep his heart under a constant interrogation, looking for any *scintilla de cinere carnis* 'spark of dying flesh', or harder to detect still, the *robur* 'enduring hardwood'.[33] But the object would not, as we have suggested, be to rescue the pristine child Augustine. In a work from this time, the *Soliloquiorum*, we find the following reflection: '. . . what death would not be preferable if the soul so lived as we see it in a boy newly born? Not to mention the life lived in the womb, which I suppose must be called life'.[34] In his first work against the Pelagians, *De peccatorum meritis et remissione*, Augustine would amplify his thoughts on the myth of innocence and the singular character of Original Sin. He would write that from the ethical point of view infants are, without question, sinless: '. . . only recently come into the world, they continue to live within themselves, in a state that escapes the cognizance of human perception; indeed, we can arrive at no data, or facts, to sustain controversy on the subject'.[35] Yet some would have it that they are culpable in order to bring original sin within the human categories of good and evil. They would say this so as to remove the Christian obstacle to salvation through good works. Augustine refutes this with copious evidence from the Scriptures, especially from the Gospels and the Epistles of St Paul.[36] Infants may be sinless – that is, excused from any rational ownership of their wills – but they already possess that love of self that distinguishes the Earthly City.[37] As Augustine explains, possibly from his own experience of fatherhood, 'I myself have seen and had the experience of a jealous infant; it was not able to speak, but it was pale and bitter in face as it watched its little fellow nursing at the same breast'.[38]

In the meantime Augustine envisaged a complete withdrawal from public life and its trappings. At the beginning of the *feriae vindemiales* (end of August, AD 386), he retreated to the rural villa of a fellow Milanese rhetorician, Verecundus. Augustine records the place as Cassiciacum, widely accepted to be the present-day Cassiago di Brianza, located to the North-East of Milan. He travelled there with family and friends for the purpose of conversing with God, for having resolved to abandon his old method of life he had, as yet, no idea how God would require him to live. Perhaps he hoped that God would allow him to continue in a life of 'leisurely retirement' – the classical ideal of the *otium liberale*. Or more likely still, he might be called to follow the example of St Anthony and the ascetic life. In the event, the months at Cassiciacum did prove decisive. Augustine wrote a number of philosophical dialogues, some of which we have already mentioned. They were the *Soliloquiorum*, *Contra Academicos*, *De beata vita* and *De ordine*. In one of these, *Contra Academicos*, he propounds a kind of mission statement: 'It is now certain to me that I must never, in any way, depart from the authority of Christ'.[39] As it turned out, this was a bold pronouncement for the young Christian to make, for the reality of living as one of St Paul's new creations[40] bore little relation to the theory. Augustine could not, after all, have been expected to dispense so easily with a private morality that included apologizing for a silent and unsophisticated god. His mature opinion was that these dialogues showed his good intentions while '. . . still breath[ing] forth the school of pride [he means Neoplatonism] . . .'[41] Scholars have long debated the credentials of these dialogues.[42] A later work, *De immortalitate animae*, written in AD 387 during the period of Augustine's baptism, is considered to exhibit a similar ambivalence between Christianity and Neoplatonism.[43] To Augustine, however, the dialogues did not have this great importance in themselves. Perhaps he did conceive them out of his long-held ambition to produce an encyclopaedia of wisdom with God as *summum bonum*;[44] but whatever the case, he would like us to treat them today as resonances of his early dealings with God, face to face: of his desire '. . . for liberty and leisure in which to sing to You out of my very marrow: "My heart said unto Thee, Thy face, Lord, will I seek."' [Ps. 27.8][45]

In fact it is this desire to seek God's Face and not His Wisdom that tells us most about the practical effect of Augustine's conversion and of the significance of the time that he spent at Cassiciacum. In the garden at Milan he had turned away from his life lived in love of self, away from any notion of his innocence, and towards a new life lived in love of God. In that moment he had died to the old man and been resurrected a new man, with a new heart oriented on God. However, this new man born of Grace would thenceforth have to battle the old man and the old nature:

> We have, then, even now begun to be like Him, having the first-fruits of the Spirit; but, by the same token, we are unlike Him according to the old nature which persists in us. We are like Him to the extent that we are sons of God by means of the regeneration of the Spirit; but we are unlike Him insofar as we are still the children of the flesh and of the world. Under the one aspect we cannot commit sin; but under the other, 'If we say that we have no sin, we deceive ourselves' [I Jn 1.8]. This must be the case until we pass entirely into adoption, and the sinner is no more: indeed, 'thou shalt diligently consider his place, and it *shall* not *be*' [Ps. 37.10].[46]

It is in this sense of an enduring struggle, between an old nature that would return him to dependence on a private morality and a new nature that would subject him to a voluntarist law, that we should interpret Augustine's final assessment of his time at Cassiciacum:

> For my memory invites me to return, and indeed it becomes sweet to

me, O Lord, to confess to You by what inward goads You subdued
me: how You brought me low by leveling the mountains and hills
of my thoughts, and also how You straightened my crookedness
and made plain my rough places [cf. Isa. 40.4; Lk. 3.4–5]. It is also
sweet to me to recall how, in like manner, You subdued Alypius (my
heart's brother) to the name of Your only-begotten, 'our Lord and
Saviour Jesus Christ.' [2 Pet. 3.18] For initially he disdained to put
that name into our writings, wishing that they should rather smell of
the cedars of the [Greek] schools – those same which the Lord had
by this time broken down for us [cf. Ps. 29.5] – than of those useful
herbs which the Church recommends against serpents.[47]

And it is not enough for a man to die to his old life once: citizenship of
the Pilgrim City obligates him to die to it continually in the actual present:

This age is the desert, and all the more so to the Christian who
has just received baptism and understood what that means. If the
process has not been superficial but has actually affected something
spiritual in their hearts, then they will understand that this world is
a desert: they will understand that they are on pilgrimage, longing
for their fatherland . . . For temptations occur that suggest something altogether different – the delights of this world, perhaps, or
another way of life. They would turn you off your road and lead
you away from your final good if you did not overcome them. But
if you do, the enemy is beaten on the very road and the people are
led to the fatherland.[48]

We have sketched a theology of discipleship with far-reaching moral and
political implications. No citizen of the Pilgrim City enjoys perfection of
nature: Grace overcomes only their self-consciousness, allowing them to
pursue a childlike submission to God. The perfection of the Pilgrim City
is correspondingly a perfect obedience. It is open to all the rational creation by virtue of their freedom to choose whom to love. We have seen
that, on the one hand, Augustine is obliged to say that this perfection is

restricted to those whom God has predestinated to receive the help of Grace. But on the other hand, he is quick to point out the impracticality of dwelling on this doctrinal construction. As C. S. Lewis would put it,

> . . . every attempt to see the shape of eternity except through the lens of Time destroys your knowledge of Freedom. Witness the doctrine of Predestination which shows (truly enough) that eternal reality is not waiting for a future in which to be real; but at the price of removing Freedom which is the deeper truth of the two.[49]

The citizenship of the Pilgrim City is in this sense universal, but the obedience that it demands is total and unqualified:

> In other words, let the number of us who are presently running perfectly remember this: that, being not yet perfected, we must continue to advance our course by the same means that has allowed us to run perfectly to this point. This is in order that, 'when that which is perfect is come, then that which is in part shall be done away.' [1 Cor. 13.10][50]

Notes

1 Fyodor Dostoyevsky, *Crime and Punishment* (Harmondsworth: Penguin, 1997), pp. 415–16.

2 See *Confess.*, XIII, 34, 49.

3 *Ibid.*, I, 1, 1 (author's translation).

4 *Ibid.*, VIII, 6, 13 (author's translation).

5 *Ibid.*, VIII, 1, 2 (author's translation).

6 *Confess.*, VIII, 5, 12. This metaphor was used by Augustine on a number of occasions. See *Contra Acad.*, I, I, 3; *De b. vita*, 35; *Solil.*, I, 2. It seems that Augustine learned it from the Bible. *See* 1 Cor. 15.34; 1 Thess. 5.6; 1 Pet. 5.8.

7 *Ibid.*, VIII, 5, 11 (author's translation).

8 *See*, for instance, what he has to say at *Serm.*, CXCVII, 1: 'However, because they were lost to pride, the proud liar and deceiver could intervene, promising them that their souls would be cleansed in some way (I do not know how) by pride. Thus he made demon-worshippers of them. This is the source

of all the rites celebrated by the pagans, which, as they say, have the power to cleanse their souls'. (author's translation).

9 *En. in Ps.*, LXXXV, 6 (author's translation). Notwithstanding this, the habit of viewing Augustine's conversion in terms of belief, or faith, has gone largely unremarked upon in Augustinian scholarship. *See*, for instance, Frederick E. Van Fleteren's presumption that, 'Augustine's notion of conversion to Christianity [is] an acceptance of faith'. (Frederick E. Van Fleteren, 'Authority and reason, faith and understanding', *AS*, Vol. 4 [1973], p. 56).

10 Baynes, *The Political Ideas of St. Augustine's* De civitate Dei, p. 16. *See* also *De div. qq. 83*, LXVI, 1, 2, 5; *Exp. q. p. ep. ad Rom.*, XXIV, 3; XXVIII, 2; XXIX, 2; XXXII, 1; *De div. qq. ad Simpl.*, I, 1, 15; 17.

11 This metaphor is Augustine's: see *Confess.*, VIII, 11, 25.

12 Nothing is known about this man other than the information which Augustine gives in his *Confessiones*: '. . . a countryman of ours, in so far as being from Africa, who held high office at court'. (*Confess.*, VIII, 6, 14).

13 Most probably the *Vita S. Antonii*, by Athanasius (ca 296–373). It was translated from the Greek by Jerome's contemporary, Evagrius (ca 345–399).

14 *Confess.*, VIII, 6, 14 (author's translation).

15 *Ibid.*, VIII, 7, 16.

16 *Ibid.*, VIII, 8, 19 (author's translation).

17 *Ibid.*, VIII, 8, 19 (author's translation).

18 *Ibid.*, II, 3, 7 (author's translation).

19 *Confess.*, IV, 15, 27.

20 *Ibid.*, V, 10, 20.

21 *Ibid.*, IV, 15, 24.

22 *Ibid.*, VIII, 10, 24 (author's translation).

23 *Ibid.*, VIII, 11, 26 (author's translation).

24 For instance, *see* the articles 'Confessiones' (pp. 227–32) and 'Conversion' (pp. 239–42) in *ATA*.

25 *Confess.*, IX, 1, 1.

26 *Ibid.* (author's translation).

27 We might now ask where this places Augustine's Pilgrim City *vis-à-vis* modern conceptions of Christian discipleship? According to G. W. H. Lampe, 'The theological revolution of modern times is centred upon changes in the Christian understanding of revelation and, in particular, upon the widespread abandonment of the traditional belief that revelation is communicated by God to man in the form of propositions, so that it is possible to speak of revealed doctrines . . . That consensus has now been broken down and can never be put together again. Doctrinal statements, that is, propositions about God and His relation to the world and to ourselves, are not commonly believed today to be communicated by God in such a way that

somewhere, in the Bible or the creeds or the authoritative teaching of the Church, they are accessible to us as a store of unchanging and guaranteed truths'. (G. W. H. Lampe, 'Athens and Jerusalem: joint witness to Christ?', in Brian Hebblethwaite & Stewart Sutherland [Eds.], *The Philosophical Frontiers of Christian Theology: Essays Presented to D. M. MacKinnon* [Cambridge: Cambridge University Press, 1982], pp. 14–15).

28 *Confess.*, X, 2, 2.
29 *Solil.*, I, 30 (author's translation).
30 Trapè, *Agostino: l'uomo, il pastore, il mistico*, p. 128.
31 *Confess.*, IX, 4, 8.
32 *Digest.*, I, 17, 35 (author's translation).
33 See *Serm.*, CCCXLIV, 4. Cf. *De cont.*, XIV, 31.
34 *Solil.*, II, 20, 36 (author's translation). Cf. *De civ. Dei*, XXI, 14: 'If anyone were offered the choice of suffering death or becoming a child again, who would not recoil from the second alternative and choose to die?
35 *De pecc. mer. et rem.*, I, 17, 22 (author's translation).
36 See *ibid.*, I, 40, 27–28.
37 See *Confess.*, I, 7, 11: '. . . at that time I did reprehensible things, but because I was not yet able to grasp the sense in which they were so, neither custom nor reason held me culpable'. (author's translation).
38 *Ibid.*, I, 7, 11 (author's translation).
39 *Contra Acad.*, III, 20, 43 (author's translation).
40 *See* 2 Cor. 5. 17.
41 *Confess.*, IX, 4, 7.
42 For a short synopsis of the received wisdom see the article 'Cassiciacum Dialogues', in *ATA*, pp. 135–42.
43 For instance, *see* John A. Mourant's comments in his article, 'Remarks on the *De immortalitate animae*', *AS*, Vol. 2 (1971), pp. 213–17. Cf. Van Fleteren's observation that, 'The optimism with which Augustine views the relationship between Platonism and Christianity is apparent. Both call men to the intelligible world. Augustine, at other times, explicitly identifies the Kingdom of God with the intelligible world [*De ord.*, I, 2, 32]. One of the effects of this identification in the early works is their pressed intellectualism. Christian Salvation is equated with the Neo-Platonic ascent of the soul to the vision of God. Salvation and the acquisition of knowledge are closely allied. These results and their cause Augustine will live to regret [*Retract.*, I, 3, 2]'. (Van Fleteren, OSA, 'Authority and reason, faith and understanding', p. 45).
44 *See* Ch. 4, n. 30 above.
45 *Confess.*, IX, 3, 6 (author's translation). Cf. *ibid.*, IV, 10, 15.
46 *De pecc. mer. et rem.*, II, 8, 10 (author's translation).

47　*Confess.*, IX, 4, 7 (author's translation).

48　*Serm.*, IV, 9 (author's translation). Cf. *ibid.*, IX, 13.

49　C. S. Lewis, *The Great Divorce* (London: HarperCollins, 2002a), p. 141.

50　*De perf. iust. hom.*, VIII, 19 (author's translation). As we began with Dostoyevsky we might then end with him. As a pilgrim Augustine would face many unexpected developments, not least his return to Africa and ordination as priest there in 391. It is possible, then, that he did not yet fully know '. . . that a new life is not given for nothing; that it has to be paid dearly for, and only acquired by much patience and suffering, and great future efforts. But now a new history commences: a story of the gradual renewing of a man, of his slow progressive regeneration, and change from one world to another – an introduction to the hitherto unknown realities of life. This may well form the theme of a new tale; the one we wish to offer the reader is ended'. (Fyodor Dostoyevsky, *Crime and Punishment*, p. 434).

Conclusion: the Pilgrim City

Now that we have reached the end of our enquiry we must sum up our findings and say something conclusive about Augustine's contribution to the history of political thought in the West. In the Introduction and Chapter 1 we took some care to set Augustine in relief against what we call the natural-law style of moral and political argument. We noticed that Augustine's political ideas do not exhibit the usual features of this style of argument. They have not, for instance, been systemized to any great extent; nor for that matter, have they been directed towards an idealistic conclusion. Yet they do share a single point of reference in relation to which they make sense. This is Augustine's insistence to seek wisdom *ex ore veritatis* 'from the mouth of [God's] truth'.[1] This is, from the moral and political point of view, an unexpected point of reference, and it correspondingly enjoins us to characterize Augustine's genius in unusual terms. Unlike other great thinkers who worked up a system and harvested its implications, Augustine maintained an original poise and perspective that he was able to bring to bear successfully on diverse subjects. This means that any unity and coherence that his political ideas exhibit is due not so much to their relationships to each other but to their participation in a common mind. This, we need hardly point out, is not the familiar beginning for a set of ideas on man, society and the state. Moral and political argument is normally carried on from *a priori* statements of value, for these imbue what follows with an aura of independence and objectivity, and, in matters moral and political, independence and objectivity has come to mean much the same thing as truth.[2] Why this should be so is perhaps not as clear as we would like, but evidently it has much to do with the development of the medieval world out of the ancient, and of the modern out of the medieval.

When ancient man first sought to understand the world in theory, he presumed to be able to relate its apparent flux and chaos to an underlying principle of justice. In time this principle came to correspond with the idea of what is natural. The world has its own way – its own order and laws of procession – and it is therefore meet that we attempt to bring our own activities in the state into line with it. This vague idea, exemplified in ancient man's preference for uniting religion and politics in a single conception, brought morality, justice and human destiny into the same theoretical universe.[3] Human association would no longer be for the sake of mere survival, but for the higher end of civilization; men would no longer allow their appetitive instincts to predominate, but act in pursuit of rational goods.[4] Out of this process of intellectual development came the now familiar theme of ethical speculation – the theme that we found it easiest to represent as a question. 'What exactly should a man do in each moment in order to secure his happiness?' Many answers have been given to this question. In ancient times the most plausible came to be that given by the Stoic philosophers. They argued that the moral and intellectual consciences of man form a single piece – that the moral intuitions of the heart are an aspect of the providentially arranged universe – and that, by their shared rational appreciation of this, men are united in a kind of cosmopolitan brotherhood. In time the Church would take this logic to a new level of sophistication.[5] Ecclesiastical thinkers such as John of Salisbury would argue that human happiness consists in conforming oneself to the traditional lights of conscience; that indeed a man might go far in this direction on his own initiative (this is the value of traditional humanism), but ultimately it is only the Church that can complete the journey for him. Classical Greek philosophy, they wrote, might well have proved that reason can set a man on the path of salvation, but without faith and Grace – the prerogatives of the Church – his efforts are wasted.[6] The effect of this argument was, as we have seen, to make the Church into the special protector and administrator of morals. When medieval ecclesiastics were arguing for the supremacy of the Church *vis-à-vis* the secular powers, it was invariably this logic that they were deploying. They argued that if the settled aim of human association on earth is to form a harmonious commonwealth, characterized by the just distribution of labour and resources, only the Church can advise how best this should be accomplished for, unlike the secular powers, she is not motivated by self-interest or tainted by fallen considerations. To the contrary, it stands to reason that her ontological superiority should qualify her to pilot all aspects of human affairs. Such, at any rate, was the essence of the more advanced arguments for a papal plenitude of power.

From the purely philosophical point of view we have so far drawn a straight line from ancient man's desire to live according to nature to the Church's claim to best be able to interpret what this should mean morally and politically. We have in addition attached great significance to the form of the natural-law style of argument that characterizes this straight line. 'The good life is properly lived when positive human laws can be shown to be the intellectual descendents of the first principles of morality'. We are here paraphrasing the Christian philosopher whose synthesis of Aristotle and Christianity came to exemplify the aspirations of the medieval mind as we have characterized it. To account for all knowledge in a system that still leaves room for a respectable Christian faith was Aquinas' aim.[7] And in one important respect it would anticipate the aims of other more modern systems of moral and political thought. Even in this age, for instance, where the contrast between the secular and the spiritual is self-consciously made, but where post-modernism has inspired new interest in the search for moral certitudes, the language of universal rights is an echo of the old need to end ethical disputes by pointing to what is natural. We have worked hard to extricate ourselves from the old dogmas and to heighten our analytical sensibilities, but a familiar fear still prompts us to base our arguments upon universal – that is, upon independent and objective – principles of right.[8] And as our enquiry has shown, it is in response to this longstanding paradox that Augustine seems to have something definite to contribute. For the fact is that he does not construct the question of human freedom in the normal way. This is in large part due to his insistence to fear scriptural authority – especially, and most spectacularly, the first three books of Genesis. He does not, as we have seen, fear it without good cause: the narrative of Scripture would, in his opinion, have been true regardless of other considerations, but in the event it came to be borne out by the narrative of his own life.

How, then, does Augustine construct the question of human freedom out of his literal reading of Scripture and his own experiences? He does so primarily by understanding the biblical narrative of the Fall of Man from the epistemological point of view. Before his sin and expulsion from the Garden of Eden, man lived according to one theory of knowledge; afterwards, he lived according to another. In his first epistemological state, all his knowledge and understanding came *ex ore veritatis*; in his second, he was his own source of truth, judging the world according to his own categories of understanding. From the moral and political point of view it is not difficult for us to appreciate the significance of this epistemological transition. Initially man experienced what we can only accurately describe as the freedom of the child: that is to say, his best interests were accounted for out of the Wisdom and Mercy of God, and his only protection was correspondingly the love of God for him. However, after he had disobeyed God, man took on the responsibility and uncertainty of calculating his own best interests and, in addition, of conceptualizing his own happiness. He moved, technically speaking, from the voluntarist law of God's Will for him to the intellectualist law of his own imagination. Furthermore, whereas the voluntarist law of God's Will had allowed him to express his love for God in perfect obedience to His judgements, the new intellectualist law of his own imagination would be directed towards his new expectations about wisdom and happiness. For Augustine, then, the question of human freedom simply has to construct itself as a paradox. The natural inclination of fallen man is to attempt to recreate the happiness that he once knew in Paradise. However, the natural equipment with which he must do this is not fit for the purpose. It is not fit for the purpose because man is a creature designed to act on the inspiration of God: standing on his own initiative he is, in Augustine's language, 'unformed'.[9] Nearly all the animate creation can receive and respond to commands, but only man can call them to answer at the bar of reason. It is, in fact, this ever-present capacity for disobedience that allows him to experience happiness on its highest plane. For unlike the rest of the animate creation, whose responses to commands and stimuli are accounted for by instinct, man can obey and then retrospectively reflect on the goodness and wisdom of what he was asked to do by God. Of course this is not always possible. Sometimes God requires men to perform actions the goodness of which lies beyond a lifetime's reflection, but this, as Augustine explains, is a point of merely intellectual interest, for obedience to God is an act of love and knowing, not understanding. As Augustine would characteristically put it in his autobiographical work,

> There is a joy that is not granted to the wicked [cf. Isa. 48.22], but to those who choose freely to worship You, and for whom You Yourself are joy. This is what the happy life consists in: to rejoice in You, over You, and on account of You: this it is, and there is no other. Those who think that it consists in something else are really pursuing another joy altogether; and it is not true joy. Yet notwithstanding this, their will is not turned away from a glimmer of [true] joy . . . Indeed they would not love [this image: this faint recollection of Paradise] unless there were some impression of it in their memory. Why then do they not rejoice in it? Why are they unhappy? It is because other things have won their affections – things which have more power to make them unhappy than has that glimmer of joy, which they recall so faintly, to make them happy. Yet a little while there is light with men. Let them walk, let them walk, lest darkness come upon them [cf. Jn 12.35].[10]

The fruits of this self-deception are, in Augustine's opinion, a number of psychological and philosophical problems, all of which have by now been well documented. Considered together, they move us closer to a

conclusive statement on Augustine's contribution to the history of political thought in the West.

Let us begin with the most obvious psychological problem. A creature
such as man – designed to delight in his unquestioning obedience of God
– is free only so long as he continues to live unencumbered, in the actual
present. Characteristics that we might normally choose to associate with
freedom – the application of forethought, self-determination, the sense of
independence – are in fact the only things that can destroy his freedom.
This means that in his ordinary moral and political progress, man chooses
to conceptualize his happiness in terms that are fundamentally opposed
to his basic psychology as a rational creature. Some thinkers have even
tried to attribute otherwise inexplicable historical events to this paradox.
For instance, in his 'fear of freedom' thesis, Erich Fromm used the biblical
narrative of the Fall as a framework to explain the underlying psychology
of mass compliance with totalitarian dictatorships:

> One particularly telling representation of the fundamental relation
> between man and freedom is offered in the Biblical myth of man's
> expulsion from Paradise. The myth identifies the beginning of human
> history with an act of choice, but it puts all emphasis on the sinful-
> ness of this act of freedom and the suffering resulting from it. Man
> and woman live in the Garden of Eden in complete harmony with
> each other and with nature. There is peace and no necessity to work;
> there is no choice, no freedom, no thinking either. Man is forbidden
> to eat from the tree of knowledge of good and evil. He acts against
> God's command, he breaks through the state of harmony with nature
> of which he is a part without transcending it. From the standpoint
> of the Church which represented authority, this is essentially sin.
> From the standpoint of man, however, this is the beginning of human
> freedom. Acting against God's orders means freeing himself from
> coercion, emerging from the unconscious existence of prehuman life
> to the level of man. Acting against the command of authority, com-
> mitting a sin, is in its positive human aspect the first act of freedom,
> that is, the first *human* act. In the myth the sin in its formal aspect

is the acting against God's command; in its material aspect it is the eating of the Tree of Knowledge. The act of disobedience as an act of freedom is the beginning of reason . . . The myth emphasizes the suffering resulting from this act. To transcend nature, to be alienated from nature and from another human being, finds man naked, ashamed. He is alone and free, yet powerless and afraid.[11]

As Fromm saw it, it is this overwhelming sense of powerlessness and fear that ultimately drives people to seek a freedom that corresponds more closely with their psychological requirements. A totalitarian state that claims to be able to legislate for every aspect of their existence is one way that they can draw closer to the original freedom enjoyed by Adam in Paradise. The longstanding conceptualization of freedom in the West – that freely chosen social obligations are the basis of civic virtue – is in actual fact an intellectual conceit. Any dictatorship appears, in the nature of the case, to be a truer representation of what men need to be happy.

Fromm's thesis is open to many obvious criticisms that need not detain us. We are interested primarily in the way that it amplifies the psychological incongruity of what Augustine came to call *libido vindicandi sui* 'love of self-vindication'.[12] In terms of his own life, he found that this love expressed itself chiefly in his desire for worldly praise. In a passage with unmistakable echoes of Machiavelli, he would write that the love of self-vindication, or pride, is in its practical manifestation the desire to be loved and feared like God:

But now, because certain official positions in society cause us to be both loved and feared by men, we are hounded by the adversary of our true happiness. He sets his snares everywhere, breathing the words, 'Well done! Well done! [cf. Ps. 35.21; 40.15; 70.3] He does this in the hope of catching us off-guard: in the hope that as we greedily gather up his words we may begin to seek our joy in the deceits of men rather than in the truth. We would do this for the pleasure of being loved and feared not on account of You, but in place of You. By this means he would have for himself those who

have become like himself; not in a freely-chosen union but for company in punishment. This is he who has aspired to put his throne in
the sides of the north, in order that men may serve him in darkness
and cold who in perverse and distorted ways seek to imitate You.
[cf. Isa. 14.13–14][13]

Augustine was not, of course, the first Christian thinker to notice this
aspect of human nature. Nor did he attempt to claim any originality for
his views. It was from the writings of St Paul[14] that he learned seriously to
suspect the motives of his heart – particularly concerning his expectations
about salvation and his conceptualization of wisdom. The philosopher
Ludwig Wittgenstein (1889–1951) would later make the disarming point
that thought is not the dispassionate tool we imagine it to be; to the
contrary, it is fully implicated in the world it purports to judge, so that
the conditions of life are, in actual fact, the selfsame categories by which
we attempt to understand it. With his eye on the developed scholastic
philosophy of the medieval period, he would write that 'It used to be said
that God could create anything except what would be contrary to the
laws of logic. The truth is that we could not *say* what an 'illogical' world
would look like'.[15] As our enquiry has now shown us, it was during this
time in his life – his reading of St Paul – that Augustine began to suspect
something similar. He had always conceived his salvation along the lines
of the classical ascent to enlightenment. After years of toil and a proper
initiation, he would embrace the obverse of this world. That is to say, in
place of misleading sensible impressions, his understanding would come
to be guided by his stable apprehension of eternal verities known all at
once. These verities would be the completion of all the fractions of truth
that he had hitherto glimpsed on earth. Like Plato he would rise above
the milieu of mere opinion and belief and achieve a proper perspective;
it would be grounded in his knowledge of the essences of things rather
than of their appearance and, perhaps more importantly still, of their true
values relative to each other. He would thus become the man who acts
not by chance, or on instinct, but in full possession of the principles of
right. He would, in effect, be achieving the dream of the Stoic imagination

and of the intellectual tradition that it represents.[16] And this, as we have described it, is to make a single city of the universe: to presume that the summit of wisdom is anticipated in the merest wanderings of the mind, so that man, though separated from the Divine by an immeasurable distance, might have his heart quickened by the thought that he participates, by his nature, in that which elevates and saves. Ernest Barker described the scheme very well:

> For the [Stoics] there is really but a single city, reaching from earth to heaven – a city in which the baser sort . . . will indeed occupy a far lowlier position, never attaining near to the outer ether, but which, none the less, includes the Divine and the *daimones* and all humanity in its wide embrace. St. Paul implies two sorts of cities – the Divine commonwealth in the heavens, and the human commonwealths on earth. (Just in the same way St. Augustine distinguishes the *Civitas Dei* and the *terrena civitas*.) And the reason for this distinction of the two sorts of cities is, in one word, 'Righteousness.' For the Divine city is the city only of the righteous; and no unclean thing may enter into it. Here, in this one word Righteousness, which in Latin is *Justitia*, we touch one of the great key-words of human thought – a key-word to the thought of St. Augustine, a key-word to the thought of the Middle Ages.[17]

It was indeed under the influence of St Paul that Augustine began to moderate his idealism with the evidence of his own life. Like his old hero the poet Virgil, he began to realize that in great matters it is not always prudent to speculate from small things to the unknown.[18]

Once again we are struck by the paradox that is the hallmark of Augustine's mature perspective on the human condition, and which we have only analysed in detail from the psychological point of view. This world – that is, the Earthly City – is such that its ironies and contradictions invite us to describe the naturalness of moral and political activity in distinctly ungenerous terms. Likewise individual human behaviour, dominated as it is by the love of self-vindication, is susceptible to analysis in ungenerous terms. These are among the reasons for the plain, scientific appeal of ordinary political realism, which bases itself upon a pessimistic conception of human nature. Yet over and against this formidable tradition there is the optimism that we have associated with the natural-law style of moral and political argument – the style of argument that estimates man from the point of view of his rational good. Both these approaches offer distinct answers to what we earlier called the main theme of ethical speculation: the question, what exactly should a man do in each moment in order to secure his happiness? However, as we have had many occasions to notice, Augustine, although he accorded a great deal of respect to both approaches (and used each as a mode of explanation when it suited his purpose), was never compelled to commit himself to either. He was not, for want of a better word, an ideologue. There were certainly many occasions when he was required to base an argument upon a point of principle found in Scripture, but we have suggested that these cases of intellectualism, or legalism, were forced upon him as conventions of their day and did not represent his favoured approach. In fact by the time of his emergence from his retreat to Cassiciacum he had already begun to accept that wisdom was not the prerogative of intellectual systems or theories, but could only be heard 'from the mouth of [God's] truth'. This realization would present him with a problem that he would have to battle for the remainder of his life: the problem of pride – the urge to attribute to himself the truths of God's judgements and, in so doing, to make them the first principles of an independent mode of understanding. As he would characteristically put it:

O Lord, Your judgements are to be feared, since Your truth does not belong to me, or to him, or indeed to any other man. In fact it belongs to all of us whom You publically call to hold it in common; and You issue us a terrible warning not to will to take it to ourselves lest we be deprived of it [cf. 1 Tim. 6.5]. This is because whoever arrogates to himself that which You gave it to all men to enjoy, and desires that to be his own which belongs to all men, is correspondingly driven from the truth that is common to all men to what is his own, namely, a lie. For, 'When he speaketh a lie, he speaketh of his own' [Jn 8.44].[19]

We might now ask to what specific end did Augustine combine these disparate elements of realism and idealism in his thought? That he was something of an eclectic is clear when we recall how he believed that the primary function of truth in the Earthly City is to reprove or disquiet. We are, in his opinion, far better off likening states to robber bands if doing so disabuses us of the compulsion to describe them in terms more favourable to us. Every man has been gifted the capacity for critical analysis: it is the highest expression of God's Mercy and the sense in which salvation is freely available to all. However, not all men choose to go through with the consequences of judging themselves and the various creations of human hands by the universal standards of justice, for to do so is to forgo all the comforts – all the reassuring comparisons with others – that allow us to see a virtue in the life lived imperfectly. Augustine is, as we have suggested, often forced into this mould by readers wanting to identify with him. That the wellspring of his political ideas exhibits so little sympathy for our plight is unconscionable to many, and this response is fortified by his descriptions of God's arbitrary justice, most especially in his doctrines of Original Sin, Grace and Predestination. That he is serious about excluding the traditional virtues from everything but the life lived in obedience to God's spoken word comes as a profound disappointment to many.

> Who am I, and what am I? What of evil is not found in my acts, or if not in my acts, in my words, or if not in my words, in my will? But You, O Lord, are merciful and gracious [cf. Ps. 103.8; Exod. 34.6]: Your right hand has had regard for the profoundness of my death, and from the very depths of my heart it has emptied out an abyss of corruption.[20]

We must now consider what has developed into the main idiom of opposition to Augustine, or indeed Augustinianism, in the moral and political

theorizing of the West. We have already suggested that the wellspring of
this tradition of theory is a profound sympathy with the human condition. Man, as Aristotle pointed out, is distinguished from the beasts by
his ability not merely to make sounds, but to express his preferences in
language. 'Language', as he puts it,

> serves to declare what is advantageous and what is the reverse, and
> it therefore serves to declare what is just and what is unjust. It is the
> peculiarity of man . . . that he alone possesses a perception of good
> and evil, of the just and the unjust, and of other similar qualities;
> and it is association in [a common perception of these things] which
> makes a family and a polis.[21]

Augustine understood this too; indeed, we have had occasion to remark
on the generosity of his definition of justice in the state, which accords to
any assembled multitude the freedom to compose their own conception
of political right. However, we have also noticed that when Augustine
makes statements of this kind he is invariably expressing realism rather
than idealism: one conception of political right is much the same as
another because they both express preferences formed apart from the
inspiration of God. This, perhaps, is the most accurate measure of his
radicalism. For where we would want him to deploy his abilities to allevi-
ate our sense of bewilderment and futility in the face of such relativism,
he steadfastly refuses. He knows that we crave certainty because it is
certainty that we gave up in the Garden of Eden, but to his mind there
is only one route back to it. And it is a route that excludes the paths
already familiar to us as students of the history of political thought in
the West. On the one hand, Augustine refuses to promote a version of
the concept of positive liberty: he refuses, in other words, to make the
types of arguments that we have associated with the aggressive papal
politics of the medieval period. And on the other hand, he refuses to
extol the virtues that we have come to associate with the concept of
negative liberty. Indeed it is arguably on this latter point that his refusal
to share our point of view can seem most betraying, for we would argue

that negative liberty – the right to self-determination within reasonable limits – is how we express a hard-won tolerance and humility. Likewise it is disconcerting for us to imagine, with Plato, that democracy is merely the institutionalized expression of our envy of the wise.[22] Either way it is true that we impose limits upon our understanding (and therefore also upon the things that we endeavour to understand) that Augustine does not.[23] He does not because these limits are, as he explains, part of a project to replace God's judgements with our own, and that it is a hopeless project given our circumstance is, he thinks, a conclusion that it is open to all men to make. As the writer of Ecclesiastes says, 'I have seen the travail, which God hath given to the sons of men to be exercised in it. He hath made every *thing* beautiful in His time: also He hath set the world in their heart, so that no man can find out the work that God maketh from the beginning to the end'.[24] To Augustine this means that the metaphysical realities of life on earth have consequences that he finds it impossible to ignore;[25] indeed, it is precisely for ignoring them that he so often castigates 'the philosophers' for being 'vain in their imagination'.[26] By refusing to seek any correspondence between his City of God and his Earthly City, he unsentimentally accepts that the human mind can, in Dyson's expression, '. . . only work in ways that are logically and historically determinate'.[27] This is what he means by estimating fallen human nature from the point of view of temporality and talking of *infirmitas moribundorum sensuum* 'the infirmity of dying sense'.[28] Consequently one fact dominates his entire perspective on the human condition: '. . . how great a difference lies between presumption and contrition . . .'[29] There is only one route back to God for men, though there are many different philosophies, gods and utopias. Each one paints a picture of a paradise that we would like to inhabit, but each one is merely the obverse of an aspect of this world. Augustine is, we suggest, the first thinker in the West to consistently draw attention to this detail. He does so in the name of a Christian philosophy. His metaphysical speculations on time and the creation of the universe, as well as his theories concerning the rational apprehension of knowledge, amplify St Paul's warnings about presuming upon 'the tradition of men' and the 'rudiments of the world'.[30]

It is, however, in his voluntarist interpretation of the Will of God (which makes the Garden of Eden an archetype for nothing on earth) that he shows himself to be the faithful expositor of St Paul rather than of the Stoics and of the intellectual tradition that they exemplify.

Augustine's contribution to the history of political thought in the West is to be measured, then, in the extent that he amplified St Paul's teachings on the distance between man and God, and on the corresponding rôle and necessity of Grace. His political ideas were, in the first instance, the impression left by a Pauline theology of discipleship upon the social and political pretensions of Rome, but they have in turn gone on to become the preeminent alternative to the kinds of moral and political argument that do not take full account of man's limitations as a rational creature. The citizens of the Pilgrim City are in this world but not of it; their independence consists in their love of God and their corresponding willingness to repeatedly die to their old lives in the actual present.[31] They are, to borrow Heracleitus' expression, 'Immortal mortals, mortal immortals; living their death and dying their life'.[32] The theological import of this statement is straightforward. But it is the secular advantage of such an independent perspective that Augustine would like us to consider as students of moral and political thought.[33] This, after all, was the message that he repeatedly gave in writing to the political leaders of his day. Christian realism is not exhausted by dogmatic pronouncements on human sinfulness; it is not in that sense unqualified. The skepticism that we customarily associate with the outlook is buttressed by an intellectually distinct answer to the question of human happiness. The languages of perfection, the certainties of virtuous action, come from another place; at any rate, they could not have been composed as reflections upon this world. The Christian citizen, better still the Christian ruler, is not encumbered with the prospect of describing his activities in their terms. The advantage of Christianity for the state is, in Augustine's opinion, an unexpected flexibility and freedom of movement.

Notes

1 *Confess.*, VIII, 1, 2.
2 We are of course referring to the so-called 'fact versus value' debate in the

social sciences. This debate is constructed upon a number of premisses, the two most important of which being 1) that moral and political philosophy consists in attempting to establish the truth of ethical propositions and 2) that ethical propositions, being value judgements, are incapable of proof by the ordinary methods of science. The idea is that facts enjoy an independent existence and are therefore trustworthy, while values are arbitrary concoctions of the mind. For a short introduction to the main themes of this debate insofar as they bear upon political theory *see* W. G. Runciman, 'Sociological evidence and political theory', in Laslett & Runciman (Eds.), *Philosophy, Politics and Society* (Oxford: Basil Blackwell, 1972), pp. 34–48.

3 Heracleitus (*Acme*, ca BC 504–501) was able to express this idea quite clearly in the sixth century BC: 'Those who speak with sense must rely on what is common to all, as a city must rely on its law, and with much greater reliance. For all the laws of men are nourished by one law, the divine law: for it has as much power as it wishes and is sufficient for all and is still left over'. (Heracleitus, fragment 253, in Kirk & Raven [Eds.], *The Presocratic Philosophers*, p. 213).

4 A sentiment most famously expressed by Aristotle: '. . . the polis [is] an association which may be said to have reached the height of self-sufficiency; or rather [to speak more exactly] we may say that while it *grows* for the sake of mere life [and is so far, and at that stage, still short of full self-sufficiency], it *exists* [when once it is fully grown] for the sake of a good life [and is therefore fully self-sufficient]'. (Aristotle [tr. Ernest Barker], *Politics* [Oxford: Clarendon Press, 1960], 1252*b*).

5 As Edwyn Bevan put it plainly '. . . the resemblance between Zeno, the Hellenized Phoenician of Citium, and Paul, the Hellenized Hebrew of Tarsus, is not purely accidental. The author of the Acts has assuredly put into the mouth of his Paul, with deliberate purpose, phrases characteristic of the teaching which went back to Zeno. Nor is the connexion made by the writer an arbitrary one; it is the index of a great fact – the actual connexion in history between Stoicism and Christianity'. (Edwyn Bevan, *Stoics and Sceptics* [Oxford: Clarendon Press, 1913], p. 14). Cf. T. R. Glover's assessment: '[Paul] slid, as we also do, into using the speech of our day, where it coincides with what we know to be true'. (T. R. Glover, *Paul of Tarsus* [London: Student Christian Movement, 1925], p. 22).

6 *See* his *Policraticus*, VII, 8: 'If all good things are, therefore, consequent upon wisdom, and philosophy is the study of wisdom, then surely contempt for philosophers is the exclusion of everything good. For this reason it is deduced that however much anyone diligently pursues philosophy, to that extent does he more faithfully and correctly advance towards happiness. For philosophy assigns the virtues according to which one proceeds in particular

duties. But because the ancients, although they believed for the most part in the mortality of the soul, had not yet received instruction about the eternal life which is to be after this one, they founded the greatest good upon virtue, than which there is clearly nothing better except the enjoyment of Him Who is good in the highest degree and is the greatest good'. John of Salisbury (tr. Cary J Nederman), *Policraticus* (Cambridge: Cambridge University Press, 1990).

7 See *HMPTW*, Vol. V, pp. 36–44, for an excellent short summary of Aquinas' aspirations as a Christian philosopher.

8 Cf. d'Entrèves, *Natural Law*, p. 115: 'Here, indeed, is where the moralist will have his word to say, and will decide whether the old speculations on the nature of law are entirely superseded. If he be the man of the *verum* he will not ignore that the certainty for which conscience craves is not that of transient laws, but that of absolute values. He will provide such grounds for obedience as are capable of carrying conviction. But he will also take into account the unrelenting quest of man to rise above the "letter of the law" to the realm of the spirit. He will draw the dividing line between mere conformity to the law and the real value of action, between the Pharisee and the truly moral man'.

9 See *De civ. Dei*, XII, 26.

10 *Confess.*, X, 23, 32–33 (author's translation). *See* also *De cont.*, III, 8: '. . . we exist under Grace, which, making us to love what is enjoined of us, really holds sway over the free'. (author's translation).

11 Erich Fromm, *The Fear of Freedom*, pp. 27–8.

12 See *Confess.*, X, 36, 58.

13 *Ibid.*, X, 36, 59 (author's translation).

14 See *ibid.*, VII, 21, 27.

15 Ludwig Wittgenstein (tr. D. F. Pears & B. F. McGuinness), *Tractatus Logico-Philosophicus* (London: Routledge & Kegan Paul, 1974), 3.031, p. 11. Cf. Pope Benedict XVI on the same theme: 'Modern scientific reason quite simply has to accept the rational structure of matter and the correspondence between our spirit and the prevailing rational structures of nature as given, on which its methodology has to be based. Yet the question why this has to be so is a real question . . .' ('Faith, Reason and the University: Memories and Reflections', lecture delivered to the Representatives of Science at the University of Regensburg, on 12 September 2006).

16 The aspirations and chief attractions of this intellectual tradition have been elegantly summarized for us by Sir Oliver Lodge (1851–1940). As he writes, '. . . we regard the sense of conscience [in man] as the most important and highest characteristic of all, the sense of responsibility, the power of self-determination, the building up of character, so that ultimately

it becomes impossible to be actuated by unworthy motives. Our actions are now controlled not by external impulses only, but largely by our own characters and wills. The man who is the creature of impulse, or the slave of his passions, cannot be said to be his own master, or to be really free: he drifts hither and thither according to the caprice or the temptation of the moment; he is untrustworthy, and without solidity or dignity of character. The free man is he who can control himself, who does not obey every idea as it occurs to him, but weighs and determines for himself, and is not at the mercy of external influences. This is the real meaning of choice and free will. It does not mean that actions are capricious and undetermined; but that they are determined by nothing less than the totality of things. They are not determined by the external world alone, so that they can be calculated and predicted from outside; they are determined by self and the external world together. A free man is the master of his motives, and selects that motive which he wills to obey'. (Sir Oliver Lodge, *The Substance of Faith Allied with Science: A Catechism for Parents and Teachers* [London: Methuen, 1907], p. 27).

17 Barker, 'Introduction', *The City of God* (tr. John Healey)(London: J. M. Dent & Sons, 1931), p. xx. This tradition would receive its fullest expression in the philosophy of the Renaissance, and in what has come to be called the 'discovery of the natural man'. As Professor Höffding would describe the mood, '. . . man is obliged as well as capable of doing good without the hope of immortality; virtue is its own reward'. (Harold Höffding [tr. Charles Finley Sanders], *A Brief History of Modern Philosophy* [New York: Macmillan Company, 1912], p. 5).

18 *See* Virgil, *Eclogae*, I, 19–25.

19 *Confess.*, XII, 25, 34 (author's translation).

20 *Ibid.*, IX, 1, 1 (author's translation).

21 Aristotle, *Politics*, 1253*a*.

22 *See* Plato, *Republic*, 555*b*–562*a*.

23 *Confess.*, X, 6, 10: 'However, through love for such things they become subject to them, and in subjection they cannot pass judgement on them'.

24 Ecclus. 3.10–11.

25 Augustine characteristically describes these consequences in terms of the necessity of language: 'The cause of the physical utterance of these words is the abyss of this world and the blindness of our flesh'. (*Confess.*, XIII, 23, 34).

26 *See* Rom. 1.21–22.

27 Dyson, *St. Augustine of Hippo*, p. 26.

28 *De civ. Dei*, XXI, 12. Is Augustine right always to refer conventional moral and political activity to the restrictions of our temporal existence?

Is the necessity to produce reasons for our activities in time actually a limitation? Is he innovative to suggest that it is? That the human condition is most flagrantly displayed in our attempts to equate eternity with the truly objective first principle of action? It is not appropriate for us to answer these questions. We can go only so far as to say this: that the evidence suggests that the Augustinian innovation in political thought occupies a distinctive place. Cf., for instance, Rawls, *A Theory of Justice* (London: Oxford University Press, 1973), p. 587: 'The perspective of eternity is not a perspective from a certain place beyond the world, nor the point of view of a transcendent being; rather it is a certain form of thought and feeling that rational persons can adopt within the world. And having done so, they can, whatever their generation, bring together into one scheme all individual perspectives and arrive together at regulative principles that can be affirmed by everyone as he lives by them, each from his own standpoint. Purity of heart, if one could attain it, would be to see clearly and to act with grace and self-command from this point of view'.

29 *Confess.*, VII, 20, 26.

30 *See* Col. 2.8: 'Beware lest any man spoil you through philosophy and vain deceit, after the tradition of men, after the rudiments of the world, and not after Christ'. Augustine cites this verse in a passage recommending the Christian religion above the arts of the philosophers: see *De civ. Dei*, VIII, 11.

31 As we have now established, the pilgrim dies to his old life by confessing the truth of his heart – not some abstract truth, some dogmatic construction of 'sinfulness', but his personal reason for not being disquieted by the realities of the human condition: what we have called his myth of innocence (or the extent to which he is compromised into acquiescing in his earthly citizenship). We have seen also that Augustine consistently refers the vexed question of the nature of truth to human pride. He thinks that what is true of us and the world is too disapproving to be faced for long (*see*, for instance, *De cont.*, V, 13); that the pilgrim only avoids this conundrum by renouncing his earthly citizenship and being fortified against the consequences of this decision by Grace. This probably explains the original Christian insistence on 'doing' or 'making' truth. At any rate, Augustine certainly thinks it does. The truth is something that we are either for or against. If we are against it, it is for ideological reasons based in pride. If we are for it, it is because we have actively renounced our old citizenship and taken on a new one: we have done and made the truth by a political decision in time, aligning ourselves with what is real. See *De mend.*, XVII, 35: '"Thou hatest all workers of iniquity;" [Ps. 5.5] but they will not be

lost if they repent by speaking the truth in confession: that by doing/making [*faciendo*] the truth they may come to the light, as indeed it is said in the Gospel according to John: "But he that doeth truth cometh to the light."' [Jn 3.21] (author's translation).

32 Heracleitus, fragment 242, in Kirk & Raven (Eds.), *The Presocratic Philosophers*, p. 210.

33 As Augustine exhorts Laurentius, in the dedication of his *Enchiridion*, to be '. . . one of those of whom it is written: "the number of the wise is the wellbeing of the earth."' [Wis. 6.24] (*Ench.*, I, 1 [author's translation]).

Bibliography

SELECTED SECONDARY SOURCES

ALLEN, J. W., *A History of Political Thought in the Sixteenth Century* (London: Methuen, 1957).

ARMSTRONG, A. H., *An Introduction to Ancient Philosophy* (London: Methuen, 1965).

———, *St. Augustine and Christian Platonism* (Villanova: Villanova University Press, 1966).

———, *Plotinian and Christian Studies* (London: Variorum Reprints, 1979).

ARQUILLIÈRE, H.-X., *L'augustinisme politique: essai sur la formation des theories politiques du moyen-age* (Paris : Librairie Philosophique J. Vrin, 1934).

BABCOCK, W. S. (Ed.), *The Ethics of St. Augustine* (Atlanta: Scholars Press, 1991).

BARKER, Sir. Ernest, *The Political Thought of Plato and Aristotle* (New York: Methuen, 1959).

———, *Greek Political Theory: Plato and His Predecessors* (London: Methuen, 1960).

BATHORY, Peter Dennis, *Political Theory as Public Confession: The Social and Political Thought of St. Augustine of Hippo* (New Brunswick: Transaction Books, 1981).

BAYNES, Norman H., *The Political Ideas of St. Augustine's* De civitate Dei (London: Historical Association, 1936).

BECKER, Carl L., *The Heavenly City of the Eighteenth-Century Philosophers* (New Haven: Yale University Press, 1969).

BERLIN, Isaiah, *Four Essays on Liberty* (Oxford: Oxford University Press, 1969).

———, *The Age of Enlightenment: The Eighteenth-Century Philosophers* (Oxford: Oxford University Press, 1979).

BEVAN, Edwyn, *Stoics and Sceptics* (Oxford: Clarendon Press, 1913).

BONNER, Gerald, 'Quod imperatori cum Ecclesia? Augustine on history and society', *AS*, Vol. 2 (1971), 231–53.

———, *St. Augustine of Hippo: Life and Controversies* (Norwich: Canterbury Press, 1986).

———, 'Augustine and Pelagianism', *AS*, Vol. 24 (1994), 27–49.

BOURKE, Vernon J., 'Voluntarism in Augustine's ethico-legal thought', *AS*, Vol. 1 (1970), 3–19.

BOURKE, Vernon J., *The Essential Augustine* (Indianapolis: Hackett, 1974).

BOYER, Charles S. I., *Essais sur la doctrine de saint Augustin* (Paris, 1933).

———, *Christianisme et Néo-Platonisme dans la formation de Saint Augustin* (Roma: Officium Libri Catholici, 1953).

BRONOWSKI, J. and MAZLISH, Bruce, *The Western Intellectual Tradition* (Harmondsworth: Penguin, 1963).

BROWN, Peter, *Religion and Society in the Age of St. Augustine* (London: Faber & Faber, 1972).

———, *The Making of Late Antiquity* (London: Harvard University Press, 1978).

———, *Augustine of Hippo: A Biography* (London: Faber & Faber, 1979).

———, *Power and Persuasion in Late Antiquity: Towards a Christian Empire* (Wisconsin: University of Wisconsin Press, 1988).

———, *Poverty and Leadership in the Later Roman Empire* (Hanover, NH: University Press of New England, 2002).

BUBACZ, Bruce, 'Augustine's illumination theory and epistemic structuring', *AS*, Vol. 2 (1980), 35–49.

———, *St. Augustine's Theory of Knowledge: A Contemporary Analysis* (New York and Toronto: Edwin Mellen Press, 1981).

BURLEIGH, J. H. S., *The City of God: A Study of Augustine's Philosophy* (London: Nisbet, 1949).

BURNET, John, 'Law and nature in Greek ethics', *IJE*, Vol. 7, No. 3 (Apr., 1897), 328–33.

BURNS, J. H. (Ed.), *The Cambridge History of Medieval Political Thought, c. 350–c. 1450* (Cambridge: Cambridge University Press, 1997).

BURNS, Patout J., *The Development of St. Augustine's Doctrine of Operative Grace*, (Paris: Études Augustiniennes, 1980).

CALLAHAN, John F., *Augustine and the Greek Philosophers* (Villanova: Villanova University Press, 1967).

CARLYLE, Sir R. W. and CARLYLE, A. J., *A History of Mediaeval Political Theory in the West*, 6 Vols. (Edinburgh and London: William Blackwood & Sons, 1962).

CARNES, John R., 'Whether there is a natural law', *Ethics*, Vol. 77, No. 2 (Jan., 1967), 122–9.

CARY, Phillip, *Augustine's Invention of the Inner Self: The Legacy of a Christian Platonist* (Oxford: Oxford University Press, 2000).

CASSIRER, Ernst, *The Myth of the State* (New Haven: Yale University Press, 1963).

CHADWICK, Henry, *The Early Church* (Harmondsworth: Penguin, 1967).

CHROUST, Anton-Hermann, 'The philosophy of law of St. Augustine', *The Philosophical Review*, Vol. 52, No. 3 (Mar., 1944), 195–202.

————, 'The function of law and justice in the ancient world and the middle ages', *Journal of the History of Ideas*, Vol. 7, No. 3 (June, 1946), 298–320.

CLARK, Mary T., *Augustine*, (London: Continuum, 2000).

COCHRANE, C. N., *Christianity and Classical Culture* (Oxford: Oxford University Press, 1943).

CONNOLLY, W., *The Augustinian Imperative: A Reflection on the Politics of Morality* (Newbury Park: Sage Publications, 1993).

COLLINGWOOD, R. G., *The Idea of History* (Oxford: Clarendon Press, 1951).

CORNFORD, F. M., *Before and After Socrates* (Cambridge: Cambridge University Press, 1932).

————, *From Religion to Philosophy: A Study in the Origins of Western Speculation* (Princeton: Princeton University Press, 1991).

CULLMAN, Oscar, *Salvation in History* (London: SCM Press, 1967).

DANIEL-ROPS, H. (tr. Audrey Butler), *The Protestant Reformation* (London: J. M. Dent & Sons, 1961).

DEANE, Herbert A., *The Political and Social Ideas of St. Augustine* (New York: Columbia University Press, 1963).

———, 'Classical and Christian political thought', *Political Theory*, Vol. 1, No. 4 (Nov., 1973), 415–25.

De COULANGES, Numa Denis Fustel, *The Ancient City: A Classic Study of the Religious and Civil Institutions of Ancient Greece and Rome* (Garden City, New York: Doubleday & Company, 1956).

D'ENTRÈVES, A. P., *Natural Law* (London: Hutchinson University Library, 1970).

DODARO, Robert, *Christ and the Just Society in the Thought of Augustine* (Cambridge: Cambridge University Press, 2004).

DODARO, Robert and LAWLESS, George (Eds.), *Augustine and His Critics* (London: Routledge, 2002).

DODDS, E. R., *Pagan and Christian in an Age of Anxiety* (Cambridge: Cambridge University Press, 1965).

DONNELLY, Dorothy F. (Ed.), *The City of God: A Collection of Critical Essays* (New York: Peter Lang, 1995).

DYSON, R. W., 'St. Augustine's remarks on time', *The Downside Review*, (July 1982), 221–31.

———, *The Pilgrim City: Social and Political Ideas in the Writings of St. Augustine of Hippo* (Suffolk: Boydell Press, 2001).

———, (Ed.), *Thomas Aquinas: Political Writings* (Cambridge: Cambridge University Press, 2002).

———, *Normative Theories of Society and Government in Five Medieval Thinkers: St. Augustine, John of Salisbury, Giles of Rome, St. Thomas Aquinas, and Marsilius of Padua* (Lewiston: Edwin Mellen Press, 2003).

———, *St. Augustine of Hippo: The Christian Transformation of Political Philosophy* (London: Continuum, 2005a).

———, *Natural Law and Political Realism in the History of Political Thought: Vol. I, From the Sophists to Machiavelli* (New York: Peter Lang, 2005b).

———, *Natural Law and Political Realism in the History of Political Thought: Vol. II, From the Seventeenth to the Twenty-First Century* (New York: Peter Lang, 2007).

EARL, Donald, *The Moral and Political Tradition of Rome* (London: Thames & Hudson, 1970).

EHLER, Sidney Z. and MORRALL, John B. (Eds.), *Church and State through the Centuries: A Collection of Illustrative Documents* (London: Burns & Oates, 1954).

ELSHTAIN, Jean Bethke, *Augustine and the Limits of Politics* (Notre Dame, Indiana: University of Notre Dame Press, 1995).

FERGUSON, J., *Pelagius: A Historical and Theological Study* (Cambridge: Cambridge University Press, 1956).

FIGGIS, John Neville, *The Political Aspects of St. Augustine's 'City of God'* (London: Longmans, Green, 1921).

FORTIN, E. L., 'Augustine's City of God and the modern historical consciousness', *Review of Politics*, Vol. 41 (July, 1979), 323–43.

FREND, W. H. C., *The Donatist Church: A Movement of Protest in North Africa* (Oxford: Clarendon Press, 1952).

FRANKFORT, Henri *et al.*, *Before Philosophy: A Study of the Primitive Myths, Beliefs and Speculations of Egypt and Mesopotamia, out of which Grew the Religions and Philosophies of the Later World* (Harmondsworth: Penguin, 1961).

FROMM, Erich, *The Fear of Freedom* (London: Kegan Paul, Trench, Trubner & Co., 1945).

GIERKE, Otto (tr. Frederic William Maitland), *Political Theories of the Middle Age* (Cambridge: Cambridge University Press, 1968).

GILSON, Étienne, *The Christian Philosophy of St. Augustine* (New York: Random House, 1961).

GLOVER, T. R., *The Influence of Christ in the Ancient World* (Cambridge: Cambridge University Press, 1929).

——, *The World of the New Testament* (Cambridge: Cambridge University Press, 1931).

——, *The Ancient World: A Beginning* (Cambridge: Cambridge University Press, 1935).

GRUEN, Erich S., *The Hellenistic World and the Coming of Rome* (London: University of California Press, 1984).

HARRISON, Carol, *Augustine: Christian Truth and Fractured Humanity* (Oxford: Oxford University Press, 2000).

————, *Rethinking Augustine's Early Theology: An Argument for Continuity* (Oxford: Oxford University Press, 2006).

KEYES, G. L., *Christian Faith and the Interpretation of History: A Study of St. Augustine's Philosophy of History* (Lincoln, NE: University of Nebraska Press, 1966).

KIRK, G. S. and Raven, J. E., *The Presocratic Philosophers* (Cambridge: Cambridge University Press, 1962).

KIRWAN, Christopher, *Augustine* (London: Routledge, 1989).

LANCEL, Serge (tr. Antonia Nevill), *St. Augustine* (London: SCM Press, 2002).

LAVERE, George J., 'The political realism of St. Augustine', *AS*, Vol. 2 (1980), 135–45.

————, 'The influence of Augustine on early medieval political theory', *AS*, Vol. 12 (1981), 1–19.

LEE, K. L. E., *Augustine, Manichaeism, and the Good* (New York: Peter Lang, 1999).

LEFF, Gordon, *Medieval Thought: St. Augustine to Ockham* (Harmondsworth: Penguin, 1965).

LEPELLEY, Claude, 'Facing Wealth and Poverty: Defining Augustine's Social Doctrine', *AS*, Vol. 38, No. 1 (2007), 1–19.

LEWIS, Ewart, 'Natural law and expediency in medieval political theory', *Ethics*, Vol. 50, No. 2 (Jan., 1940), 144–63.

————, *Medieval Political Ideas* (London: Routledge & Kegan Paul, 1954).

LEWIS, C. S., *The Great Divorce* (London: HarperCollins, 2002a).

————, *The Abolition of Man* (New York: HarperCollins, 2002b).

LLOYD, A. C., *The Anatomy of Neoplatonism* (Oxford: Clarendon Press, 1990).

LULL, Timothy F. (Ed.), *Martin Luther's Basic Theological Writings* (Minneapolis: Fortress Press, 2005).

MACQUEEN, D. J., 'The origin and dynamics of society and the state', *AS*, Vol. 4 (1973), 75–103.

MARKUS, R. A., *Saeculum: History and Society in the Theology of St. Augustine* (Cambridge: Cambridge University Press, 1970).

————, *The End of Ancient Christianity* (Cambridge: Cambridge University Press, 1997).

MARROU, H. I., *Saint Augustin et la fin de la culture antique* (Paris: de Boccard, 1938).

——, *Saint Augustin et l'augustinisme* (Paris: Seuil, 1956).

MARTIN, Rex, 'The two cities in Augustine's political philosophy', *Journal of the History of Ideas*, Vol. 23 (1972), 195–217.

McCOY, Charles N. R., 'The turning point in political philosophy', *American Political Science Review*, Vol. 44, No. 3 (Sep., 1950), 678–88.

MOMIGLIANO, A. (Ed.), *The Conflict between Paganism and Christianity in the Fourth Century* (Oxford: Clarendon Press, 1963).

MOMMSEN, T. E., 'St. Augustine and the Christian idea of progress: the background of the City of God', *Journal of the History of Ideas*, Vol. 12 (1951), 346–74.

MORRALL, John B., *Political Thought in Medieval Times* (London: Hutchinson University Library, 1960).

NASH, Ronald H., 'Some philosophic sources of Augustine's illumination theory', *AS*, Vol. 2 (1971), 47–67.

NIEBUHR, Reinhold, *Christian Realism and Political Problems* (London: Faber & Faber, 1954).

——, (Ed. with an intr. R. M. Brown), 'Augustine's Political Realism', in *The Essential Reinhold Niebuhr: Selected Essays and Addresses* (New Haven: Yale University Press, 1986).

O'CONNELL, R. J., *Images of Conversion in St. Augustine's Confessions* (New York: Fordham University Press, 1995).

O'DONOVAN, Oliver, *The Desire of the Nations: Rediscovering the Roots of Political Theology* (Cambridge: Cambridge University Press, 1999).

O'MEARA, J., 'Neo-Platonism in the conversion of St. Augustine', *Dominican Studies*, Vol. 3 (1950), 334–43.

——, *The Young Augustine: The Growth of St Augustine's Mind up to His Conversion* (London: Longmans, 1954).

——, 'Augustine and Neoplatonism', *Recherches augustiniennes*, Vol. 1 (1958), 43–66.

O'MEARA, J., *Charter of Christendom: The Significance of the 'City of God'* (New York: Macmillan, 1961).

PAOLUCCI, Henry (Ed.), *Political Writings of St. Augustine* (Chicago: Henry Regnery Company, 1962).

PORTALIÉ, E., SJ (tr. R. J. Bastian, SJ), *A Guide to the Thought of St. Augustine* (London: Burns & Oates, 1960).

RAU, Catherine, 'Theories of time in ancient philosophy', *The Philosophical Review*, Vol. 62, No. 4 (Oct., 1953), 514–25.

RIST, John M., (Ed.), *The Stoics* (London: University of California Press, 1978).

RIST, John M., *Augustine: Ancient Thought Baptized* (Cambridge: Cambridge University Press, 1994).

ROMMEN, Heinrich A. (tr. Thomas R. Hanley), *The Natural Law: A Study in Legal and Social Philosophy* (London: B. Herder Book Co., 1955).

ROSE, H. J., *Religion in Greece and Rome* (New York: Harper & Brothers, 1959).

SIGMUND, Paul E., *Natural Law in Political Thought* (Cambridge, Mass.: Winthrop Publishers, 1971).

——, *St. Thomas Aquinas on Politics and Ethics* (New York: W. W. Norton & Company, 1988).

SPARROW SIMPSON, W. J., *St. Augustine's Conversion* (London: SPCK, 1930).

STEAD, Christopher, *Philosophy in Christian Antiquity* (Cambridge: Cambridge University Press, 1995).

SYKES, Stephen, *Power and Christian Theology* (London: Continuum, 2006).

TeSELLE, Eugene, *Living in Two Cities: Augustinian Trajectories in Political Thought* (Scranton: University of Scranton Press, 1998).

——, *Augustine* (Nashville, TN: Abingdon Press, 2006).

TRAPÈ, Agostino, *Agostino: l'uomo, il pastore, il mistico* (Roma: Città Nuova Editrice, 2001).

TROELTSCH, Ernst (tr. Olive Wyon), *The Social Teaching of the Christian Churches*, Vol. I (London: George Allen & Unwin, 1931).

ULLMANN, Walter, *Law & Politics in the Middle Ages: An Introduction to the Sources of Medieval Political Thought* (London: Sources of History, 1975).

Van der MEER, Frederick (tr. Brian Battershaw and G. R. Lamb), *Augustine the Bishop: The Life and Work of a Father of the Church* (London: Sheed & Ward, 1961).

Van FLETEREN, Frederick, 'Authority and reason, faith and understanding, in the thought of St. Augustine', *AS*, Vol. 4 (1973), 33–73.

WILES, Maurice and SANTER, Mark, *Documents in Early Christianity* (Cambridge: Cambridge University Press, 1975).

WOLIN, Sheldon S., *Politics and Vision: Continuity and Innovation in Western Political Thought* (London: George Allen & Unwin, 1961).

Index